D1593374

A Legacy of Wisdom

*The thirtieth chapter and colophon of Amenemope (27:1-28:1),
sixth century B.C.* Courtesy of the British Museum *(B.M. Papyrus
10474).*

A Legacy of Wisdom

The Egyptian Contribution to the Wisdom of Israel

Glendon E. Bryce

Lewisburg
Bucknell University Press
London: Associated University Presses

48261
026084

© 1979 by Associated University Presses, Inc.

Associated University Presses, Inc.
Cranbury, New Jersey 08512

Associated University Presses
Magdalen House
136-148 Tooley Street
London SE1 2TT, England

Library of Congress Cataloging in Publication Data

Bryce, Glendon E
  A legacy of wisdom.
  Bibliography: p.
  Includes index.
  1. Wisdom literature—Relation to Egyptian literature. 2. Bible.
O.T. Proverbs—Criticism, interpretations, etc. I. Title.
BS1455.B79   223'.7'06   74-4984
ISBN 0-8387-1576-1

PRINTED IN THE UNITED STATES OF AMERICA

To my wife, Sylvia

Contents

46261

0260847

Preface

Just a half-century ago Adolf Erman and Hugo
Gressmann discovered the composition entitled "The
Sayings of the Wise" in Proverbs 22:17-24:22 and established a clear connection between the thirty sayings that
it contained and the Egyptian instruction of
Amenemope, which consisted of thirty chapters. A year
before this Sir E. A. Wallis Budge had already noted two
parallels between this Egyptian instruction and the book
of Proverbs in the original publication of Papyrus 10474
of the British Museum. What some scholars had suspected about the relationship between the wisdom of
Egypt and the book of Proverbs had now apparently
been confirmed. A period of intense discussion about

the significance of this new discovery followed. Unfortunately, this dialogue and its implications for understanding the wisdom of Israel were largely confined to specialized studies appearing in journals and monographs. In fact, with the exception of a brief period a decade ago resulting from a new study of the relationship between Amenemope and Proverbs by the French Egyptologist Etienne Drioton, interest in this subject had waned. A comprehensive study of the relationship between Egyptian and Israelite wisdom in the form of a book has never been written in English. For such a study we are indebted to Paul Humbert, whose book appeared in French in the year 1929.

With the current revival of interest in the wisdom literature of the Old Testament, the question of the relation of Israelite wisdom to extra-biblical sources has become important. In fact, the general subject of the relation of Israel to the cultural matrix of the ancient Near East and the way in which literary forms and ideas are transmitted from one culture to another is a critical issue, having considerable bearing upon our understanding of the religious heritage of Israel. It is, then, just fifty years after the important discovery about the relationship between the wisdom of Israel and the literature of Egypt was made that this study is presented. It seeks to give the relation between Egyptian and Israelite wisdom a wider relevance by the development of a particular literary theory concerning the way in which a cultural and literary heritage is transmitted, also by extending this to include the important subject of the religion of Israel. It also brings into greater prominence the role of the king and the royal court in the formation of the religious and literary traditions of Israel that were received and subsequently canonized by the Jewish people.

For careful scrutiny of the manuscript and helpful suggestions I am especially indebted to Professor George R. Hughes of the Oriental Institute of the University of Chicago, and also to Professor J. Coert Rylaarsdam, formerly at the Divinity School of the University of Chicago and presently at Marquette University in Milwaukee, Wisconsin.

Princeton Theological Seminary
Princeton, New Jersey

1976

Acknowledgments

Grateful acknowledgment is made to the following persons and institutions for the use of the material indicated:

The Trustees of the British Museum and the British Library Board for the frontispiece and figures 3 and 4.

Professor Joseph A. Fitzmyer, S. J., Editor, for portions of my article "Another Wisdom-'Book' in Proverbs," *Journal of Biblical Literature* 91 (1972):145-57.

Professor B. J. Peterson and the Egypt Exploration Society for figure 2.

Professor Georges Posener for figure 1.

For assistance in bibliographical and other details, I am grateful to Graham Ogden, a graduate student at Princeton Theological Seminary, and James Irvine, the Assistant Librarian at Princeton Theological Seminary.

A Legacy of Wisdom

1

The Theory of Semitic Dependence

The work of Sir E. A. Wallis Budge in the discovery, publication, and evaluation of the Hieratic papyrus copied by the scribe Senu, Papyrus 10474 of the British Museum, known as "The Teaching of Amenemope," had two effects. First, it made scholars aware of the close parallels that existed between the text of Amenemope and the book of Proverbs. Second, it signaled one of the possible directions that could be followed in attempting to explain the close relationship between the two documents. In the official publication of the manuscript, *Facsimiles of Egyptian Hieratic Papyri in the British Museum*, which appeared in 1923, Budge drew attention to the first two parallels between Amenemope and Proverbs in two separate notes on his translation of the Egyptian document.[1] In the second note he recorded the first parallel between Amenemope and the collection of proverbs contained in the third section of the book of Proverbs (22:17-24:22).

Amen. 10:4-5

Prov. 23:5

(Or) they have made themselves wings like the geese
And flown up into the heavens![2]

For *riches* certainly make themselves wings; they fly away as an eagle toward heaven.[3]

In his book *The Teaching of Amen-em-Apt, Son of Kanekht,* published the following year, Budge also proposed a theory to explain the striking similarities between Amenemope and the Old Testament.[4] Impressed by the high character of the religious teaching found in Amenemope, Budge suggested that this could be accounted for by Asiatic influence that found its way into Egypt during the Middle Kingdom period. Although Budge did not pursue his theory further, other scholars accepted it as a working hypothesis. As a result, his proposal led to a number of theories that sought to interpret the wisdom of Amenemope in terms of Semitic influences upon Egypt.

The first comparative study between Amenemope and Prov. 22:17ff. was done by the Egyptologist Adolf Erman.[5] Prior to the work of Erman the dependence of Hebrew wisdom upon its Egyptian parent had been assumed on the basis of general similarities of thought and form. Now for the first time in a detailed analysis of a number of the close verbal parallels between the two texts, Erman attempted to document the dependence of the Hebrew proverbs by showing the specific words and phrases that had been borrowed. The result of his work was to temporarily displace the theory of Budge. In the ensuing discussion most scholars followed the theory of Erman, presupposing Egyptian influence and emending the Hebrew text with reference to it.

The work of Budge and Erman represents the two main divisions that came into being in the attempt to assess the precise relationship of Egyptian and Hebrew wisdom. Therefore, to trace the history of the interpretation of this problem is largely to follow these two approaches. Accordingly, the first chapter of this work will deal with the results of those studies which posited Egyptian derivation of the Hebrew proverbs in Prov. 22: 17ff., particularly up to 23:11, where the close similarity ends. After a study of the verbal parallels, together with the various theories to explain the dependence, the chapter will conclude with a review of the reactions against a theory of Egyptian derivation. Then, in the second chapter, the interpretations of those who proposed a theory of Semitic derivation will be presented.

In his study of the relation between Amenemope and Prov. 22:17ff., Erman discovered seven close parallels.[6] Accepting the priority of the Egyptian text, he concluded that the Hebrew text had not only borrowed from the Egyptian source but had also misunderstood it and distorted it in places. For this reason Erman tried to bring the text of Proverbs into a closer conformity to its source by emending it where it appeared to diverge from the original. His examination of the parallels between Amen. 9:14ff. and Prov. 23:4-5 revealed that the Hebrew text was an adaptation of the Egyptian passage.[7]

9:14. Do not labor to seek out excess.

23:4a. Do not toil to become rich.

9:19b. They are no longer there.

23:5a. It is not there.

10:4-5. They have made themselves wings like geese, and they have flown to the heavens.

23:5b. It makes itself wings like an eagle and flies to the heavens.

Erman regarded the Hebrew abbreviation of the Egyptian text as corrupt because the noun antecedent for the pronominal references in the third person in 23:5 was missing in 23:4.

Consequently, Erman proposed a series of corrections to improve the text of Proverbs and to bring it into closer conformity to the Egyptian original. In Prov. 22:17 he proposed the deletion of the word "wise" (ḥkmym) in the phrase "the words of the wise" (dbry ḥkmym) since it properly belonged to the superscription. In its place he read "hear my word" (dbry).[8] Also, by changing the phrase "to my knowledge" (ld'ty) to the meaning "to know them" (ld'tm), he achieved an exact reproduction of Amen. 3:10 ("to understand them") in the Hebrew text.[9] In Prov. 22:21, since the Egyptian word "report" (smi) in Amen. 1:6 was represented by the Hebrew "words" ('mrym), he deleted the second word ('mt, "truth") from the phrase "words (of) truth."[10] Rejecting the Masoretic text of Prov. 22:20, which contained the reading šlšwm (translated "excellent things" in the older English versions), Erman explained its meaning by referring to the number of chapters mentioned at the conclusion of the Egyptian source (Amen. 27:7). The written form šlšwm was a corruption of the Hebrew word for "thirty" (šlwšym), alluding to the thirty chapters mentioned in Amenemope.[11]

Erman's explanation of this parallel not only provided

a cogent argument for his theory of dependence but also illuminated his own hypothesis about the relation of the two texts to each other. According to Erman, the editor of the proverbial collections had before him a Hebrew or Aramaic form of the text of Amenemope that was in a fragmented condition.[12] The beginning of this book is found in Prov. 22:17-18. Its conclusion, which contained the number thirty, was also in the possession of the editor. However, because he did not understand it, no doubt due to the corrupt form of the text and also because of the methods of the tradents (i.e., those who transmitted and interpreted the tradition), who often dismantled such collections, it was placed at the beginning of this collection in Prov. 22:17-24:22. Thus, without any apparent reason, the number thirty was mediated through another source and was subsequently inserted into the introduction of this wisdom book. The Masoretic text, then, represented an adaptation of a lost Hebrew source that contained portions of Amenemope, particularly its introduction and conclusion. Erman believed that with the discovery of Amenemope the original source had been located, and it was now incumbent upon scholars to emend the Masoretic text with the aid of the original.

In his preliminary discussion of the subject, Hugo Gressmann noted two other parallel passages, which Erman had not recorded.[13] Accepting the emendations proposed by Erman, he used the text of Amenemope even further in an attempt to restore the corrupt Hebrew text to its original state. In Prov. 22:18 Gressmann suggested that the word "together" (*yḥdw*) was really a corruption of the Hebrew word for "peg" (*ytd*), so that the verse should correspond with the Egyptian clause "that they may be a peg (*n'y-t*) on your tongue" (Amen. 3:16).[14] In Prov. 23:7 he translated the Hebrew word *š'r* as *š'r*, "storm," corresponding to the Egyptian word *šn'* in the clause "it is a storm" (Amen. 14:7)[15] and interpreting the Hebrew phrase to mean "as a storm in (your) greed"(!).

Yet, the most striking correspondence between the two texts, recorded by Erman but left without a satisfying explanation, was the number "thirty." It was Gressmann who first pointed out that the third collection in Proverbs (22:17-24:22) not only contained the number "thirty" but also the exact same number of sayings, corresponding to the thirty chapters of Amenemope.[16] This number itself was further evidence of Egyptian derivation, since it stemmed from a very ancient Egyptian tradition, the college of the thirty judges.[17] Gressmann suggested that this tradition, adopted by Amenemope and used as a literary device, was subsequently employed by the editor of the third collection for his own book, entitled "The Sayings of the Wise."

Following the proposal of Erman, Gressmann also concluded that the evidence was in favor of the Egyptian origin of Prov. 22:17-23:11.[18] The content of the two books was the same. The agreements between the two were in large part verbal, even without textual emendation. In fact, Gressmann observed that the only saying in the first part of the third collection of Proverbs not found in some form in Amenemope was the statement about pledges (22:26-27). In addition, there was other evidence to support his theory of derivation.[19] For Gressmann it was obvious that Egyptian influence was evident in other sayings, such as in Proverbs 24:12, where the Egyptian imagery concerning the weighing of

the heart was employed with reference to the Israelite
deity, Yahweh. As far as cultural traditions were concerned, the scribal office was much older in Egypt than
Israel, where there was no scribal bureaucracy until the
development of the monarchy. Therefore the cultural
context also favored the Egyptian origin of a scribal
tradition such as the book of Proverbs reflected. Although the materials in Proverbs that had been borrowed had not been mechanically or senselessly translated, as Erman had implied, in the final analysis the
correspondence between the two sources was clearly a
case of Israelite dependence.

To the ten parallels between Amenemope and Prov.
22:17ff. already adduced by Erman and Gressmann,
Sellin contributed one more, comparing Proverbs 23:9
with Amen. 22:11-14, where caution in speech is ad-
monished.[20] He also added to the number of emendations already proposed. In Prov. 22:19 he emended the
reading of the Septuagint "his way" (τὴν ὁδὸν αὐτοῦ) to
"ways of life" (*drky ḥyym*) and placed it after the verb in
the second clause to read "to cause you to know the ways
of life."[21] In this way he provided an antecedent for the
reference contained in the word "thirty" that followed in
v. 20. In v. 21 he proposed that the whole verse was dependent upon the introductory infinitive "to cause you
to know" (*lhwdyʿk*), so that the two phrases "true sayings"
(*'mry 'mt*) and "to reply" (*lhšyb 'mrym*) were its rightful objects. In Prov. 23:10, contrary to Erman, he adopted the
Egyptian phrase "the boundary of the widow" (*sic*) (*t3š·w
n ḥ3r·t*, Amen. 7:15) instead of the Hebrew "ancient
landmark" (*gbwl ʿwlm*).[22] Similarly, in Prov. 23:4 he reinterpreted the phrase "desist from your understanding"
with the aid of the Egyptian parallel that referred to

46261

"robbery" (*ḥwrʿ*, Amen. 9:16), reading in place its Hebrew equivalent *mbṣtk*, "desist from your 'robbery.' "[23] Another important change that he proposed was the translation "Make an enclosure against your swallowing . . ." for the Hebrew words *wśmt śkyn blʿk* in 23:2 with reference to the clause "it is an 'obstruction' (*śnʿ*) to the throat" in Amen. 14:7.[24]

Sellin concluded that, with reference to both content and form, the direct dependence of Prov. 22:17ff. upon Amenemope was a matter of complete certainty.[25] The Hebrew editors had thoroughly studied the Egyptian source material, had eliminated what was unacceptable to Israelite thought, had assimilated those facets of the instruction of the Egyptian courtiers that were serviceable within the framework of Israelite piety, and then, having exhausted the relevant material, had turned to other sources to complete the collection. Sellin emphasized the fact that the adoption of foreign material, though much greater than anyone had previously dared to accept, was not a mere "reproduction" of ideas but involved a "transformation" of the material. Thus, Sellin came to a new understanding of the wisdom movement in Israel. No longer was the relation between Israelite and foreign wisdom literature a matter of mere ideological influence nor a borrowing of an individual proverb here or there. Rather, it was a matter of direct literary dependence, a fundamental association derived from the interchange of literary documents.

In his second contribution to the subject Gressmann provided a list of all of the parallels between Amenemope and Prov. 22:17ff., including one that had not been previously recorded, the parallel between Proverbs and Ahiqar.[26] In Prov. 22:19 for the Hebrew phrase "even you" (*'p-'th*), emended by Sellin to "ways of life," he proposed "your ways" (*'rḥtyk*), pluralizing the reading of the Greek versions.[27] Similarly, in 23:4 he read "desist from 'your unjust gain' " (*mbṣ'k*), conceding that the word "robbery" proposed by Sellin might be preferable.[28] In place of the usual interpretation of *lhwdy'k*, "to cause you to know" in 22:21, he proposed that the second person pronoun be translated as subject of the verb and take as its object *'mr* "so that you cause to know the truth (*qšṭ*)—the one who commands" (*'ōmēr*), deleting *'mt*, "truth", as a marginal gloss.[29] In Prov. 22:29 Gressmann made two further deletions. The verb "you see" (*ḥzyt*) at the beginning of the verse, which was not found in the Egyptian parallel (Amen. 27:16), was to be deleted as an editorial addition, reflecting the same phrase that appears in Amen. 27:7 (*ptr·n·k*, "see for yourself").[30] The third line of this verse, which refers to men of low estate, Gressmann suspected as a republican addition made in the post-exilic period.[31] In both of these instances the original form of the Hebrew text was determined by its Egyptian source.

The emendations that Gressmann proposed for Prov. 23:2, 5, and 7 were based on the same principle of following the Egyptian original. For the enigmatic Hebrew *wśmt śkyn bl'k*, usually rendered "and put a knife to your throat" (Prov. 23:2), he proposed "and you make a joy of what you swallow" (*wśmt śśn bl'k*) to correspond to Amen. 23:16, "it is a delight in your spittle" (*st ḏ3y-ḥr m t3y·k pgs*).[32] Likewise, in 23:5, instead of the translation "your eyes light upon it" (*ht'wp 'ynyk bw*) of the Masoretic text, he suggested that the Hebrew should correspond with the parallel in Amen. 9:19, which simply employed the verb "see" (*ptr*); therefore he rendered it with the

Hebrew verb *ttbwnn*, "your eye regards it attentively."[33] Since Prov. 23:7 lacked any parallel to the Egyptian clause "it is bitter (*shy*) for the throat" (Amen. 14:8), Gressmann added the phrase "like bitterness in the throat" (*wkmw mr bṣw'r*) to complete the correspondence in the second half of the verse.[34] Sellin's proposal, that in Prov. 23:10 the phrase "boundary of the widow" was more appropriate, he rejected because the meaning was quite general, not an exact reproduction of the Egyptian parallel.[35] Almost without exception Gressmann's changes in the text were premised upon a Hebrew text that was dependent upon Amenemope. Although the nature and condition of the text of Amenemope were not introduced in a way that affected the question of Hebrew dependence, Gressmann did raise the general question of possible textual displacement in Amenemope itself with his suggestion that Amen. 27:16-17 and 1:5-6 needed to be placed in correct order.[36]

To the textual parallels already recorded, Grimme added one more from the Greek version of the Old Testament. Since the Greek proverb did not stand in close connection to its own context, he surmised that it was a marginal addition later placed in the text of the Septuagint. The correspondence of this new parallel was between 24:22b of the Septuagint and Amen. 20:8-9.[37]

24:22b. Utter no falsehood by word of mouth to a king, and let no falsehood of his go out by word of mouth.	20:8-9. Do not enter the court of justice before a prince, and render no false statements.

Besides his suggestions that "his ways" (*'rhtyw*) be read in place of "even you" (*'p-'th*) in Prov. 22:19 and "like a peg" (*kytd*) in v. 18, Grimme put forth three additional emendations.[38] In Prov. 22:20 he divided the phrase "in counsels" (*bm'ṣwt*) into two words (*bm 'ṣwt*), thus eliminating the negative connotation attached to the word "counsel" (*mw'ṣh*) with the translation "in them are (wise) counsels." Rather than delete the verb "you see" (*ḥzyt*) in 22:29, he read in its place the verb "maintain" (*ḥzq*), transferring it to the end of the preceding verse so that it provided the main injunction, "maintain that which your fathers have made" (i.e., established), and eliminated the phrase not found in the Egyptian parallel in the verse that followed. In place of the phrase "from your understanding" in 23:4, he suggested "from your gain" (*mtbw'tk*) as an alternative. The emendations of Grimme were determined by his effort to maintain the consonantal Masoretic text, where it provided a parallel. Amenemope, he believed, was the source of the content of Proverbs, reformulated by the Hebrew editor.

Although the lack of unity in the whole section from 22:17-24:22 had previously been perceived, particularly the noticeable break at 23:12, Grimme divided the whole collection into three sections, corresponding to the breaks in the sources.[39] The first section, which was derived from Amenemope, was taken over by an Israelite as an expansion of those proverbs in the second section of the book (10:1-22:16) which were attributed to Solomon. The second part of the collection began with the group of sayings derived from another source, one of which has come to us through the Aramaic version in the sayings of Ahiqar. The third group began with the introductory saying in 23:19 and extended to the end of 24:22. Thus, the whole section known as "The Sayings of the Wise" consisted of three individual collections of sayings, marked by breaks at 23:12, 23:19, 24:22.[40]

In the most complete study of the relation between Israelite and Egyptian wisdom up to this time, Paul Humbert asserted that Hebrew dependence upon the Egyptian sources was primitive, original, and permanent, extending throughout the wisdom literature.[41] The clearest
evidence of this dependence is found in Prov. 22:17-
23:11, an extraction and adaptation of maxims found in
Amenemope achieved in the pre-exilic period. Although
no proverb outside of this collection could be certified as
a direct, verbal adoption, in this section all of the
maxims, with the exception of 22:19, 23, 26, and 27,
were derived directly from Amenemope. To bring the
Hebrew text into its actual direct dependence upon its
source, Humbert was not only willing to accept many of
the emendations proposed but also to suggest a series of
other changes in conformity with the Egyptian source.

Using the text of Amenemope as a guide, Humbert
proposed the following emendations. In Prov. 22:20 he
suggested the translation "they are counsels and knowledge" (ḥm ꜥṣwt wdꜥt) in correspondence with Amen. 27:8,
where the Egyptian pronoun "they" (st) appears in the
initial position in the clause "they instruct."[42] In v. 21 in
place of "truth" (qšṭ) he proposed the reading "refute"
from the intensive verb qaššēṭ, equivalent to the Egyptian
word ḥsf, "oppose," in Amen. 1:5. By following
Gressmann's emendation of ’mt to ’mr (sic!), he was able
to reproduce his interpretation of Amen. 1:5, "to refute
the charges of the one who utters them" (r ḥsf wšby·t n ḏd
sw) in the Hebrew qšṭ ’mr, "to refute the charges of the
one speaking." In Prov. 22:25 he replaced "lest you
learn his ways" (pn-t’lp ’rḥtw) with "lest you reproach
him" (tḥrp ’wtw), eliminating the tautology in the two
verbs rꜥh and ’lp, and bringing the clause into close cor-

respondence with the word "slander" (*w'3*) in the passage "beware of slandering him" in Amen. 11:16.

By accepting several proposed emendations of Prov. 23:7-8, Humbert was able to bring these verses into almost exact correspondence to Amenemope.[43] He translated Prov. 23:7 as "For this would be like a 'hurricane' (*š'r*) in the 'throat' and a 'vomiting for the gullet.' " For *bnpšw* he suggested *npš* meaning "throat," since the context concerned something put in the throat, not a miserly action. Removing the suffix from *bnpšw*, he attached it to the second clause of the verse, which he changed to read, not "thus he" (*kn-hw'*) but "and a vomiting for the throat" (*wlgrn qy'*), parallel to Ecclus. 31:12, "do not open your throat at it" (*'l tpth 'lyw grnk*, LXX μὴ ἀνοίξῃς ἐπ' αὐτῆς φάρυγγά σου'). In the second half of the verse Humbert sought to find a parallel for the Egyptian clause "his desire is perverted in his body" (*iw ib·f sh3 m h·t·f*, Amen. 14:10) by reading *wlbw ynbl 'mw*, "but, in himself, . . . 'his heart will act insultingly' " for the usual rendering "for his heart is not with you" (*wlbw bl-'mk*). In 23:8, by taking *dbr* to mean "thing," he completed the correspondence of this section, the clause "you would have lost your good things" being parallel to Amenemope's "you are emptied of your good" (14:18).

With the work of Humbert we have reached the point where the dependence of Israelite wisdom upon its Egyptian prototype is considered to be almost total. The process of emendation is now carried out, not only on the basis of the coincidence of words and phrases, but by the use of phrases from various verses in a similar context in Amenemope. Consideration is given primarily to the possibility of reproducing the alleged original correspondence because the priority and influence of the

0260847

source are almost absolute. Hereby, a patchwork of
Egyptian phrases from different verses may be used to
reconstruct the text of Proverbs. The use of the text of
other versions, such as the Septuagint, other wisdom literature, or even other contexts in the Old Testament, is
limited to its capability of producing evidence in favor of
readings that correspond to the Egyptian source. According to Humbert, Egypt was a principal source for
the forms and content of Israelite wisdom, and
Amenemope was the one source for the phrasing and
wording of the text of Prov. 22:17-23:11. Although
many scholars had adopted this approach and many
others would also follow it, in the work of Humbert the
theory of Egyptian influence upon Proverbs had reached
its zenith.

Up to this point only the linguistic and philological aspects of the relation between Amenemope and Proverbs
have been discussed. Of course, scholars who adopted a
theory of Egyptian influence did not limit their consideration to purely philological matters. They also
theorized about the actual process by which Egyptian
wisdom penetrated the wisdom movement in Israel. The
initial difficulty, which all historical reconstructions encountered, was provided by the original source itself.
Until the date of Amenemope was settled, little could be
said about the conditions in which it originated and then
came to be circulated. The proposed dates for this work
covered a span of almost a thousand years, from the
twentieth dynasty in Egypt (twelfth century) to the Hel-
lenistic era (fourth century).[44] Nevertheless, in spite of
the difficulties, several scholars made proposals seeking
to illuminate the possible conditions in which the wisdom
literature of Israel could have come into contact with
and thereby assimilated Egyptian materials.

Erman had recognized in Proverbs 22:17-22:22 an adaptation of Amenemope.[45] Unfortunately, the original book was dissected by the collectors of Hebrew wisdom, men who in his view pursued their work with little understanding. In their hands the book was so completely divided that we would not have recognized it if the Egyptian original had not been discovered. The original book, a translation of the Egyptian book into Hebrew or Aramaic, was done by a Jew living in Egypt, who discovered Amenemope because it was being used as a school text. Wishing to make it available to his contemporaries, he adapted it to the Jewish faith, retaining the original division into thirty chapters. By the time it reached the Old Testament, however, it had been so dismantled by the collectors of proverbs that the significance of the number was lost and only a few places in the text, beyond what one would imagine to be possible, retained their original form. Since Erman dated Amenemope quite late, possibly as late as the sixth century, he assigned the original Hebrew adaptation to the Persian or Saitic period.

Gressmann did not accept Erman's post-exilic date for the collection in Proverbs, nor his negative judgment on the state of the Hebrew adaptation of Amenemope.[46] He attempted to trace the connections in a broader sphere, particularly in the international character of the wisdom movement. The origins of this movement were in the royal courts whose emissaries were scribes, particularly men of foreign origin. Previously, evidence for the existence of such a movement had been confined to testimony dating from a very late period, the era in which the wisdom of Ahiqar was produced. Gressmann drew attention to evidence that indicated that such a movement may have been in existence from a very early period. The presence of Canaanite scribes in the court of Egypt in the Amarna period, the letter of Hori concerning the Egyptian scribe in Palestine during the thirteenth century, and the universality of the wisdom tales associated with King Solomon attested an international exchange of scribal personnel and ideas at a very early age. It became quite apparent to him that the principal mediators in such exchanges were those scribes who traveled from one court to another.

The first evidence that this phenomenon was present in Israel in historical times dates from the era of David. One of David's scribes, Sausa (= Shavsha, 1 Chron. 18: 16) bore a Babylonian name.[47] From the time of Solomon the Hebrew tradition gave unanimous testimony to the participation of all nations in the production of wisdom literature. Egyptian influence, and more particularly, Amenemope itself, confirmed Gressmann's thesis that the wisdom movement was already international some five hundred years before Ahiqar. With regard to Proverbs, Gressmann concluded that its middle portions, representing the older collections of wisdom, dated from the seventh or eighth centuries, when it was most probable that a collection of Assyro-Egyptian literature was made. Included among those older collections of wisdom was Prov. 22:17-24:34, located just prior to the section assigned to Hezekiah (25:1). Although individual elements in it might be dated as early as 1000 B.C., in its final form it also dated from the later period of kingship. However, Gressmann did leave the question of the amount of gnomic poetry that Israel appropriated from foreign sources unanswered, at the same time suggesting for its solution a thorough study of the influence of foreign cultures and of the prophetic movement in Israel.

Sellin also accepted a pre-exilic date for the collection in Prov. 22:17ff.[48] Associating it with the tradition of Hezekiah, he assigned the collection to the end of the eighth century. Evidence from the prophets Hosea and Isaiah, where images of Osiris and wise men are mentioned, led him to conclude that this was attestation of a new penetration of Egyptian culture. Sellin was not certain as to precisely how this influence was articulated within the context of Israelite thought. He also left the question of the relation of this section to the rest of Israelite wisdom literature unresolved. He surmised that it could merely have been a case of cultural exchange achieved on the basis of the admiration of Egyptian wisdom on the part of an Israelite.

According to Humbert the *Sitz im Leben* of Israelite wisdom was the royal court and the diplomatic circle.[49] In its origins the movement was to be associated with the birth of the Israelite monarchy, the appearance of a politically astute king in the person of Solomon, and the intense development of a civil service. It was at this time that Israel was open to religious and cultural influences from Egypt, with which she had close political relations. For these reasons Humbert was willing to assign a very early date to the origins of the wisdom movement.

As in Egypt, the development of wisdom in Israel arose out of the practical necessity of recruiting and educating young men for positions at court, particularly the sons of high officials. Yet, what had taken centuries to develop in Egypt developed more quickly in Israel owing to this foreign influence. Israelite wisdom rapidly achieved a high stage of development. Whereas Egyptian wisdom had focused upon the scribal office and the work associated with it, Israelite wisdom gave its attention to the man himself, the person and not the office.

By the time of Hezekiah its concerns had moved from a professional interest to a moral characterization of the individual representing a high religious achievement. It was this stage of wisdom that Humbert regarded as its most evolved form, its highest attainment. Of course, this tendency was confirmed by the moral tone of the compilation ascribed to the men of Hezekiah. It was also apparent in the democratization of wisdom contained in Prov. 22:17ff., where the injunctions usually associated with the scribal bureaucracy in Egypt are lifted out of their professional context and universalized. The scribe and the tradition associated with him are now related to the "man" in Proverbs (22:29).[50] Although Humbert set a very early date for some of the materials in the collection in Prov. 22:17ff., it was to the stage of the development represented at the time of Hezekiah that the whole work was to be assigned.

Although Kittel agreed with Gressmann and Humbert that the wisdom movement in Israel was dependent upon foreign influences to some degree, especially evident in the use of Amenemope by Proverbs, he separated those elements which he deemed unessential in the development of Israel's thought from those which he felt had played an integral role.[51] Among the former he included important elements related to the older collections of wisdom, particularly the professional ethic and the characterization of men into certain types. Kittel considered these to be subsidiary elements, not embedded in the mainstream of Israelite thought. Of course, in the collection contained in Prov. 22:17ff., which Kittel assigned to the period between the time of the reigns of Solomon and Hezekiah, these two elements were very prominent (22:29, 23:1-3, 6-7).

On the other hand, Kittel admitted that characteristic traits of Israelite wisdom were a result of foreign influence.[52] But the wisdom movement was not unrelated to other influences. In the Old Testament the connection between the scribe and the royal archive is paralleled by the relation of the prophet to the royal archive, just as the priest and prophet are also mentioned in connection with the wise man. Thus, as a result both of foreign influences and the influence of the prophetic movement, Israelite wisdom attained its zenith in the latest period of Israelite-Jewish spiritual life. The role of the wisdom movement in this was to provide moral and ethical direction, thus laying a foundation leading up to the final and ultimate construction of Hebrew thought, represented in the moral achievement of the prophets and the wisdom of the later period (Prov. 1-9). For this contribution Israel was indebted both to the older collections of wisdom contained in Proverbs and to the influence of Egyptian thought, in spite of the fact that this influence apparently played no substantive role in the development of Israel's later traditions.

In his review of the work of Humbert, the Egyptologist Posener was among the first to reject the idea that the Hebrew collection was dependent upon Amenemope.[53] Apart from those who posited a Hebrew original for Amenemope, he and Herzog attempted to qualify the theory of Israelite dependence without resorting to any theory of Egyptian dependence.[54] Using Humbert's own admissions, that the Hebrew text is not an exact reproduction of Amenemope but rather a resumé, that often the perspective is quite different, and that there are numerous modifications of details, Posener maintained that the two texts were too distant from one another to be able to speak of direct dependence. Particularly in the religious concepts the influence of Amenemope was negligible. Moreover, Humbert's theory that the Hebrew editor had carefully adapted essential Egyptian materials was vitiated by the reduplication of ideas contained in Prov. 22:28 and 23: 10.

Herzog himself moved one step further than Posener and objected *in toto* to the theory of Egyptian derivation.[55] He regarded the attempt to clarify the Hebrew text with the aid of the Egyptian parallels as a failure. The parallels were not only far too general but overlooked decisive differences in the standpoint of the two documents. The egoistic tone of Amenemope was not to be found in Prov. 22:17ff. To explain how other sections of Proverbs, which contained sayings similar to those of Amenemope but do not use it as a source, Herzog suggested that Babylonian influence was probably greater than had been assumed by these scholars.

To show the improbability of any Egyptian source for Proverbs, Herzog studied the differences in detail, adducing parallels from elsewhere in the Old Testament to support his thesis.[56] In Prov. 22:17 the phrase "give ear" (*nṭh 'zn*) was singular as in 2 Kings 19:16 and Ps. 17:6, whereas the Egyptian parallel was in the plural. The emendations of "to my knowledge" (*ld'ty*) by Erman ("to know them," *ld'tm*) and Gressmann ("to know" *ld't*) were erroneous because the infinitive construct, which requires an object in this construction, receives a direct suffixial ending only when the suffix is in the first person singular. The two idioms "the words of the wise" (*dbry ḥkmym*) and "set (the) heart" (*šyt lb*) were common in Hebrew. Thus, the parallelism between Amenemope and

Proverbs was only apparent. Without emendation the Hebrew verse consisted of idioms that were thoroughly rooted in Semitic usage.

In many cases proposed emendations were considered by Herzog to be unnecessary or unduly complicated. In the case of the latter he found the change of "altogether" (*yḥdw*) to "peg" (*ytd*) in Prov. 22:18 to be incorrect idiom or grammatical usage. Since *yknw* ("they may be ready") was a stative verb here, the improvement to "like a peg" (*kytd*) was unnecessary, for it was simpler merely to read the verb as a passive.[57] In 22:19, by rearranging the words "even you" (*'p-'th*) to "you even today" (*'th 'p hywm*), this phrase read very naturally in the context. The phrase "in your belly" (*bbṭnk*) in 22:18 was not to be credited to Egyptian influence as its equivalence to "heart" in Prov. 4:21 showed. Since *qšṭ* ("truth") could be parallel to *'mt*, there was no reason for the deletion of any words in 22:21. Sellin's emendation of *mbyntk* ("from your understanding") to *mbztk* ("from your robbery") in 23:4 was beset with difficulties. It was not in accord with the gender of the masculine references (*bw, w'ynnw,* and *lw*) in the following verse. Also, this word was found mostly in parallelism to *šby* and *šll*, being used exclusively of booty taken in war. The proposal of Grimme, to read "from your gain" (*mtbw'tk*), was problematical because of its lack of accord with the gender of the pronouns following and the absence of the connotation of "gain" in its usage. Although Herzog regarded Gressmann's original proposal of *mbṣ'k* ("unjust gain") as better, he asserted that the text as it stood made perfectly good sense. Similarly, *dbryk* ("your words") in 23:9 provided an acceptable sense, particularly with the parallels in Proverbs 15:26 and 16:24.

Herzog also found that where the Egyptian text could be used as a source for the emendation of the Hebrew text, it offered no real solution to the difficulties.[58] In 22:22 the Egyptian text offered no equivalent to the Hebrew phrase "because he is poor" (*ky dl-hw'*), none at all to the second half of the verse. In reality, the Hebrew text was closer in meaning to a saying found in the wisdom of Ptahhotep. In 23:5 Herzog found no reason why the Hebrew writer should avoid mentioning a goose or duck because it was native to Palestine. In any case the image of a bird for wealth was so common in the ancient Near East that an assumption of dependence was unnecessary. Herzog also suggested that the "man" (*'yš*) mentioned in 22:29 was a Hebrew artisan, having no connection at all with the exemplary Egyptian scribe. The deletion of "you see" (*ḥzyt*) from this verse, and the addition of "maintain" (*ḥzq*) to verse 28 would force acceptance of a Germanism in a Hebrew text!

Nevertheless, the *crux interpretationis* was the word *šlšwm* in 22:20.[59] Herzog admitted that this was the most important support for the theory of dependence upon Amenemope. On grammatical and contextual grounds he rejected any connection of this word with the number thirty, and with this he also rejected Gressmann's attempt to explain away the lack of a determinative with the number, insisting that such a construction was linguistically impossible. In cases where no determinative was present, the number followed some word in the context that clearly indicated what was meant. The attempt to relate the number to "the words of the wise" (*dbry ḥkmym*) did not change the grammatical difficulty, nor would the substitution of any other word, such as "words" (*'mrym*), be permissible. Herzog insisted that the number could not stand there because there was no way to determine its reference.

As for the context, it scarcely provided any help in determining what was meant. The collection of sayings numbered thirty-three; an approximation of the number could hardly be used if it was being employed to explain the section. Moreover, only a third of the sayings had any real relation to the alleged Egyptian source. Herzog's query about this factor, as well as his obvious demand for proof of the relationship of the two texts, was the only strong opposition that the theory of Semitic dependence encountered at its inception.

In assessing the history of the interpretation of the relationship of Prov. 22:17-24:22 and Amenemope, certain limitations in the way in which scholars approached the relationship between the two sources are observable. Very little consideration was given on the part of those who assumed Israelite dependence upon Egyptian materials to the degree to which the assimilation was accomplished. By failing to isolate the possible stage or stages of the assimilation of traditions, the whole question was severely restricted to the one issue, namely, whether one could or could not "prove" dependence. Thus, the long history of the discussion has been accurately characterized by Ruffle as "a kind of academic parlor game . . . 'Spot the Parallel,' with marks being awarded for each ingenious parallel suggested and bonuses for emendations of the Masoretic text on the basis of the Egyptian book."[60] Only by careful observation of the process by which literary materials flow from one culture to another is it possible for us to assess the nature and degree of the dependence. Of course, such an analysis will include a thorough study of Hebrew proverbs within

their own context to determine whether the idiom and
literary form are part of normative West Semitic usage.
Following the second chapter, which deals with the possibility that such questions could be answered by means
of a theory of Egyptian influence, the investigation will
pursue these aspects of the problem.

2

The Theory of Egyptian Dependence

Although most scholars favored the view that Prov. 22:17-23:11 was dependent upon the Egyptian wisdom contained in Amenemope, the suggestion of Budge, that the Egyptian material itself was influenced by Semitic ideas, was adopted by a few scholars. Budge had been deeply impressed by the high character of the ethics and morality of Amenemope and sought to explain this by reference to Asiatic influence. These considerations prompted others to entertain the possibility of a Semitic original for Amenemope.[1] Oesterley was the first to make a case for the theory that Amenemope, at least in part, was dependent upon a Hebrew original. Subsequently, Kevin and McGlinchey sought to substantiate his thesis by detailed comparative studies of Amenemope and Proverbs. Finally, the Egyptologist Drioton raised the issue anew by the introduction of further evidence in favor of a Hebrew original.

In his first article on the relation between Amenemope and Prov. 22:17ff., Oesterley concluded that both documents had made use of an older Hebrew wisdom collection.[2] Quite unlike Budge, Oesterley did not attribute this to diffused cultural influences, nor did he date it in the period before the establishment of the Hebrew monarchy. In its early history Israel was unprepared for such influence; its soil was not receptive, nor was its literature sufficiently advanced to accept any Egyptian contribution. Later, when Israel did enter into the concourse of the nations, it was not in a position to accept foreign ideas because of the dominant influence of the prophetic movement. However, with the fructification of prophetic religion, including the development of a high ethic, Israel and Egypt were in close mutual relations, particularly from the time of Hezekiah to the fall of the Assyrian empire. It was in this period, during the Assyrian eclipse and the restoration of Egypt at the beginning of the sixth century, that Amenemope was written. Since Egypt had already been under the influence of the ethical ideals of Israel for some time, Amenemope not only utilized a common stock of oriental wisdom but also unconsciously reproduced the religious and ethical fruits of Hebrew genius. Like Budge, Oesterley assumed the superiority of the religion of the Semites, located a period in history when mutual relations were most probable, and then posited a theory of Egyptian dependence.

Oesterley adduced historical, religious, and literary support for his theory of Egyptian dependence.[3] Historically, the existence of Semitic loan words in Egyptian documents, as in the case of Papyrus Anastasi, the presence of Aramaic materials in Proverbs, and the testimony of the Old Testament (1 Kings 4:30) pointed toward the accumulation of a mass of wisdom material which had become common property among the peoples of the ancient Near East. In the case of Amenemope he felt that its religious ideas, particularly its conception of God and duty to fellow man, were unlike anything in the literature of the pre-Christian period, with the exception of the Old Testament. Oesterley was notably impressed by the way in which the whole of Amenemope was imbued with a religious ethic of a high order. These two factors, combined with the close parallelism between Amenemope and Prov. 22:17ff., convinced him that both sources derived from a common Hebrew original.

The literary evidence itself, which Oesterley accepted as favoring a common Hebrew original for the two collections, was based primarily on the consecution of parallels in the two books.[4] The parallels themselves could only demonstrate a close relationship. For this reason Oesterley could accept emendations of the Hebrew text, such as the reading "thirty" in Prov. 22:20, without admitting direct dependence. Only at one point, in Prov. 22:21, did Oesterley assert that the author of the original source, or the compiler, copied directly from Amenemope. With reference to the order of verses, Oesterley detected a difference between those portions of Amenemope which appeared in Prov. 22:17ff. and those which were found in the rest of the book of Proverbs. The proverbial material scattered throughout the book of Proverbs appeared consecutively in chapters 10 and

21 of Amenemope. The sayings similar to Amenemope in 22:17ff., appearing consecutively in Proverbs, were dispersed throughout the book of Amenemope. Oesterley deduced from this that if the compiler of Proverbs had used Amenemope, we should expect a consecution of sayings in both books. The rather terse and arbitrary use of·Amenemope by Proverbs required by a theory of Egyptian dependence led him to the conclusion that both Amenemope and the compiler of Proverbs made use of an older Hebrew collection. In this way both the religious content of Amenemope and the similarities to the collection in Proverbs could be most satisfactorily explained.

Whereas the evidence adduced by Oesterley in favor of Egyptian dependence was of a more general nature, it did lay the foundation for the work of Kevin. He was the first scholar to seriously attempt to demonstrate the actual dependence of the Egyptian text upon the Old Testament by an analysis of the literary parallels. The chief evidence for this dependence was the many Semitisms scattered throughout Amenemope, which were to him clear indications of an Egyptian adaptation of a Hebrew original.[5] According to Kevin this adaptation had taken place in the post-exilic period in Egypt in the milieu of the Jewish colonies that had been founded in Egypt.

Although considerable work had been done in the study of the relation between the Semitic and Egyptian languages, the number of Semitisms in this text was so great that Kevin could account for it only by the assumption that the Egyptian writer was acquainted with a book of Hebrew proverbs. Five Semitisms had already been noted, to which Kevin added thirty others.[6] All of them, with one exception, were previously unobserved and therefore absent from the lists of Erman, Ember, and Albright.[7] No other Egyptian moral papyrus employed so many Semitisms as Amenemope.

Kevin was convinced that a satisfactory reconstruction of the original Egyptian text could be made on the basis of the Hebrew parent text. Therefore, he sought to reconstruct the Egyptian text on the basis of the Hebrew version.[8] In Prov. 22:29, the Hebrew clause "you see a man" (*ḥzyt 'yš*) really referred to a "man of vision" (*'yš ḥzyt*; LXX ὁρατικὸν ἄνδρα). In Amen. 27:16 the borrower read "a watchful man" (*'yš s3wy!*) as its equivalent, but this was obviously a misinterpretation of the parallel sense of the correct Egyptian adaptation which according to Lange was "who is clever" (*iw·f šs3*). Similarly, the Hebrew clause in Prov. 23:1, "Consider well who is before you," would originally have been reproduced in the Egyptian clause, "Apply yourself to the man who is before you" (*w3ḥ rḫ·w r ḥ3·t·k*). But the Egyptian translator misinterpreted the Hebrew phrase "before you" (*lpnyk*) and read "your mouth" (*pyk*), thus giving rise to the Egyptian *r(3)·k*, an incorrect interpretation "Apply 'your mouth' at the beginning" (Amen. 23:14).

Thus Kevin could justify his reconstructions of the Egyptian text because he believed that the Egyptian translator had misunderstood the Hebrew original in various places.[9] In Prov. 23:4 the translator had interpreted the Hebrew phrase "from your wisdom" (*mbyntk*) by the erroneous root *byt*, meaning "house," and by separating the prefix from it and equating it with the Egyptian word for "property" (*ḫr·t·k*), had read the clause in Amen. 9:15 to mean "when your property is at rest." In place of the Hebrew idea "grudging" (*r' 'yn*,

Prov. 23:6) he suggested that the translator had misread
"eye" for the word "humble" (*'ny*) by mixing up the consonants, and had misinterpreted the word "evil" for
"friend, fellow citizen." Combining these two ideas produced the Hebrew phrase "humble fellow citizen," thus
effecting the translation "poor man" (*tw3*) in Egyptian
(Amen. 14:5). Likewise, in 23:10, the scribe interpreted
the Hebrew "ancient boundary" (*gbwl 'wlm*) as "boundary

*The Turin Writing-Tablet of Amenemope (24:1-25:9), seventh or
sixth century* B.C. **Courtesy of Georges Posener (Cat. 6237).**

of the widow" (*gbwl 'lmwn!*), reproduced exactly in the Egyptian phrase *t3š·w n ḫ3r·t* "boundaries of a widow" (Amen. 7:15).

The hypothetical nature of Kevin's method and the erroneous results that can be obtained with his approach are strikingly revealed in his interpretation of 24:4, "Verily, the heart of man is the 'lamp' of God."[10] He understood this proverb, as usual, in terms of its Hebrew original found in Prov. 20:27, which used the word "lamp." His justification for substituting "lamp" for "nose" was that the Egyptian scribe had misread or misinterpreted "lamp" (*nr*) for "nose," ('*p*), Actually, the peculiar Egyptian image "nose of god" may be a textual corruption in the British Museum papyrus, where *fnḏ* ("nose") was read instead of the word *fḳ3* ("gift"), a reading attested in the Turin Tablet (fig. 1, right side).[11] What the original saying may have affirmed, then, was that the heart of man was a gift of God. Unfortunately, Kevin's theory of Egyptian dependence and interpretation of the text by a translation process eliminated the most important source for the understanding of Amenemope— Egyptian texts themselves. His attempt to demonstrate the dependence of Amenemope was vitiated both by his methodology and by his misunderstandings of the Egyptian language.

Up to now studies of the relation between Proverbs and Amenemope had been largely limited to the collection beginning in Prov. 22:17, where the similarities were most pronounced. In McGlinchey's study, which also attempted to demonstrate Egyptian dependence, the collections preceding this in Prov. 1-9, 10-15, and 16:1-22:16 were also taken into consideration.[12] In all these sections McGlinchey found the similarities to be too great to deny the existence of some relationship between them and the teaching of Amenemope. Although actual verbal parallels were few, the resemblances of thought, the similarity of phraseology, and the order of words were too many to be a result of chance. However, this did not necessitate a theory of Semitic dependence. In fact, consideration of parallels between Egyptian ideas and other parts of the Old Testament and between Proverbs itself and the Old Testament led McGlinchey to conclude that the influence was from Israel to Egypt.

McGlinchey assumed that where Egyptian materials have close parallels both to Proverbs and to other portions of the Old Testament, they themselves may be reflecting Hebrew idiom.[13] For instance, Amenemope is the only Egyptian wisdom book that deals with landmarks and boundaries, yet this subject is common in the literature of Israel. The eudaemonism of Proverbs, strongly present in Amenemope, is also found in older biblical writings. For example, $st3$ (Amen. 22:3), an Egyptian word deemed to be unknown to Egyptologists, with its parallel $ḥr\ nḫt$, "strong chief" (22:1), was interpreted by McGlinchey to mean "redeemer," akin to the Hebrew $g'l$. This showed that Amen. 22:1 was dependent upon Prov. 23:11.

In other instances ideas that were already a part of the Old Testament milieu needed no special Egyptian source by which to account for them. Phrases such as "pay attention to" ($ḥqšb\ l$), "incline the ear" ($nṯh\ 'zn$), and "hear" ($šm'$) were frequent in wisdom literature.[14] The expression "way of life" ($mi·t\ n\ 'nḫ$), found only twice in Amenemope as well as in some very late Egyptian texts, where Jewish influence could be assumed, was quite common in the Old Testament. In this one case McGlinchey favored Hebrew priority. Nor did the Hebrew word *tkn* (Prov. 24:12) need the Egyptian concept of the judgment of the dead, as Gressmann had asserted, to explain it. Not only was the normal word for "weigh" *šql*, but the Septuagint did not interpret *tkn* to mean "weigh."

Besides long lists of words and phrases showing how frequently certain ideas appeared in the Old Testament, McGlinchey produced one example that apparently revealed its precedence over its Egyptian counterpart.[15] Prov. 23:6-8, though originally belonging after 23:1-3, as the doublet in 23:3a and 23:6b showed, quite appropriately used the words "swallowing" and "vomiting" in a context that concerned dining. In Amen. 14:7-8, these two words, as applied to the property of the dependent, had to be interpreted figuratively. The literal interpretation of these Hebrew words had given way to a figurative one in the Egyptian context, showing that in this case Amenemope was the borrower. Furthermore, other materials that represented normal Hebrew idiom obviously needed no Egyptian source to explain them. In fact, McGlinchey maintained that in such cases Egyptian parallels might well be dependent on influences emanating from the Old Testament.[16]

More than two decades were to elapse before the work of Oesterley, Kevin, and McGlinchey was to be resumed. The majority of scholars had rejected these attempts to show Egyptian dependence as unconvincing, merely reflecting the predilection of their proponents.[17] Now for the first time, however, an Egyptologist presented a series of studies supporting the position represented in their work. The proposals of Etienne Drioton were based on linguistic, literary, cultural, and religious con-

siderations. Together they represent the most careful
and complete treatment of the subject from this perspective.

Drioton was unsatisfied with the linguistic and literary
analysis done by Kevin and McGlinchey. The Semitisms
in Amenemope, which Kevin used to demonstrate dependence, were not confined to a few passages but affected the whole work.[18] Nor was it possible to solve the
problem, as McGlinchey had done, by a superficial comparison of ideas common to the Hebrew and Egyptian
books. Since the language of Amenemope was uniform,
and the Semitisms were distributed throughout the
work, by this method the scholar was restricted to a
comparison of ideas, and this Drioton regarded as an
unsatisfactory way of solving the problem.

In his study of the language of Amenemope, Drioton
observed a peculiar *"sémitisation"* of vocabulary.[19] As well
as numerous cases where Egyptian words were replaced
by Semitic ones, he discovered some seventy Egyptian
words that were not being used with their normal sig-
nification.[20] Nor could their meaning be explained simply as a case of inaccurate linguistic transmission. What
other scholars, such as Griffith, had suspected, pointed
to the real solution of the problem.[21] The peculiar Egyptian words and phrases in Amenemope resulted from
what Drioton called *"une sémitisation de leur sémantique."*[22]
Egyptian words that were normally used in one sense
were found in Amenemope with another, more "isolated" meaning, one that corresponded to a similar Hebrew word in its normal usage. These semiticized Egyptian words pointed to a translation process in which
Hebrew was being translated into Egyptian.

Although Drioton had clearly struck on a new method

with regard to meanings conveyed by individual words, in the matters of idiom and phraseology his approach did not differ greatly from that of McGlinchey. Both scholars sought to show that certain phrases that appeared in Egyptian wisdom literature had already had a long and possibly even more remote ancestry in Hebrew literature. For example, the expression "way of life" (*mꜣ·t n ꜥnḫ*) was regarded as Semitic in origin by McGlinchey because it was found outside the Old Testament only in late Egyptian texts.[23] In the same way Drioton accepted this fact as evidence of Hebrew priority. Likewise, parallelisms such as "give ear, hear" (*nṯh ꜣzn, šmꜥ*) were common in oriental literature, allowing no special pleading as regards their source. Apart from the new interpretation of the significance of Semitic influence upon Egyptian words, Drioton's approach differed from that of McGlinchey only in apparent expertise and extent of application.

Frequently, however, Drioton combined the two approaches. For instance, in Amen. 1:2 the phrase "precepts for well-being" (*mtr·w(t) n wḏꜣ*) contains Egyptian words used with Hebraic connotations reflecting Hebrew idiom.[24] According to Drioton *mtr* normally means "testimony" in Egyptian. The corresponding Hebrew word "testimony" (*ꜥdwt*), can also mean "precept" in Hebrew, a meaning that it has only rarely in Egyptian. In this context, however, "precepts" is the required meaning, corresponding to the phrase "counsels of salvation" (*ꜥdwt šlwm*) found in the Latin of Tob. 1:15 (*monita salutis*). The second Egyptian word, *wḏꜣ*, which normally means *bonne santé*, is also being used with the normal Hebrew connotation of *šlwm*, physical and spiritual "well-being." In this way Drioton perceived in the Egyptian expression "precepts for well-being" the work of a translator seeking an approximation for the Hebrew phrase *'dwt šlwm*. Both the presence of Egyptian words with Hebrew connotations and the existence of Hebrew idioms similar in meaning attested a Hebrew original.

Besides this, Drioton found support for his thesis in certain grammatical and linguistic usages that were rare in Egyptian. Phrases such as the "chest of your body" (*hn n h·t·k*, Amen. 3:13; Prov. 18:8), "storehouse of life" (*wd3 n 'nh*. Amen. 4:1; 1 Chron. 27:27) and "the hands of god" (*·wy p3 ntr*, Amen. 5:4; Ps. 31:5) were considered by Drioton to be, respectively, "unknown, unusual," or "uncommon" in Egyptian literature, yet quite common in Hebrew usage.[25] Such grammatical phenomena as the use of the participle as a verb or the juxtaposition of nominal phrases appeared quite frequently in Hebrew but were only theoretically possible in Egyptian. In Amen. 17:7 the use of the particle *ir* to introduce a nominal phrase, which was acceptable Hebrew usage (i.e., *'m*), was impossible in Egyptian when the second part of the sentence lacked the copula *pw*.

Drioton also discovered natural and cultural phenomena mentioned in Amenemope that did not suit Egypt. The north wind, referred to as an agent of destruction in Amenemope (4:14), was considered to be a bearer of benefaction to the Egyptians.[26] It was the tempestuous south wind that was feared. Both this observation and the mention of the opening of the earth (Amen. 9:20-10:1) clearly reflected the coloration of Amenemope by Semitic thought. Several of the temple customs appearing in Amenemope also had closer parallels to the Old Testament than to Egyptian religious practices (Amen. 6:14-15; 11:3). Finally, the treatment of the elders described in Amenemope was quite contrary to Egyptian custom. Since Egypt was not a patriarchal society, elders were never mentioned in a way that would arouse pity toward them (4:6; 25:8). This portrayed Hebraic, not Egyptian, culture.

Not content merely to demonstrate the existence of Semitic influences, as McGlinchey was, Drioton proceeded to elaborate the conditions under which it would be possible for Hebrew wisdom to be adopted and presented in the form of an Egyptian wisdom book. Since Amenemope contained allusions to Jewish religion and religious affairs, Drioton was able to reconstruct the circumstances surrounding the Egyptian edition.[27] The possible translation of the name "Yahweh" in Amen. 17:5 (Egypt. *wnw*, The One Who Is!) and mention of "the anger of God" (11:4-5) indicated that the book of the thirty sayings was a product of a Jewish community that was aware of the religious controversy surrounding the demand òf the Deuteronomists for the purification of Israel's religion. It was about this time that the Hebrew original, which eventually circulated to Egypt, was composed. This primitive version continued to circulate in Palestine, however, and was eventually incorporated into the book of Proverbs.

Taking this book with them, a group of Israelites made an exodus to Egypt and introduced the tradition of the thirty sayings there. Since this community practiced a form of sun worship free of speculations attaching to Heliopolitan practices, Drioton surmised that they must have left Palestine some time after the fall of Samaria (Ezek. 8:6, 16).[28]

Having settled in Egypt, the community became thoroughly naturalized. They followed Egyptian customs, adopting a good-neighbor policy even in matters of religion (Amen. 11:4-5).[29] Mutual relations with the

Egyptians were good, and the governors of Egypt found among these Jews a good supply of agents for the exchequer (Amen. 17:20-21; 18:15-16). Thus, the community, aware of its need for continuing mutual relations, was quick to censure the zealot, whom they called "the hot man of the temple" (Amen. 6:1-6). In such circumstances prophetic proclamations, such as the prophecy about the eventual subjection of Egypt to Israel (Isa. 19:1-25), were not only premature but could have a detrimental effect. These Jews preferred to live as a community of "silent men" with a quiet trust in the providence of Yahweh.

Some time before or during the period of Persian occupation, an admirer of wisdom, wishing to codify Jewish ethics and to produce a book for this Jewish community living in Egypt, translated the volume of proverbs into Egyptian.[30] Of course, as he did this, he amplified them and adapted them for an Egyptian audience. The only part of Amenemope that was not genuinely Hebraic was the prologue (1:1-3:7). However, this pseudepigraphical introduction, attributing the sayings to a local Egyptian wise man, did give the book a permanent place in the scholarly literature of Egypt. Thus, Jewish moral doctrines were introduced to Egypt and began to exert their influence, as their appearance in Pétosiris several centuries later attests. In Drioton's opinion the translation of the Hebrew version into Egyptian was poorly done by an amateur whose rendition was rather mechanical. How such a literal translation could assume such an important place in the literature of Egypt was not explained by him.

It was not long before it became very evident that the attempt to derive Amenemope from Hebrew sources, at least in the form in which it had been presented up to

the present, was doomed. Even the comprehensive
treatment of Drioton was quickly exposed as inadequate.
Both his theoretical reconstruction and his linguistic and
grammatical analysis were challenged by further discoveries revealing more accurately the place of Amenemope
in Egyptian literature. To verify this assessment, it is important that the evidence deriving directly from Egyptian sources themselves by presented.

Both Williams and Couroyer undercut the work of
Drioton by pointing out several misinterpretations of the
language and syntax of Amenemope, as well as numerous instances of alleged Semitic phrases found in other
Egyptian literature, where no foreign influence could be
assumed.[31] As for the latter, Williams pointed out three
instances of the phrase "way of life" in Egyptian literature outside of Pétosiris. Obviously, no Hebrew priority
could be assumed here as McGlinchey and Drioton had
urged. Drioton's theory of the "semiticization" of Egyptian words was shown to be based on insufficient evidence. The phrase "precepts for well-being," which did
not exist in Hebrew at all, represented a very normal use
of *mtr* meaning "precept" and *wḏ3* signifying "well-
being" in Egyptian. The phrases "chest of your body,
storehouse of life," and "in the hands of God" were also
attested elsewhere in Egyptian literature. Even the
phrase "give ear" (*ỉmỉ 'nḥ.wy.k*), which Drioton asserted
was unknown in Egyptian, appears at least four times in
late Egyptian texts.

Williams also cast serious doubt on the ability of
Drioton to identify Semitic influences.[32] The use of *ỉr*
with a nominal phrase and without a predicative *pw* in
the second clause, identified by Drioton as a Semitism, is
a common construction in late Egyptian as well as in
Amenemope. Drioton's participial construction was also

a misinterpretation of a normal late Egyptian tense. In Amen. 1:3 the reference was not to elders (*3w*) but to "magnates" (*wr.w*), a text that Drioton adduced in support of his reference to the treatment of elders. Finally, Drioton's peaceful north wind hardly befitted the watchful peasant in the *Lebensmüde*, who kept an eye upon his boats as the north wind approached.[33]

Although Williams presented other considerations to support his assertion that Drioton's "thesis of translation from Hebrew or Aramaic has little to recommend it," the theoretical reconstruction of Drioton, that Amenemope was produced by a translator in the sixth or fifth century, collapsed in the face of discoveries published by Peterson and Posener.[34] The ostracon fragment of Amenemope in the Cairo Museum, assigned to the tenth century by Černy, was now augmented by additional fragments of the text. A small sheet of papyrus, pieced together from several fragments and containing a small section of Amenemope (12:7-14:5) as well as a few words from the portion immediately preceding (10:18-12:6), was published by Bengt Peterson from a collection of antiquities that had been brought to Stockholm at the end of the nineteenth century (fig. 2). At the same time the French Egyptologist Georges Posener published separate portions of Amenemope from three writing tablets, each with a few lines on them. His publication of the contents of another wooden tablet, discovered in 1905 or 1906, though not significant for the text or interpretation of Amenemope, at least reveals how popular this instruction had become in Egypt during the twenty-fifth or twenty-sixth dynasty, that is, the eighth to the sixth centuries B.C.

Of course, Amenemope could be dated strictly on paleographic evidence or more generally on the basis of

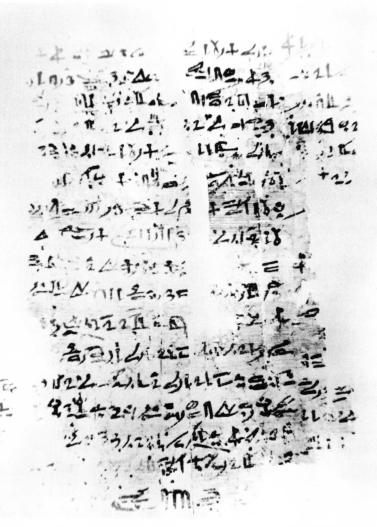

The Stockholm Fragment of Amenemope (10:18-14:5), eleventh to the eighth centuries B.C. Courtesy of Bengt Julius Peterson *(MM 18416).*

thematic considerations. The former more objective method allowed a *terminus ad quem* as early as the eleventh century, certainly the eighth century at the latest (twenty-second dynasty). A thematic approach permitted a *terminus a quo* as early as the Rameside era.[35] Posener maintains that by the vertical position of the Egyptian hieroglyph for the numeral ten, appearing in a cultic calendar on the back of the British Museum papyrus of Amenemope, this particular text cannot be dated earlier than the middle of the sixth century B.C.[36] It is now quite evident, of course, that the reconstruction of the circumstances surrounding the composition of Amenemope presented by Drioton is impossible.

For these reasons further consideration of the theory of a Semitic original for Amenemope in the forms in which it has been presented by scholars is unnecessary. This does not mean that the general question of the influence of West Semitic culture upon the language and literature of Egypt is unimportant. To deal with the larger subject of the mutual relations between Syria, Palestine, and Egypt in the areas of language, literature, art, architecture, and religion is beyond the scope of this study. The presence of West Semitic peoples in Egypt and the general influence of the cultures of the Levant upon Egypt, reaching back as far as the Old Kingdom, strengthens the case for mutual dependence. But it is not decisive with respect to the question of a Semitic original for the text of Amenemope. Only by a detailed study of the literary forms and idiom can it be determined which particular culture was the heir that received the literary heritage. It is to this study that we now turn in order to determine the way in which these literary materials were transmitted and how they were assimilated by the scribes who received them.

3

The Adaptive Stage

The indebtedness of the wisdom literature of Israel, and
especially the proverbial literature, to sources that derive
from an international wisdom movement in the ancient
Near East has been variously estimated.[1] Since Egypt
played an important role in this movement, it has been
assumed, especially since the discovery of Amenemope,
that Israelite wisdom was dependent upon an Egyptian
prototype.[2] The object of this study is to analyze this assumption with reference to the content and forms of the
literature found in the book of Proverbs. Its central
thesis, growing out of a study of the history of the tradition, is that we can isolate three stages marking the fixation and development of Egyptian materials appearing

57

in this book.[3] These three stages are characterized by the degree of the assimilation of these elements in the wisdom literature of Israel, whether they have been *adapted* with few changes, *assimilated* with important modifications, or *integrated* into Hebraic literary traditions so that little remains of the original contribution.

Previous attempts to demonstrate the dependence of Israel's wisdom literature upon foreign influences have been vitiated, in some cases, by an approach that was too rigid. Scholars have sought to demonstrate the presence or existence of derived elements by emending the Hebrew text to make it correspond to the original source. When such attempts have been proved to be artificial, the presence of external influences has been denied. The unfortunate dichotomy that such an approach had engendered is quite evident in the study of the history of the interpretation of the relation between Proverbs and Amenemope. Literary dependence has been affirmed or denied without sufficient consideration of the degree to which foreign elements have been assimilated into the literary traditions of Canaan. Sometimes such traditions and usages, whether cultural or religious, have affected the process of transmission before such materials have reached the Old Testament. In other instances this process has continued in the Old Testament itself even after they have been fixed in one form. With regard to the content and forms adopted from Egyptian sources, a comparison of these with similar materials in the wisdom literature of Israel helps to determine the degree to which they have been affected in the process of transmission and to mark their place in the history of the tradition.

The first stage in the process of transmission is one of

adaptation. In this case a word, idiom, grammatical usage, or literary form appears in the new language in a form closely approximate to what it was in its native tongue. In some cases the correspondence will be very precise; in other cases, however, since a process of literary reproduction is always very flexible, minor changes will be made. The important matter, denoting the process of adaptation, is that essential literary elements, whether material or formal, are not naturalized so that they appear to be products of their new environment. Where changes do occur, they do not affect the essential usage or structure found in the original. Of course, to trace foreign elements back to their source involves detailed literary comparisons combined with a study of the history of the tradition. Only in this way is it possible to observe where the essential contribution of the original source, even though foreign, has been left unchanged.

Although Egyptian materials appearing in such a form in Canaanite literature are few, it is important that one observe the process where it is clearly at work. In a letter to Abimilki, king of Tyre, to Akhenaton, one of the kings of Egypt during the Amarna period, we have one example of Egyptian hymnic expressions being adapted in a letter written in Canaanitized Akkadian.[4] They occur in two parts of the letter and are noticeably present in the first part, which is cited below. As early as 1918 Gressmann had identified the Egyptian background of these sections, and in 1932 Alt demonstrated that one expression in the second part of the letter was a pure Egyptianism. It appears in line 53, where Pharaoh is described as a "wall of bronze" (*dūri siparri*), an expression frequently used of Egyptian monarchs but not found in Assyro-Babylonian sources, at least, not in reference to a king.[5] Although more recent study has somewhat eroded the view that the hymn contains numerous Egyptianisms, in the first part three expressions appear to be directly dependent upon Egyptian sources.

```
 5  bēlī
     šamaš ša ittaṣṣi ina muḫḫi
     mātāti ina ūmi u ūmima
     kīma šīmat šamaš abūšu damqu
     ša iballiṭ ina šēḫīšu ṭābi
10  u isaḫḫar ina ṣa-pa-ni-šu
     ša it-ta-ṣa-ab gabbi māti
     ina pašāḫi ina dunni ZAG ḫa-ap-ši
     ša iddin rigmašu ina šamê
     kīma ᵈAddi u . . . ku-ub gabbi
15  māti ištu rigmīšu[6]
```

```
 5  My Lord
     is the Sun-god who rises over
     the lands day by day
     according to the decree of the Sun-god,
        his gracious father,
     who gives life by his sweet breath
10  and who becomes young when he hides,
     who has set the whole land
     at rest by the power of his arm (? might),
     who thundered in the heavens
     like Hadad, and the whole land . . . (? quakes)
15  from his thunder.
```

For purposes of comparison, without maintaining that the following reconstruction represents an actual Egyptian *Vorlage*, some clue to possible idiomatic correspondences and difficulties may be given by an Egyptian rendition.

5 p3-Rʿ (*or* p3 'Itn) nb·ỉ p3y wbn (*or* ḫʿ) ḥr
   t3·w rʿ nb
   mỉ wḏ·t p3-Rʿ ỉt·f nfr
   dy ʿnḫ m t̠3w.f nḏm
10 rnp m ỉmn·f sw
   dy ḥtp t3 r ḏr·f
   m wsr ḫpš·f
   ḫrw m p·t
   mỉ Stḫ . . . (? ktkt) t3
15 r ḏr·f ḫr ḫrw·f[7]

It is difficult to determine whether the scribe was translating directly from an Egyptian hymn or freely creating his own composition, using Egyptian idiom and expressions. In view of the unusual combination of elements, it is probably a new hymnic composition suited to the context of the letter. The presence of actual Egyptian words in Akkadian, with the exception of titles, which merely show precision, is difficult to determine. As early as 1909 Böhl suggested that the Akkadian word for "might" *ḫa-ap-ši*, which has been regarded as an Egyptianism from the word *ḫpš* ("arm, might"), was a Canaanite gloss, derived from the root *ḥbš* ("bind"), which is used of coercive action (Job 40:13).[8] Since a legitimate Canaanite root (*ḫpt̠*, "soldier") exists for this word, these proposals may have to be set aside. Nevertheless, the phrase "by the power of his might" is unusual in Akkadian and hardly Egyptian, whereas "by the might of his arm" is good Egyptian idiom, suggesting the possibility that this word is an actual Egyptian gloss or a wordplay on the common meaning of the root. The other expression that Albright regarded as an Egyptianism is found in the second part of the letter, the word *a-ru-ú*, which appears in line 28 in parallelism with the verb *hadiāti*, "I am happy." For this word he proposed the Egyptianism *hrw*, "being contented" or "satisfied," an old perfective form in the third person. However, the Egyptian *h* is normally rendered into Akkadian by *ḫ*, leading us to expect *ḫarû* if it were an actual Egyptian word.[9] Moreover, the lack of agreement between the proposed Egyptian word, which is in the third person, and the verb in parallelism, which is in the first person, makes the construction quite awkward and unlikely.

In the adaptive stage the matter of dependence does not, of course, rest only on the direct borrowing of words. We do possess examples of idiom that show the process of adaptation. For instance, although the idea contained in the phrase "make alive by the breath," referring to a deity, is found in Assyro-Babylonian sources, weakening the force of the more general Egyptian parallels adduced, the combination "make alive by the *sweet* breath" is an Egyptianism.[10] Also, the appearance of the Canaanite word *ṣa-pa-ni-šu* in line 10 reproduces an association common in Egyptian hymnic materials where there is a play on the name of the sun-god Amon, which refers to his being as *imn*, the one who is hidden, and his activity as he disappears each day.[11] The verb immediately preceding this, however, has not yet been fully understood. Albright suggested for *isaḫḫar* the meaning "diminishes," from the root *ṣeḫērum*, "be small." However, in Egyptian mythology the sun-god may rest at night, but he is not thereby considered to be diminished as a deity. If we take the Akkadian root that has been proposed in its second sense, "to be youthful," this meaning reproduces a motif in Egyptian hymnic literature that is somewhat paradoxical yet nevertheless was used by the Egyptians. Just as the sun-god is born anew and is youthful when he rises, by a transfer of this idea to his entrance into the underworld he is also regarded as becoming youthful when he sets.[12] Since this verb can also signify "become young," as in the meaning of a name in the Gilgamesh Epic, the idea expressed is an Egyptian one, that the sun-god becomes youthful when he sets. The two ideas of youthfulness and hiddenness are found together in Middle Kingdom hymnic materials.

'Imn R' m ḥwn rnpy ỉmn ḏ·t·f m 'Imn wr[13]

Amon Re is a rejuvenated youth whose body is hidden as Amon the Great.

Finally, we observe that the hymn contains a motif that appears several times in Egyptian sources and is also found in Canaanite literature. This motif may be traced back to the Middle Kingdom period in Egypt, appearing in the story of the struggle between Horus and Seth in the historical records of Ramses II, and in the report of the journey that Wenamon made to Byblos. It refers to the activity of Seth who, when he is defeated in the struggle with Horus, is given the right to dwell with Re and thunder from the sky. The motif appears in the three sources in the following lines, respectively.[14]

Mtw·f ḫrw m t3 p·t

And he shall thunder in the sky.

hmhm·t·f mỉ Bʿr m t3 p·t

His battle cry is like (that of) Baal in the sky.

Mk ỉ ỉr ʾImn ḫrw m t3 p·t
ỉw dỉ·f Stḫ m rk·f

Behold, it was after he had appointed Seth in his time that Amon thundered in the sky.

The same motif is found in Canaan in the religious texts of Ugarit, where Baal is the equivalent of the Syrian Hadad and the Egyptian god Seth. In this case the reference is to Baal.

wtn . qlh . bʿrpt

He gives forth his voice in the clouds.[15]

In this occurrence of the motif at Ugarit we observe that the last element refers to the "clouds," not the heavens as in the Egyptian examples. In the Amarna hymnic material, where this same idea occurs, the scribe follows the Egyptian word, not the Canaanite one. Hadad thunders in the *heavens*. Although this difference is very slight, given the other Egyptian materials in the passage we must conclude that this provides further evidence of the dependence of the Amarna writer upon his Egyptian sources. Of course, with respect to the deities themselves, this adds nothing new to either of them, since they were both regarded as heavenly beings.[16] In view of the long period of time during which the two gods were equated, it is not at all surprising that this function should be assigned to both of them. In fact, it is possible that in Egypt it might eventually have been more exclusively associated with Seth as the result of Canaanite influence. What is important here, however, is to show that the particular form in which the motif appears represents Egyptian influence upon the scribe.

Having studied carefully one example that clearly shows how Egyptian hymnic themes are being adapted into Canaanitized Akkadian, we are in a position to make some deductions that will help us in the identification of a similar process occurring elsewhere. The most obvious mark of adaptation, of course, is the presence of transliterated words. With the exception of technical words, which merely show scribal precision, it is doubtful whether any such words appear in this letter, but if they are present, they simply strengthen the case for dependency. Another earmark of adaptation is the presence of unusual meanings or idioms in the dependent text. It may be that the use of *ṣeḥērum*, in the meaning "become youthful," is an example of this. Somewhat harder to identify are words and phrases that correspond to usages current in the literature of the source but not native to the idiom of the dependent document. Although unusual syntactical constructions may well indicate a process of adaptation, they are hard to identify in our case because we already have a Canaanitized form of Akkadian being used. Yet, unless they are clearly identified, they cannot be of assistance in determining whether or not dependence exists. Stereotyped phrases and clauses, where several elements are found in frequent association, also indicate motifs that have developed in the process of adaptation but have remained rather fixed. Most important for the identification of adapted materials is the fact that the correspondence need not be verbal but merely ideological. Thus, minor changes, such as the substitution of other words with equivalent meaning, changes in word order, or even the introduction of individual new elements, for example, the name of a deity, together with necessary adjustments to accommodate tenses of verbs, subordinate clauses, and pronouns, are part of the process of adaptation. Even with these modifications, the essential elements, indicating foreign origin, remain.

Two further observations, which may play an important role in such a process, concern the connection between the literary type and the appearance of borrowed elements. A perusal of Egyptian sources reveals that phrases such as "who gives life" (*dỉ 'nḫ*) or "sweet breath" (*ṯ3w nḏm*) are frequently found in Egyptian hymnic literature. Thus, it is not unusual that they appear in other sources in the same type of literature. This does not mean that they could not appear elsewhere, but the fact that they are reproduced in the same literary genre indicates that there was a fund of stock phrases available to the writer or translator working with a given literary form. Strengthening this conclusion is the fact that borrowed materials often appear in clusters, so that the identification of foreign elements is facilitated. Where a conglomeration of such materials appears in a specific literary genre in Egyptian and reappears in the same literary type in another culture, the case for dependence is considerably strengthened. Although these factors have often been overlooked, they serve as ancillary guides, aiding in the task of locating the original sources of derived materials.

With these criteria as guides, we may now study the proverbial literature of Israel to determine whether we can show a process of adaptation at work in the adoption of Egyptian materials. In Prov. 22:24 we have an example of Israelite adaptation of a common Egyptian theme found in Amen. 11:13.

אל־תתרע את־בעל אף
ואת־איש חמות לא תבוא

Make no friendship with a man given to anger,
nor go with a wrathful man.[17]

m ỉr snsn n·k p3 šmm
mtw:k ḫnḫn·f r sdd

Do not associate with the hot man,
and do not approach him to converse.[18]

In the first line the correspondence between the two
admonitions is very close. The unusual use of *rʿh* in the
Hithpaʿel stem to signify "make friends with" may be accounted for by its close equivalence to the Egyptian
word *snsn*, which also means "befriend."[19] In the second
line the Egyptian idea of approaching this man to "converse" is absent, probably because of the modification of
the verse according to the structures of Canaanite-
Hebrew parallelism. However, we may note that the second element "go to" (*tbwʾ ʾt*), which is parallel to the idea
"befriend" (*ttrʿ*), closely approximates the Egyptian
meaning "approach" (*ḫnḫn*). The idea expressed in the
phrase "wrathful man" (*bʿl ʾp*) is Egyptian, not Israelite,
as the parallel in Prov. 29:22 (*bʿl ḥmh*), which is an exact
equivalent of the Egyptian image, shows.[20] Therefore,
we may conclude that this admonition was inspired by
the Egyptian prototype.

In this Hebrew adaptation of an essentially Egyptian
type, the parallel phrase *bʿl ḥmh*, "a man of heat," that is,
"anger," clearly marks the correspondence. Prov. 29:22,
using the very same phrases, only in juxtaposition, characterizes this man in essentially Egyptian terms, as is
shown by other Egyptian parallels.

אישׁ־אף יגרה מדון
ובעל חמה רב־פשׁע

A man of wrath stirs up strife,
and a man given to anger causes much transgression.

sw dỉ·t sn·w ṯṯṯ

He causes colleagues to quarrel.[21]

m-ỉr nhb ṯṯṯ [ỉ]-r-m p3 t3-r[22]

Do not seek a quarrel with the hot-mouthed man.

This association of the hot-tempered man with disputa-
tion and wrongdoing traces back to the earliest Egyptian
wisdom literature and becomes one of the principal
themes in Amenemope. Although the concept "hot" is
also employed figuratively in Semitic sources, the use of
this image to characterize a well-known type of person is
peculiarly Egyptian, whence it came into the book of
Proverbs.[23]

In other proverbs, where a process of assimilation is
beginning to take place, the hot-tempered man is contrasted with his counterpart, the "silent man."[24] It is important to note, however, that this typical Egyptian characterization is not directly represented by any single
Hebrew concept. A series of phrases are used to present
the attributes of this character-type.[25] That these descriptions do actually represent an Egyptian model is attested by the description qr rwḥ, "cool of spirit," which is
found in parallel to ḥwśk 'mryw, "he who restrains his
words," in Prov. 17:27. For the silent man, in contrast to
his hot-tempered rival is "cool of body." A Theban tomb
inscription describes him as "silent, calm (= cool) in
temperament . . . calm in expression."[26] As this concept
is naturalized, the Semitic phrase 'rk 'pym, "slow to
anger," is introduced as an equivalent.

However, in one text we have a wordplay in which the central characteristic of the "silent" man is directly introduced. Of course, plays on words and ideas are a feature of proverbial literature. One such example is found in the poem concerning the "hot man of the temple" in Amen. 6:1.[27] Even though the imagery facetiously depicts this "hot man" as a wild tree drowning in water, his end is presented in imagery that is not only a play on his name but also strikingly contradicts the context.

t3 st3 t3y·f ḳrs·t[28]
The flame is his burial shroud.

A similar wordplay on the two types is found in Prov. 15:18, which contrasts the man who is "slow to anger" with the "man of heat."

איש חמה יגרה מדון
וארך אפים ישקיט ריב

A hot-tempered man stirs up strife,
but he who is slow to anger quiets contention.

The verb šqṭ, "be quiet," which is very close in meaning to the Egyptian word gr, "be silent," does not appear as an exact equivalent, although it is clear that other idioms present essentially the same idea. Nor is this Hebrew verb ever used in connection with "strife," except in this one instance. But just as a "man of heat" stirs up strife, so a man who is slow to anger "silences" (= silent man) contention. Compare with this the statement of the Kmyt:

'Ink gr ḫnty d3r srf m ḳm3 sp·ty
I am silent, superior in controlling
(my) temper (= warmth) as one who is close-lipped (?).[29]

COLUMN IX.

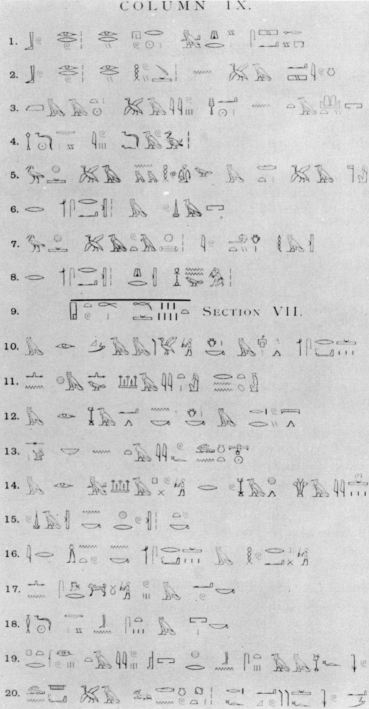

In this one instance the similar Hebrew word presents the equivalent function of the "silent man."

As well as adapting ideas from Egyptian wisdom literature, it is possible to demonstrate at least one instance where a whole proverb has been taken over from the book of Amenemope. A comparison of Prov. 15:16 with its Egyptian antecedent, found in Amen. 9:7-8 (= 16:13-14) is an example of this (fig. 3).

3ḫ p3wty·w ỉw ḥ3·ty nḏm
r wsr ḫr šnn[30]

Better is bread when the heart is glad
Than riches with vexation.

טוב־מעט ביראת יהוה
מאוצר רב ומהומה בו

Better is little with the fear of the LORD
than great treasure and trouble with it.

The comparative form of these sayings is common in Egyptian and Israelite literature but is lacking in Sumero-Babylonian sources.[31] We can observe the development of the form of this saying in the one of the oldest Egyptian wisdom books, the instruction of Ptahhotep.

gr·k 3ḫ st r tftf
If you are silent, it is better than flowery speech.[32]

The appearance of this form in the wisdom of Merikare from the Middle Kingdom period marks a transitional

The Hieroglyphic Transcription of Amenemope (9:1-20) by E.A. Wallis Budge. **Courtesy of the British Museum.**

stage in which it is becoming a fixed literary form in wisdom literature.

šsp bỉ·t nt ʿḳȝ ỉb
r ỉwȝ n ỉsf·ty

> More acceptable is the character of the trusted man
> than the ox of the evildoer.[33]

The substitution of ȝḫ ("better") for šsp in the Papyrus Moscow 4658 indicates that in the late period this had become a standard literary form. Each of these two earlier proverbs contains one of its two essential elements, the introductory formula ȝḫ . . . r and the nominal elements comprising the comparison.

A comparison of these two proverbs reveals that they are employed in independent statements, are complete units in themselves, and are brief and balanced. In the example cited, the Hebrew version is similar both in form and content. Although the comparative form is frequently used in the Old Testament, as a *Weisheitsspruch* it is marked off by its independence and nominal structure, precisely as the Egyptian is.[34] With regard to content, the two words describing wealth are cognates: both of them are used particularly of treasure that is stored. The Hebrew word ʾwṣr ("treasure") also means "storehouse," and the Egyptian word wsr ("riches") makes its implied meaning explicit in other contexts by adding the phrase m wḏȝ, "in the storehouse."[35] The two words "vexation" (šnn) and "trouble" (mhwmh) are also similar in meaning. Coincidentally, the Egyptian form derives from the verb meaning "be ill, suffer" (šnỉ), and in one context the parallel

Hebrew word (*mhwmh*) is used of distress caused by illness.[36]

In two places, however, the Hebrew version is different. It has substituted the word meaning "little" (*m't*), which usually refers to agricultural produce when used as a noun, for the Egyptian word (*p3wty·w*), which may refer to "sacrificial loaves," reflecting the priestly vocation of the author of Amenemope. A more significant change is found in the substitute of the phrase "with the fear of Yahweh" (*byr't Yhwh*) for the Egyptian clause "when the heart is glad" (*iw h3·ty ndm*). Since the Egyptian word *ndm* literally means "sweet," and the cognates of the words with this meaning in Hebrew are not used with heart except *twb* ("good"), which already appear at the beginning of the line, this may have led to the choice of a phrase that lacked correspondence.[37] It is difficult to explain, however, why a word like *śmh*, "joyful," which is used in connection with the word "heart," was not employed.

Another possibility is that the Hebrew writer fused the Egyptian proverb and its companion, which immediately precedes, into one.

3h p3 nmhw m dr·t p3 ntr
r wsr m wd3

> Better is the poor man in the hand of the god
> than riches in a storehouse.[38]

This would explain the reason for the substitution of the phrase *byr't Yhwh* in Prov. 15:16. This Hebrew equivalent comes close to the idea contained in the Egyptian prepositional phrase *m dr·t* (lit. "in the hand of"), as its use in Amen. 24:11 shows. The poor and afflicted were thought to be in the charge of God. The phrase "with the fear of Yahweh" would have been chosen to express the religious aspect of the Egyptian saying. In either case the essential elements representing the Egyptian version are present in the Hebrew adaptation.

There are other factors that suggest a direct relationship between these two sayings. The currency of this saying, found twice in Amenemope, as well as in three versions of Proverbs, once in the Psalms, once in Ecclesiasticus, and once in Demotic wisdom, exhibits its popularity.[39] Moreover, the association of content and form, both in Egypt and Israel, is evidence for an associated development. In Amenemope, where five different proverbs are found utilizing this form, four of them are concerned with riches and poverty. In the older collections of Proverbs, where thirteen are found, seven deal with the contrast between poor and rich. Of course, once this form was adopted, it is not unusual that it would inspire numerous other sayings of related content.

On instance of this is found in Prov. 15:17. As in the case of Amenemope, this literary form has attracted a second proverb of the same type as a companion. This leads to the conclusion that we are dealing here with a cluster of borrowed materials. Already we have observed how Prov. 15:18 has been minted from Egyptian materials. Therefore, it is not unusual to discover that Prov. 15:17 has recast in embellished form the idea of Amenemope 9:7-8.

טוֹב אֲרֻחַת יָרָק וְאַהֲבָה־שָׁם
מִשּׁוֹר אָבוּס וְשִׂנְאָה־בוֹ

Better is a dinner of herbs where love is
than a fatted ox and hatred with it.

Of course, the presence of the poetic parallelism, as is not the case with Prov. 15:16, as well as the Semitic derivation of the phrases, points toward a creative process in which an essentially Egyptian idea and form are inspiring a new but related proverb. The association of these three proverbs, one of which is a direct adaptation and the other two of which more or less paraphrase Egyptian ideas, strengthens the case for dependency. Although the degree of identity fluctuates from one proverb to another, this is not unusual, as we have already observed in the case of the letter of Abimilki. Furthermore, the possibility that these sayings may have circulated independently and been brought together here by an editor helps to explain this unevenness.

The existence of Hebrew proverbs utilizing the same form as their Egyptian prototype means that the process of adaptation involved not only ideas and content but also forms. As already observed, a purely grammatical form eventually evolved, in Egyptian wisdom literature, into a distinctive kind of artistic saying (*Weisheitsspruch*). The adaptation of a proverb or proverbs bearing this form obviously gave rise to new proverbs of the same form. Thus, the twofold criteria, form and content, are employed to identify sayings that may show some dependence upon Egyptian wisdom literature. Form, then, becomes a very important consideration in the whole matter of identifying the sources that have brought about an enrichment of the wisdom traditions of Israel.

Although the number and variety of forms are much greater than have previously been estimated, it is true that the two principal forms of the older wisdom of Israel were the proverb (*Weisheitsspruch*) and the admonition (*Mahnrede*), as the divisions in the collections of proverbs show. Attempts have been made to trace the admonitory form back to Egyptian influence. Since the admonition, easily identified by its negated jussive form, is characteristic of Egyptian wisdom in all of its periods, Hermisson asserts that it is not a genuine Israelite form but was originally derived from Egypt or Mesopotamia.[40] On the other hand, in his thorough study of the admonition and related forms Richter concluded that they had originated in Israel and reflected the *Sitz im Leben* of the school and court. A fundamental reason for the divergence is the definition of "form" on the part of each scholar. Richter limited his study to an analysis of purely formal elements and thus was able to observe what he thought were the origin and development of the admonition within the Israelite ethos. Therefore, he assumed that the form of the admonition need not go begging for its birthright. On the other hand, Hermisson objected that *"eine begründete Mahnung ist noch kein Mahnspruch.*[41] The sharp contrast between the two older collections of Israelite wisdom, one containing almost entirely declarations and the other consisting of admonitions and imperative utterances, led Hermisson to limit Richter's wider use of purely formal elements when it came to the wisdom literature.

That the form is rooted in Canaanite Hebrew tradition is attested by its occurrence in Ugaritic literature (2 Aqht 6:34-35a).

al tšrgn . ybtltm.
dm . lǵzr . šrgk . ḫḫm (?)

Do not beguile, O Virgin!
For to a hero thy lies are loathesome![42]

This old form, employing a negated jussive and a corroborative causal clause with *ky*, "because," is found not only in various contexts and usages over one hundred and fifty times in the Old Testament but is also attested in the ancient poetic traditions of Israel (1 Sam. 2:3).

אל־תרבו תדברו גבהה גבהה
יצא עתק מפיכם
כי אל דעות יהוה
ולא נתכנו עללות

Talk no more so very proudly,
   let not arrogance come from your mouth;
for the LORD is a God of knowledge,
   and by him actions are weighed.

This example is interesting because the verb *tkn* occurs three times in Proverbs.[43] It has been assumed that this term is directly connected with the Egyptian cult of the dead where the heart is weighed. However, this is quite obviously incorrect since *tkn* is a broader term and is used of the knowledge of Yahweh, not the judgment after death.

In any case, the use of the form elsewhere in Hebrew poetry, as well as at Ugarit, attests an independent origin within the Hebrew-Canaanite milieu. In the older declarative wisdom of Israel in Prov. 10:1-22:16, the vetitive ('*l*) is used three times and the corroborative causal clause with *ky* is used in one clause following an imperative, as well as in numerous other declarative proverbs.[44] The vetitive ('*l*) with a corroborative *causal* (*ky*) clause occurs eleven times in Prov. 22:17-24:22, closely corresponding to its use in the poetic passages cited from 1 Samuel and in the Ugaritic literature.[45] Furthermore, the presence of the admonition in Assyro-Babylonian wisdom, where corroborative causal clauses follow without an introductory conjunction, corresponds to Egyptian and Ugaritic usage. This evidence predisposes the matter of origin in favor of a common tendency of Oriental wisdom and does not require special pleading concerning derivation and use.

This discussion of form does not exhaust the possibilities in this area, for form also pertains to literary criticism involving the larger compositions. Unfortunately, consideration of the wisdom movement is often vitiated by a failure to isolate the literary forms and perceive the audience and intent of larger compositions. Because we can perceive several different literary genres included under the rubric "instruction" in Egyptian wisdom, it can help in this regard. Among these literary compositions we may distinguish the traditional form, as in Ptahhotep, propagandistic wisdom, such as in the case of Ammenemes I, what has been called the "panegyric," a type of composition that eulogizes the king and sets forth the mutual responsibilities of king and people, and also a model school book for scribes.[46] Of course, all of these are possible sources for the types of forms we perceive in the larger literary compositions present in the book of Proverbs.

Up to now the one instance that has been singled out as an example of the adaptation of an Egyptian literary form is the composition in Prov. 22:17ff. The principal evidence that has been introduced in favor of this interpretation is reading of the Qere, *šlšym* in 22:20, and the discovery of thirty sayings in the composition, which ends at 24:22. This has been compared with the conclusion of the book of Amenemope, which contains thirty chapters (27:7-8; frontis.).

Ptr n·k t3y 30 n ḥ·t
St sḏ3y-ḥr st sb3y

Regard for yourself these thirty chapters;
they amuse; they instruct.[47]

Of course, ancillary support has been found in the close
parallelism between the admonitions in Prov. 22:17ff.
and the content of Amenemope. As I have already observed, with few exceptions scholars have assumed that
Amenemope has played a large role in the formation of
this small book of precepts.

Unfortunately, the larger question that concerns the
distribution of the forms of the sayings in Proverbs has
not been brought up in this connection. Since the first
four parts of the book are obviously divided according
to the forms of the proverbs, respectively, the wisdom-
sentence (chaps. 1-9), the proverb proper (10:1-22:16),
the admonition (22:17-24:34), and mixed forms (admonitions and proverbs, chaps. 25-27), one is inclined to look
for some explanation for this editorial rationale.
Whereas Egyptian wisdom shows a preference for the
admonition, mixing other forms with this type, Assyro-
Babylonian sources tend to separate them and use only
one form in a book.[48] The mixing of these forms, together with the use of an introductory study, is characteristic of the later period. It would appear, therefore,
that the editors of the book of Proverbs have followed a
similar pattern. This would explain the sharp break at
22:17, where the *Weisheitssprüche* abruptly cease and the
introduction to a collection containing mostly *Mahnreden*
begins.

If one can perceive Semitic influences at work in the

shaping of the form of the book of Proverbs, the same question may be raised concerning the precept-collection in 22:17ff. Unfortunately, with the exception of one notable book, the introductions to most Sumero-Babylonian collections of this type have been lost. However, the discovery of a precept collection at Ugarit, the wisdom of Šube'awilum, makes it possible to compare its form with that of Prov. 22:17-24:22 and Amenemope.[49]

	Šube'awilum	Proverbs	Amenemope
Intro.	I:1-8	22:17-21	I:1-III:7
	Author Book Addressee	Book (Anon. Author-Addressee)	Book Author Addressee
Body	I:9-III:22	22:22-24:20	III:8-XXVII:6
	15 sections	30 (?) sayings	30 chapters
Concl.	IV:1-11	24:21-22	XXVII:7-17
	Treatise Source	Admonition	30th chapter: character and object of book
Colophon	IV:12-16		XXVII:18-XXVIII:1
	Number of lines Scribe Service		Ending Scribe Service

A study of these three books of precepts shows that this literary genre is international. Regardless of its original development, whether by spontaneous parallel development or by international exchange, this type of collection became the property of both Mesopotamia and Egypt. Therefore there can be no doubt that the general conformity of the collection in Prov. 22:17ff. to this genre is the result of such an international literary tradition. All three commence with an injunction to "hear," mention the nature of the book, present their precepts, and finish with a brief conclusion. Like the wisdom of Šube'awilum, Proverbs begins the very first line with a plea for a hearing. Yet, in a way similar to that of Amenemope, the author continues with a description of the object of the book before introducing the matter of authorship and audience. Although the form of the collection in Proverbs bears a close resemblance to the general form of the other two books, it is anonymous, lacks a separate conclusion, and the final admonition concludes with a summary of the general context of the work, not a separate treatise (Šube'awilum) nor a characterization of the book (Amenemope).

Because of this free use of the tradition on the part of each writer, it is not possible to plead for a special derivation of the collection found in Prov. 22:17ff. on the basis of general similarities in form. Whether an Israelite author has or has not adapted a specific Egyptian model of the general literary form that goes under the rubric "precept-collection" depends on the interpretation of *šlšym* in Prov. 22:20. Should it be read *šlšwm*, "formerly" (*Kethib*), *šl(y)šym*, "noble things" (*Qere*), or *šlwšym*, "thirty" (Amenemope)?

A series of objections have stood in the way of a confident acceptance of the reading "thirty," even though it has been adopted by most scholars.[50] As regards the literary unit, it has been urged that thirty sayings cannot be found there but must be produced by an artificial

manipulation of the count. Grammatically, the number
was considered an anomaly without individual or contex-
tually defining element. Proposed emendations have
been rejected because they violate Hebrew grammar or
do not improve on the adverb contained in the present
consonantal Masoretic text of Prov. 22:20. Finally, the
parallelism with *hywm* in the preceding line (22:19) and
the desire to avoid needless emendation of a text that
showed remarkable preservation have been presented as
decisive objections to such proposals, which seek to connect Proverbs with Amenemope.

Excessive confidence in the Masoretic Text as regards
the number "thirty" is not warranted. A case in point is
the use of the number to describe the famous thirty
warriors of David. The text is full of ambiguities, reading "three," or "thirty," or "captains."[51] In 2 Sam. 23:13
the Masoretic Text has "thirty" (*Kethib*), where "three"
(*Qere*) should be read. In 23:18 an erroneous numerical
ending, which is read "three," is preserved in most Hebrew manuscripts in obvious contradiction to the context.
These errors may trace back to the ambiguous *hšlšy* at
the beginning of the section in 23:8, which is best interpreted "three" (LXX). The later tradition does not improve upon this, for the parallel passage in 1 Chron.
11:11 simply increases the confusion. Both the *Kethib*
("thirty") and the *Qere* ("captains") are inferior readings,
and the original number of enemies is changed from
eight hundred to three hundred! Moreover, it is apparent that where the context does not require it, the tradition tends to remove the number in favor of the word
"captains" (*Qere*: 1 Chron. 11:11, 12:19).

Nor is the grammatical objection that a number must
appear with its defining element insuperable, even

though in most cases in the Old Testament this is true. In 2 Sam. 24:12, when the heart of David "smites" him after he has numbered the people, and he confesses his error to Yahweh, the word of Yahweh comes to him through Gad, the prophet, who declares,

שלש אנכי נוטל עליך

Three things I offer you.

Although the context of the later parallel tradition in 1 Chron. 21:10 is clarified by referring the verb "smote" (*wyk*) in v. 7 to the intention of Elohim, not to the heart of David, the number stands alone in 2 Samuel without any defining element. No word in the preceding passage indicates what is meant by the "three," and the two references in the rest of the verse, a number and a pronoun (*'ḥt-mhm*), are dependent upon it. The meaning is supplied by the context, particularly the verb "choose" (*bḥr*). It refers, of course, to the three kinds of divine punishment.[52]

Likewise, the "thirty" of Prov. 22:20 could stand alone, receiving its implied meaning from the verb (*ktbty*) or simply referring to "thirty things." That this is not the case, however, is suggested by its clear reference to a well-known Egyptian wisdom tradition related to the number. Just as 1 Chronicles introduces the "thirty" (2 Sam. 23:18-19) as a kind of renowned group, even though "mighty men" have been mentioned in the context, the "thirty" judges/chapters/sayings could well have passed into the Canaanite wisdom schools from Egypt without needing a defining element with it. In any case it is clear that no objection can stand in the way of the grammatical usage of the number here.

The conjectural consideration that would interpret the Hebrew text as a number is strongly supported by the versions. The Septuagint, the Syriac Peshitta, the Latin Vulgate, and the Sahidic Coptic version of Proverbs attest a numerical interpretation.[53] Although the versions have misread the person of the verb as second, instead of first person, they preserve the adverbial use of the number "three times." The peculiar τρισσῶς of the Septuagint appears to be an interpretation, not a literal translation of the Hebrew. The normal Hebrew expression for "three times" is either šlš rglym or šlš p'mym.[54] In its adverbial usage this expression of time is rendered by several Greek expressions in the Septuagint τρεῖς καιρούς, τρίτον, and τρίς but never by τρισσῶς.[55] This would suggest that possibly only one word appeared in the Hebrew text. The Greek translators could have read the consonantal text as an erroneous dual form šlšym, meaning "three times," or interpreted the present text, šlšwm, as an error for "three." Obviously, when the meaning of the "thirty" chapters of Amenemope had been lost, they would be puzzled if such a number appeared, and without a tradition to guide them they would be inclined to interpret it to make some sense of the verse.

The Latin Vulgate, which corresponds more closely to the present Masoretic Text, also reads the number adverbially, "in a threefold manner." Both the Palestinian and Egyptian traditions must have preserved the wāw between the second and third consonants of šlwšym. Otherwise, there would have been no point to their substitution of such a number in place of a very natural adverbial usage in parallelism with another such temporal element in the preceding verse (hywm). Whereas the Septuagint omits *hywm* in Prov. 22:19 and interprets *šlšym* numerically, the Masoretic Text displays the adverbial usage in verse 19 and brings *šlšwm* into agreement with it. Jerome, on the other hand, attests a point in the tradition midway between these two, reading the adverbial use of the noun (*hodie*) in v. 19 and the numerical usage (*tripliciter*) in v. 20. If the adverbial interpretation had been a firmly rooted tradition, understood and accepted, it would be much more difficult to substantiate the connection between the thirty chapters of Amenemope and Prov. 22:20.

Therefore, we must conclude that the author of the collection of sayings in Prov. 22:17 ff. has adapted an Egyptian wisdom tradition around which to develop his book. The fact that the book can be generally divided into thirty small sections, dealing with approximately twenty-four to twenty-eight subjects, provides a general guide for understanding the way in which the composition has been shaped around the number of sayings.[56] If in the process of the tradition the number was lost, as appears to be the case with the Masoretic Text of Prov. 22:20, the exact number of sayings would become meaningless. Additions or subtractions could, and apparently did occur. The fluctuations of the text are shown by the doublets and the presence of an additional saying in the Septuagint (24:22b).[57] Of course, it is possible that the tradition of "thirty" chapters or sayings became a numerical catchword, just as the tradition of the "thirty" (judges) in Egypt referred to the law court, not the precise administrative arrangement.

Also, the allusion in the rhetorical question of Prov. 22:20 is best understood in this sense. The meaningless reading of the *Qere* "noble things," or the general in-

terpretation of the Vulgate "in a threefold manner"
empties this rhetorical question of its pertinent force.[58]
It is possible that the division of the book into general
precepts (22:22-23:18), warnings about evil kinds of
people (23:17-24:2), and wisdom and government
(24:3-24:22) provided a kind of general scheme for the
interpretation of Jerome, and this must remain as
another possible way of dealing with the question.[59]
However, the divisions between the sections are not that
sharp, and no such tradition seems to be preserved from
the early period. Moreover, the Masoretic Text obviously
retains the plural ending in both the *Kethib* and *Qere*. It
is simpler to explain its text and the interpretation of the
versions from an original number in the plural. Thus,
the author of this collection begins with an appeal to an
ancient and revered tradition of Egyptian wisdom, which
was mediated through the wisdom schools of Palestine,
to give to his book the authority and weight of tradition.

    An analysis of the literary form of this little book of
precepts shows that the variegated materials are subordinated to a scheme that is based upon the Egyptian
tradition of thirty. The fact that we cannot identify each
of the elements with certainty is not a decisive objection
to this. For instance, the simple question as to whether
the introduction (22:17-21) or last verse of the book (24:
22) is to be included in the count of sayings or forms a
separate conclusion is hard to decide. The creative use
of such literary traditions is too free to allow us to place
an imprimatur on any one enumeration. However, the
broken alphabetical pattern in Prov. 24:1-5, which ends
with the third letter of the Hebrew alphabet (ג), is evidence that the materials collected are being subordinated
to a larger scheme.[60] As already observed, adaptation

does not imply rigid conformity. What it does signify is that the content and form are not native to the literary traditions of the culture in which they appear. In this case the form of this book, and some of its important elements, are being provided by an Egyptian model.

In this chapter we have observed how the Israelite wisdom schools adapted Egyptian ideas, proverbs, and literary forms in the development of their own traditions. But it has also become evident that as these materials were shaped to the patterns of the existing culture, they were altered. In the cases studied, a careful attempt has been made to observe this process, so that Egyptian materials could be clearly identified. The results gained have been small, but sufficient to demonstrate a connection. Where such materials have not been preserved in a form close to the original, their assimilation to the culture of Syro-Palestine can be observed. It is this process that must next be studied in order to determine what further Egyptian materials may have been preserved in a different state and what influence they may have exerted on the development of Israelite wisdom.

4

The Assimilative Stage

The second step in the adoption of Egyptian wisdom by Israel involves a process of assimilation. This may simply be a continuation of the adaptive stage, in which foreign materials are further modified in accordance with the literary traditions of Israel, or it may be an independent stage that has occurred in Syro-Palestine prior to the adoption of such Canaanitized elements by the Old Testament.[1] In some cases the form representing the adaptive stage has been lost and the original cannot be determined. In other cases, however, it is clear that a proverb that originally appeared in one form has been recast into a different form. By comparing these with the Egyptian original, it is possible to trace the adaptive and assimilative stages and observe the effect that they have had upon the adopted materials. Unfortunately, only a small amount of material is available, and it affords us only a brief glimpse into the total process.

For this reason the assimilation of foreign materials and their use in the tradition depends, to some degree, on factors that are not easily determined. What knowledge the tradent had of the source of a proverb, whether dependent upon or independent of its original context, the setting into which he placed it, and the effect that poetic traditions have in stereotyping utterances—these make it difficult to identify assimilated materials. Later stages of the tradition may represent the independent production of new proverbs utilizing older forms, or simple changes of older proverbs to fit them into new contexts. However, a study of the history of the tradition shows that certain changes in the materials can be observed that manifest a stage midway between adaptation and integration, where direct dependence is scarcely demonstrable but unusual similarities suggest some relationship. This may be called the assimilative stage.

In the assimilative stage the form and content of the proverbs and precepts are modified so that they appear in a naturalized state. Egyptianisms have undergone a process of "semiticization" so that correspondences may no longer be verbal but merely ideological.[2] The same ideas are now conveyed by natural Hebrew idioms chosen because of their approximate correspondence to the Egyptian idea. Similar forms are now modified by Canaanite-Hebrew literary traditions, causing alterations in the original. Larger literary units are no longer directly borrowed and applied but are inspired on the basis of Egyptian models so that the correspondences are more general, though not yet fully identifiable on the basis of Canaanite-Hebrew literary forms. Such correspondences are too close to deny literary influence yet scarcely precise enough to affirm direct dependence.

In the study of the adaptation of Egyptian themes on the part of Israelite wisdom, the unusual use of certain Hebrew expressions, which were exact equivalents of the Egyptian terms, pointed to the presence of certain Egyptian motifs embedded in the proverbial traditions of Canaan. Of the seven proverbs dealing with the "hot" and the "silent" man in Proverbs, four verses provide almost exact equivalents, Prov. 15:18, 22:24, 29:22, and 17:27. In the second stichos of Prov. 15:18, however, a natural Hebrew expression conveying an equivalent idea is introduced as a contrast to the hot-tempered man. Instead of "cool of spirit" (qr rwḥ, Prov. 17:27), which provides a verbal correspondence, the phrase "long of visage," that is, slow to anger ('rk 'pym), an equivalent Hebrew idea, is introduced.[3] Elsewhere its contrast is provided by a Hebrew idiom that is parallel to this expression, "short of spirit," that is, impatient (qṣr-rwḥ, Prov. 14:29). What was originally represented by equivalent words is now being rendered by equivalent ideas, such as "one who rules over his spirit" (mšl brwḥw) in Prov. 16:32. Of course, as long as the essential motif is present, that is, the depiction of a particular type of man, and the Hebrew expressions approximate the Egytian characterization, we are still at the assimilative stage. Only when the text begins to move away from the essential motif, and new parallels, which no longer embody the same idea, are introduced, are we moving from the assimilative to the integrative stage.

Another mark of the assimilative stage is the modifica-

tion of Egyptian proverbs and precepts by the
Canaanite-Hebrew traditions of *parallelismus membrorum*.
Although Egyptian poetry also uses this literary device, it
is not so rigidly employed.[4] We have already observed
that Prov. 22:24, which adapts the idea contained in
Amen. 11:13, changes the Egyptian form to effect the
parallelism of the two lines. This is an important criterion for the determination of adapted and assimilated
materials. In the case of the adapted form in Prov. 15:
16, the Hebrew text does not show the precise parallelism often found in such proverbs, because of the close
correspondence in the second line to the Egyptian original.

If Prov. 15:16 reveals the initial adpative stage, marking the fixation of this Egyptian proverb and its form in
Hebrew wisdom, the history of the tradition shows how
the saying developed. Prov. 16:8 displays a fully assimilated saying.

טוב־מעט בצדקה
מרב תבואות בלא משפט

Better is a little with righteousness
than great revenues with injustice.

In this example the proverb has been modified in accordance with Hebrew poetic forms. "Righteousness" and
"justice" are frequently found in parallelism, and with
the use of this pattern the correspondence between the
Hebrew and the Egyptian (Amen. 9:7-8) in the second
line is lost.[5] Also, it may be that the substitution of *tbw'h*,
"revenue," for *'wṣr*, "treasure," effects a closer correspondence to *m't*, which also refers to agricultural produce.[6]

Of course, the assimilation of a proverb does not occur without some effect upon the meaning. It has been suggested that Israel's superior religious heritage brought into being an intensified ethical insight, which shows itself in a study of the proverbs.[7] That this proverb represents any superior "ethicizing" tendency, however, must be seriously questioned. From a study of the context of Amen. 9:7-8, two important considerations emerge. First, it is clear that Egyptian proverbial literature is to be interpreted by its context, particularly where themes are developed.[8] The context of chapter 6 of Amenemope develops the subject of the unjust acquisition of riches, and moves to a climax in the comparative proverb:

3ḫ ỉp·t ỉw dỉ·s n·k p3 nṯr
r 5000 m gns

Better is a measure which the god gives to you
than 5000 (gained) by means of violence.[9]

This theme is continued with a statement concerning the transiency of unjust gain, to which the two sayings related to Prov. 15:16 are appended.

Therefore, in the second place, the context supplies the ethical meaning that does not appear to be present in Amen. 9:7-8. The "glad heart" is a result of a way of life that is in conformity to divine law, and the vexation is caused by the trouble accompanying the unjust acquisition of wealth. For this reason the interpretation of this theme found in Ecclus. 30:14, though apparently consonant with the meaning of Amen. 9:7-8, is really quite different.

κρείσσων πτωχὸς ὑγιὴς καὶ ἰσχύων τῇ ἕξει
ἢ πλούσιος μεμαστιγωμένος εἰς σῶμα αὐτοῦ.

Better off is a poor man who is well and strong in con-
stitution
than a rich man who is severely afflicted in body.[10]

At this late stage in the tradition, this form has been integrated into a context treating the subject of health and
illness. The original subject, the superiority of honest
poverty to unjust riches, has disappeared altogether.

Thus the assimilation of a proverb is not without its
effect upon the history of the tradition. The introduction of the terms "righteousness" and "injustice" in Prov.
16:8, whether representing a modification of Prov. 15:
16, or an independent creation inspired by the similar
forms, has produced a proverb that actually makes more
explicit the meaning suggested by the context of Amen.
9:5-8. This saying also reflects Canaanite-Hebrew patterns of thought in its form and content. Consequently it
has become the bearer of the tradition, not Prov. 15:16.
Therefore, Prov. 28:6 and Ps. 37:16, which represent a
later stage of the tradition, develop from Prov. 16:8.
The assimilation of a proverb to Canaanite-Hebrew
modes of thought represents the decisive step over
which the movement of foreign materials into Israel
must flow before they are fully absorbed into the tradition.

However, it is not always the case that later traditions
will develop from earlier ones in a way that is consonant
with the original intent. Ecclus. 30:14 is an example of
this. The treatment of the matter of riches and poverty
in Demotic wisdom also exhibits this tendency. In fact,

with reference to the two moral papyri entitled "The Instructions of 'Onchsheshonqy" and "The Papyrus Insinger," one can illustrate the movement in both directions. Papyrus Insinger 27:3 strengthens even further the attitude toward riches presented in Amenemope.

> ne-'n mw(t) n 3yt a 'nḫ n tm šyp
>
> Better to die in poverty than to live without (a sense of) shame.[11]

In this saying the question is one of honor and shame. For death by poverty is to be preferred to a life without a sense of shame wherein its possessor is willing to do any shameful thing in order just to live. This is not a movement toward asceticism but simply the development of a theme current in wisdom literature.[12]

On the other hand, the wisdom of 'Onchsheshonqy exhibits a contradictory tendency. In a cluster of comparative proverbs, a saying about poverty completes a series that derogates a foolish son and an evil brother.

> n-'n mwt a 3yt
>
> Better death than want.[13]

The influence of the context is decisive in the interpretation of this proverb. The triad of sayings is completed by one that reflects on the utter wretchedness of poverty. It stands in tension with two other proverbs in the same book.

> mn 3byn m-s p e:'r-mwt
>
> There is none wretched except him who has died.[14]

n-nfr tp(?) n ḥq' a mwt n 3yt

Better to grow accustomed to (?) hunger than to die of
want.[15]

Obviously, these proverbs are reflecting upon aspects of
human experience. The sharp focus upon this one negative aspect makes it impossible to have a clear view of
other dimensions of the same problem. In this case the
free and creative use of wisdom traditions in association
with a particular assessment of life has created sayings
that run counter to the more generally accepted attitude
toward poverty and death on the part of Egyptian wisdom.

In the case of the number "thirty," however, the tradition does preserve a continuity with its earlier stage. In
one sense the versions do mediate a form that is midway
between the original number and the later Masoretic
tradition.[16] If the Hebrew tradition misunderstood or
lost the meaning of the original number, and a corruption of the text occurred, as far as the Hebrew manuscripts are concerned, no stage half-way between the two
is preserved. Only by a comparison of the text of the
versions, particularly the Septuagint and the Vulgate,
can we detect a modification in the text that could be
regarded as a midpoint. Apparently the versions contain
an interpretation that is closer to the original intent of
the word than the Masoretic Text. This interpretation
attests a more accurate vocalization of the text. What
these tradents did was to interpret the number according to the sections in the collection (Vulg.), or recast the
verse so that it made sense to them (LXX, Syr., Coptic).
Therefore, it is only by a conflation of the numerical
reading of the Septuagint and the plural of the Masoret-

ic Text that the original "thirty" can be evinced. In a somewhat looser sense, then, we can speak of the assimilation of the "thirty" sayings to the "threefold" tradition of the versions.

This review of the adapted materials that have been assimilated into the Old Testament really posits a stage of tradition from which one can move both backward and forward. In some cases it is possible to propose a hypothetical text upon which a missing adaptive stage was based. In other cases, however, because the equivalents are too general, though it is possible to perceive a parallel, it is not possible to demonstrate any direct dependence. What can be claimed as direct dependence, in some instances, may well be free creations developing, not from the original but from the familiar idea represented in the assimilative stage. Likewise, as we move forward in the tradition, there is a dual movement, both toward and away from the original. Themes may be strengthened by the later tradition; they may be rejected by it. In either case it is still quite apparent that it is the tradition that is the catalyst, bringing forth new forms, even if they are mutations.

In Prov. 22:17-23:11, for which direct dependence upon Amenemope has been claimed by most scholars, a cluster of materials is found that appear to have been assimilated into the Hebrew tradition. In fact, as I have just observed, in one case the original number has been fully integrated by the Masoretes.[17] Since the process of assimilation and integration is very fluid, this unevenness is not surprising. Some materials that have been adapted, particularly literary forms, may never change. Others appear only in their final stage. Where such a conglomeration of materials appears in a modified form,

to demand that one justify dependence only on the basis
of precise equivalences is unreasonable. Also, to insist on
reconstructing a hypothetical original on the basis of alleged parallelism, even where the words of the original
text are not understood, is fallacious.[18] In the final
analysis, only by a careful study of the parallels in the
context of the Hebrew tradition can one determine the
degree of dependence and raise the question concerning
an intermediate (in this case, assimilative) stage. Where
the case is not clear, it may rest simply upon the sheer
number of coincidences, each of which lessens the possibility that they were "accidental" and increases the presumption in favor of dependence.

The introduction to "The Sayings of the Wise" in
Prov. 22:17-21 shows a close correspondence to
Amenemope. The introductory appeal that formally begins both the Egyptian and Hebrew collections of wisdom typifies this close connection (Amen. 3:9-10; Prov.
22:17).

'Imỉ 'nḫ·wy·k sḏm ỉdd·tw
ỉmỉ ḥ3·ty·k r wḥ'·w

Lend your ears, hear what one says,
apply your mind to interpret it.[19]

הַס אָזְנְךָ וּשְׁמַע דִּבְרֵי חֲכָמִים
וְלִבְּךָ תָּשִׁית לְדַעְתִּי

Incline your ear, and hear the words of the wise,
and apply your mind to my knowledge.

Although in the Old Testament the parallelism between
"incline the year" (*nth 'zn*) and "hear" (*šm'*) occurs only a
few times, the two words are associated in at least a

dozen contexts.[20] To this *parallelismus membrorum* a third element ("apply your mind") has been added to complete the correspondence to the three members of Amenemope.

The dependence of Prov. 22:17 upon Amenemope has been denied on various grounds. Herzog objects that the Egyptian word for ears is plural, whereas the Hebrew word is singular.[21] The Hebrew phrases "incline the ear" (*nṭh 'zn*) and "words of the wise" (*dbry ḥkmym*) are not Egyptian. Since "set your heart" occurs frequently, the phrase "set your heart to my knowledge" (*lbk tšyt ld'ty*) does not imply borrowing. In this analysis Ruffle sets the individual words of each language in parallelism, for example, "give" (*imi*) and "incline" (*nṭh*), and denies any dependence because their meanings are not the same. He urges that the similarity of content is due to the similar function of the two passages.

As regards the function of such passages, the tradition of introducing books of precepts with injunctions to "hear" is international. Like the Egyptian and Hebrew books, the wisdom of Šube'awilum, a Canaanite collection of precepts discovered at Ugarit, begins with the same appeal to "hear."

ši-ma mil-ka š[a](?) šu-be-[e](?)-awîl [im^{li}]^m

Hear the counsel of Sube'awilum.[22]

With these we may compare the Ugaritic parallel, which itself precedes a plea concerning the judgment of the orphan and the widow, a theme that is quite common in oriental wisdom.

sm' m' . lkrt t̲'.
ištm' . wtqǵ udn
Hear, O Krt of T̲'
Listen, and be alert of ear.²³

These similarities make it clear that the introductory
form of such books was part of a standard international
tradition.

This, however, does not gainsay the dependence of
Prov. 22:17 upon Amenemope. What it does make quite
evident is that each culture has its own idioms for rendering such an appeal. Although the Egyptian, Hebrew, Mesopotamian, and Ugaritic injunctions all contain
the word "hear," each has its own idiomatic way of employing a verb with the noun "ear" in order to express
attentiveness. Egyptian uses the verb *rdỉ* "give"; Hebrew
makes "ear" object of the verb *nṭh*, which means "turn"
or "bend"; and Ugaritic employs *qǵ*, "bow." It is quite
erroneous to insist upon an exact equivalent in each
case, especially in view of the various idioms that may
exist in any one language for a single idea. Herzog's
demand that the Hebrew word "ear" be plural to agree
with the Egyptian text is also mistaken, because the
Egyptian word is dual, not plural, and the customary
vocalization of the suffixial form of this Hebrew idiom
in the second person is singular.²⁴

Moreover, the decisive matter is not the fact that the
expressions in Prov. 22:17 are native to the Old Testament, but that when one compares the Ugaritic and
Egyptian parallels, it is obvious that the order of the
words lends credence to the assumption of dependence.
It is true that the Hebrew phrase "set your heart" (*lbk*
tšyt), corresponding to the Egyptian "give your heart"

(*imî ḥ3·ty·k*), is found in numerous other contexts.[25] But the important fact is that it is never found in association with the previous set of parallels. Nor is the additional phrase "to my knowledge" (*ld'ty*) ever used in such a context. Since the Hebrew equivalent of the Egyptian *ḥ3·ty·k* ("your heart") is found in *lbk*, the three words "ear, hear," and "heart" occur in exactly the same sequence in the Hebrew version. The parallelism between these two introductory injunctions is too close to allow these sayings to be classified as coincidences under the rubric of international wisdom.[26]

On the other hand, various emendations of the text have been proposed to bring it into closer correspondence to the Egyptian precept. The principal one, proposed by Erman, was the removal of the word "wise" (*ḥkmym*) in favor of the phrase "my word" (*dbry*) and the change to "to know them" (*ld'tm*) in the second line to complete the parallelism.[27] Although the latter form is grammatically permissible, the translation "to my knowledge" offers a simpler alternative. However, there is a good presumption in favor of the emendation to "my word" (*dbry*). First, it would create a natural parallelism with the phrase "to my knowledge" (*ld'ty*) in the second line. Second, the Egyptian precept also begins with a verbal expression and continues with two verbs having objects in agreement with each other. Third, in twelve other contexts in the book of Proverbs where similar injunctions are found, there is always an agreement between the personal pronouns or the nouns in the two lines.[28] Since the title and the colophon, if there was any, appear to be lost, and the section begins with the same expression as is found in the introductory title of Prov. 24:23, Erman's emendation appears to be a very sound one.

A comparison of Prov. 22:17-18 with Amen. 3:9-16 discloses a series of unusual coincidences in usage and word order, which suggest that the Hebrew version is a kind of précis of the Egyptian original. Of course, we have already noted the three words "ear, hear," and "heart" in Prov. 22:17. The next verse begins, just as the Egyptian saying does, with an adjectival verb meaning "good." Ordinarily, the Hebrew word "good" (*ṭwb*) renders the Egyptian term *3ḫ*, but since the word "pleasant" (*n'm*) is the normal parallel to this word, it is not unusual that it is used here, especially in view of its frequent appearance in this collection.[29] The usage of the phrase "in your belly" (*bbṭnk*) in Prov. 22:18, which is a *hapax legomenon* in the Old Testament, picks up the expression "in the casket of your belly" [*i.e.*, "body" (*ḥn n ḥ·t·k*)] in Amen. 3:13. Its strange companion "on your lips" (*'l-śptyk*) at the end of the verse is best understood as rendering the Egyptian "on your tongue" (*m ns·k*) in 3:16.[30] Without having to contrive parallels we discover the following words and phrases appearing in the same successive order in the two verses of Proverbs as they do in the introductory appeal of Amenemope:

Amenemope	*Proverbs*
Your ears	Your ear
Hear	Hear
What one says	Words of
Your heart	Your heart
It is beneficial	It is pleasant
In the casket of your belly	In your belly
On your tongue	On your lips

The most satisfactory explanation of these coincidences is that they represent condensation of the Egyptian text assimilated in the Hebrew version.

At the same time, the differences between the two texts cannot be overlooked. In four places the Hebrew shows no real correspondence. Moreover, since most of the text of Amenemope has been dropped, the attempt to contrive emendations that will bring them closer together is unconvincing. Gressmann's emendation of "together" (yḥdw) to "a peg" (ytd) in order to create an equivalent for the Egyptian word n'y·t, "peg," is an example of this. Since we have observed the addition of the adverb "today" in 22:19, it could well be that the word "together" was also added to emphasize the correspondence between the phrase "in your belly" and "upon your lips." Furthermore, contrary to the proposal of Gressmann, the normal preposition used with the term "peg" is "in" (b) not "upon" ('l).³¹ That this case against emendation is not purely conjectural is confirmed by the text of the Vulgate, which omits this word altogether.

With the introduction of the divine name in Prov. 22:19, there is a break in the connection with Amenemope. Unfortunately, there is no unanimity in the tradition concerning the correct reading of v. 19b. If it is parallel to v. 20a, then some direct object following the verb hwd'tyk "to show you" is to be expected. Since the parallelism between hywm "this day," and šlšwm, "heretofore"(!), has been removed, the direct object is represented either in hywm, or 'p-'th. The Greek versions attest two readings, ζωήν, "life," obviously derived from the former Hebrew word (ḥyym, "life"), and τὴν ὁδὸν αὐτοῦ, "his way" (or in some versions, "your way").³² Together with the Vulgate, these versions do preserve the parallelism between v. 19b and v. 20a. The only connection with

Amenemope in v. 20 is the important parallel *šlwšym*,
"thirty." This is the eighth parallel between the two
texts, and it brings to an end the consecution of thought.
Of course, the change in thought in the Hebrew text at
this point is not unusual in view of the fact that this
parallel does not belong to the introduction of
Amenemope but comes from the last chapter. With this
one exception, then, the Hebrew writer pursues his own
thought independently of the Egyptian material. The
evidence of the versions, which employ an introductory
particle corresponding to the interrogative at the beginning of the verse and conclude with prepositional
phrases, supports the reading of the Masoretic Text in v.
20.[33]

The last parallels to Amenemope in the introduction
are found in v. 21. The tautology of this verse and the
shift to a four-unit parallel structure raise the presumption in favor of some emendation. Toy's deletion of *qšṭ*,
"truth," supported by the reading of the Septuagint, and
Erman's removal of *'mt*, "truth," in the second part of
the verse, a word not found in the Vulgate, not only
eliminates the redundancy, but also brings the last clause
into closer conformity to Amen. 1:6.[34] Of course, the
Masoretic Text and the readings preserved in the versions ought not to be set aside in favor of a hypothetical
connection to Amenemope, as Humbert does.[35] But the
correspondences between this verse and Amen. 1:5-6 are
too striking to be overlooked. The Egyptian text makes
reference to knowledge that enables one to answer an al-
legation and the ability to return a report to superiors
who have sent one on a mission. The second part of
Prov. 22:21, which speaks of bringing back a report (lit.
"words") to the senders, is almost an exact parallel.
Moreover, the grammatical structure and the sequence

of the verbs "know," "bring back," and "send" correspond precisely to the Egyptian text. The probability that these similarities are not coincidental but originally represent an attempt to carefully preserve important aspects of the introduction and conclusion of the original source is in accord with earlier observations about the nature of this section.

This comparative study of the introduction of the two collections reveals that the assimilative process involves a creative use of source materials. The blending of the two is so skillfully achieved that only such a careful analysis reveals the relationship between them. The Hebrew ideas have not been fitted into a rigid scheme provided by the Egyptian model, nor do the elements derived from this source appear in a contrived manner. The opening plea appears to be a perfectly natural example of Hebrew parallelism. However, upon closer analysis it proves to be a remarkable fusion of Hebrew parallelism with Egyptian word order. The rest of the introduction moves progressively through the precepts of Amenemope, picking up the key words yet shaping the whole into a unique introductory appeal. Apparently, the delicate balance between these two was lost when the tradents could no longer understand the development of the passage. Their attempt to integrate it into the Hebrew tradition obliterated its principal referent and apparently corrupted other important elements.

In the rest of the section from Prov. 22:22-23:11 we may distinguish between three types of material. In some cases there is a close verbal correspondence between Proverbs and Amenemope, such as in 22:24. Certain sections, where the theme is the same but the thought different, words and phrases appear that reflect the original. This is particularly true of the two sections in 23:1-5. In other cases there is only a corresponding thought without close verbal equivalence. Before scrutinizing these three types of relationship, however, another important factor must be mentioned.

A survey of the whole passage reveals that many of the sayings begin with a stichos, or a few words that show a close correspondence to Amenemope. As the thought continues, however, the Hebrew version departs from its source. This departure may be a result of the assimilation of the verse to Hebrew parallelism, or the desire of the author to introduce a different idea. An example of this in Prov. 22:24 has already been seen. Another striking coincidence is the close correspondence between Prov. 22:22 and Amen. 4:4-5. In both cases, at the commencement of the main body of the collection the subject of the first moral precept is the same, robbing the poor.[36] The first two concepts are identical [*gzl* (Heb.), *ḥwr'* (Egypt.), "rob"; *dl*(Heb.), *i3d* (Egypt.), "poor man"]. The idea in the second part is also similar, that of doing violence. The Hebrew admonition does differ, however, in adding a third element to each part.

Of the nine sections dealing with different subjects in Prov. 22:22-23:11, six begin with a word or phrase that corresponds exactly to its counterpart in Amenemope. The following list shows the key words that coincide in the injunctions.[37]

Proverbs		*Amenemope*	
22:22	rob the poor	4:4	robbing a poor man
24	befriend a man of heat	11:13	befriend a hot man
29	skillful in his occupation	27:16	skillful in his occupation
23:1	eat . . . ruler	23:13	eat . . . ruler
4	labor to gain wealth	9:14	labor to seek to gain wealth
10	remove . . . landmark	7:12	remove . . . landmark

In Prov. 22:22 and 22:24 the second part is closely parallel to the first and in 23:10 the parallelism, though not word for word, presents the same thought. This accounts for the differences between the Hebréw and the Egyptian admonitions. The other three examples cited treat themes that are the same as those in Amenemope. Therefore, it would appear that the basic source of the content in this passage is the Egyptian wisdom book. This does not mean, of course, that the injunctions have been copied directly from Amenemope itself. However, it does imply that they have been selected from a collection of sayings that have been reformulated and used in the production of this new literary work.

Two of the sayings appear to correspond quite closely to their prototype in Amenemope. In Amen. 4:4-5, if the phrase *nˁš s3w-ˁ*, literally, "being strong [against] the weak of arm," was read *ngˁ* (or *ngỉ*) *s3w-ˁ*, "crush the weak," it would correspond precisely to the second stichos of Prov. 22:22.[38] In this case, with the exception of the additional phrases at the ends of the two stichoi in the Hebrew version, the precepts are identical. Prov. 22:29 also appears to be a reproduction of the idea in Amen. 27:16. However, aside from the phrase "skillful in his occupation" and the mention of king or courtier, there is no word-for-word correspondence. Gressmann's equation of the Egyptian phrase the "man who is skilled" (*sš mhr*) and the "ready scribe" (*swpr mhyr*; Ps. 45:1; Ezra 7:6) cannot be used to explain this verse.[39] The *mhr* of Papyrus Anastasi I was a technical name, probably the equivalent of an Egyptian chariot warrior (*snny*), as the descriptions of the two seem to indicate.[40] For this reason, only the context of the phrase "the man who is skilled" (*ỷs mhyr*) and the parallel usage of *mhyr* with "scribe" (*swpr*) corroborates the ideological connection between these two sayings. Certainly these factors, including the wide usage of the phrase "skillful in his occupation" and the apparent use of Egyptian imagery in reference to scribal activity in Canaanite-Hebrew tradition (Ps. 45:1; Amen. 17:7), indicate that the two sayings may be related (fig. 4).[41]

The two subjects treated in Prov. 23:1-5 are similar to

Advice to Scribes in chapters fourteen to seventeen of Amenemope (17:1-18:23), sixth century B.C. Courtesy of the British Museum (B.M. 10474).

Amen. 23:13-18 and 9:14-10:5. The subject of table etiquette, particularly in relation to superiors, is treated similarly as in Ptahhotep, Amenemope, and Ecclesiasticus. In all three cases it is introduced with a reference to a person of superior rank.[42] The meaning of Prov. 23:1b is clarified by a similar reference in each of the other texts.

> gmḥ·k r ntt m b3ḥ·k
> Look at what is before you.[43]

> inw r p3 ḳ3y nty m b3ḥ·k
> Look at the bowl that is before you.[44]

> בין תבין את־אשר לפניך
> Give your full attention to what is before you.[45]

> φάγε ὡς ἄνθρωπος τὰ παρακειμενά σοι
> Eat like a human being what is set before you.[46]

Together Ptahhotep and Amenemope clarify the reference in the Hebrew phrase *byn tbyn*. A man of good taste pays attention to his own portion, and in accordance with the ancient counsel of Kagemni, he does not quarrel but accepts the food given to him.[47] Prov. 23:2, of course, shifts immediately to the question of greed, which is treated quite directly in Ecclesiasticus but more obliquely in Ptahhotep and Amenemope.

Of course, it is apparent that the subject is being treated with reference to the tradition. Once again there is a free and creative use of the tradition. The only close resemblance between Proverbs and Amenemope, which is not found in the other texts, is the phrase "bread of deception" (*lḥm kzbym*) (Prov. 23:3), which appears to render "chewing falsely" (*wg3y n 'd3*, Amen. 23:15).[48] If direct dependence cannot be assumed as regards the relation between Proverbs and Amenemope, the identity of theme and the similarity of treatment, at least, place them both in the same stream of tradition.

The passage dealing with the acquisition of riches appears to be more directly related to Amenemope. To deny the connection between them is to disregard the creative utilization of the source on the part of the Hebrew poet. The Egyptian writer has employed two images to depict the sudden disappearance of wealth, the descent of something into the ground, and the ascent of birds into the heavens. The Hebrew poet has integrated this imagery and modified the meaning so that the whole section centers in the image of the bird. The possession of wealth appears to be a reality when the eye descends upon it.

Ptr·w t3y·w st ḫr bn st
One sees their place, but they are not.[49]

התעוף עיניך בו ואיננו
Your eyes light upon it, but it is not.[50]

The phrase "your eyes" is derived from the first word of the Egyptian line. Like a bird swooping down upon something (Isa. 11:14), so the eye falls upon wealth. Just as quickly as it alights upon this wealth, however, riches themselves take wings and fly into the heavens far out of sight. With considerable skill the Hebrew poet has integrated the imagery of descent and ascent, using the bird as his focal point. The remarkable similarity between these two passages in phraseology and use of imagery is, no doubt, a result of the influence of the Egyptian passage upon the Hebrew poet.

Although the subject of the two passages is different, Prov. 23:6-8 has been compared to Amen. 14:7-8, 17-18.[51] The sequence of the ideas "swallow" (i.e., eat), "vomit," and "good" (i.e., pleasant things) is the same in Prov. 23:8 as Amen. 14:17-18. The *crux interpretationis*, however, is the Hebrew word, *š'r*, in v. 7. Gressmann's interpretation of it ("storm"), supported by Dürr's equation of *npš* with the Akkadian *napištu*, "throat," seemed to place the connection of the two texts on firm ground.[52] However, the parallel, which seemed somewhat forced, did not convince scholars of their connection. The Ugaritic cognate, *t'r*, "arrange" or "prepare," first identified by Gray, offered another alternative that was more proximate to the Hebrew text.[53] Therefore Dahood proposed the translation "like one serving his own appetite," based on the identification of these two roots and the interpretation of *npš* as "appetite" (Prov. 23:2). Unfortunately, Dahood's interpretation runs aground on the following preposition, for the Ugaritic verb takes a direct object. Neither the Egyptian imagery, which is not found in the Old Testament, nor the Ugaritic parallel, which is syntactically dubious, offers a satisfactory explanation of the problem.

Since the root *š'r* appears in a context that deals with food, and this root is used in one other passage with such a reference, a more natural alternative is already at hand. In Jer. 29:17 the prophet refers to figs that are *š'rym*, "so 'bad' that they cannot be eaten."[54] Since the delicacies that are eaten are later vomited and the good things are "spoiled," a verb that is used with reference to pollution, the interpretation "foul thing" provides a natural connection between verses 6 and 8. Although this does not solve all of the problems in the verse, particularly, whether *bnpšw* refers to the miser in his appetite," or the foul thing "in the throat," it does prove to be an important transitional concept, which the passage needs. The food that is eaten in the presence of a miser is as deceptive as his attitude. Just as he encourages the guest to eat and drink though he is really hostile toward him, so the food seems tasty though it is really foul. Thus, the delicacies eaten in the presence of such a man are like bad food that makes the guest sick in the end.

Like Prov. 23:6-8, the rest of the collection is unrelated to Amenemope. Prov. 22:26-27 is not treated by Amenemope, and v. 28 appears to be a gloss (Deut. 19: 14). Prov. 23:9 and 24:11 treat subjects dealt with in Amenemope, but no close correspondence can be demonstrated. The few parallels in these verses are no more or less unusual than one would find in any text treating the same subject. At these points the author has turned to other sources for his subject matter.

It may be concluded, then, that the section of the collection entitled "The Sayings of the Wise" contained in Prov. 22:17-23:11, was originally derived from a source that was ultimately dependent upon Amenemope. Of course, there is no way of proving or disproving the presence of an intermediary text. To affirm that this is the case is no more or less demonstrable than to assert that the Hebrew writer borrowed from Amenemope directly, particularly in view of the scant evidence that is available to us. However, considering the form in which the sayings are found in Proverbs, the presence of an intermediary source seems more probable. In either case, however, it is very difficult to move back from this stage to an earlier stage of the text where a more original form was preserved. Hypothetical emendations, based on Amenemope alone without support of any other source, must be carefully scrutinized and for the most part rejected. Only where one can show a very natural process of interpretation in the history of the tradition can the present text be set aside in favor of the original contained in Amenemope, for the assimilative stage has moved one step away from that obvious correspondence which makes possible a reasonable conjecture concerning a more original form of the text.

In this chapter I have traced the adaptation of Egyptian materials on the part of Israel one stage further, from adaptation to assimilation. What one observes is that this is not a uniform process nor a simple substitution of Israelite idiom for the Egyptian expressions. Rather, it involves a creative utilization of the source materials in the formulation of genuine Israelite literary works. Where verbal correspondences do appear, they are found in contexts that have modified the original by changing its reference or meaning or by assimilating it to Canaanite-Hebrew literary patterns. Of course, this explains why the correspondences occur in the first lines of the proverbs and admonitions containing two stichoi and is an important factor in demonstrating the process of assimilation. It also involves the combination of the Egyptian motifs with other materials to produce something that is uniquely Israelite. Although the religious perspective is thoroughly Israelite, and although the materials have been assimilated to the faith of the people of Yahweh, this does not necessarily signify a superior ethical perspective but merely a reformulation in the context of a different religion. The controlling factor at this point is not only the particularity of the faith of Israel but also the common subject matter. What happens to this material as it is integrated into the traditions of the religion of Israel can be determined only after studying the final stage of this process.

5

The Integrative Stage

The final phase in the history of the adaptation and assimilation of Egyptian source materials, the point at which the flow of tradition comes to rest in the Old Testament, is the integrative stage. Except in a few cases no direct relationship between these materials and the original can be postulated, and sometimes even when the original source has been discovered, it may not be possible to demonstrate a connection. It is only through the intermediate stages, the phases of adaptation and assimilation, that a link can be forged to show the connection. For the themes that appear at this stage have already been adopted into the Hebrew tradition at an earlier time. They have been shaped, not by Egyptian influence, but by those motifs which are already a part of Hebrew thought, even though they have originally been occasioned by external influences. Consequently, they have no special marks by which they can be identified, so that their ancestry must be traced to Egyptian sources, not directly, but by their similarity to related materials that have already been assimilated into the Old Testament.

In the integrative stage several types of material may be distinguished. In a few instances elements have been integrated into the Old Testament directly from the adaptive stage. Because they have not been assimilated, this has been accomplished by changing their form so that it embodies a meaning that is in accord with Hebrew tradition. It is possible that this has occurred as a result of textual corruption, or deliberate changes in the text may have been made because the original was not understood. This reformulation of the tradition has had two effects. It has preserved the text in a form that is close to that of the original, and it has also reinterpreted the text in a way that has made it intelligible to the interpreters of the Old Testament. Thus, it has played a paradoxical role, both preserving and transforming the tradition.

The source for such changes in the text is the Masoretic Text, particularly, the *Qere* and *Kethib* readings. We have already studied the change of the Hebrew word for "thirty" to *šlšwm*, "formerly," and the effect this has had upon the context. Of course, this is a very natural change, considering the frequent appearance of this word together with *'tmwl* as an adverb in the Old Testament, although it does not overcome the syntactical objection that can be raised in regard to its appearance here alone.[1] Moreover, since the key consonant in this word would only appear in a *plene* writing, its disappearance from the text is not unusual. Thus, two alternate interpretations arose, one accurately preserving the plural ending and the other changing the consonants to make it an adverb. As already observed, in such cases the versions of the Old Testament play an important role in helping to restore the original.

Another important example of the integration of a Hebrew word into the tradition is found in Prov. 17:27. Of course, the parallel to the phrase "cool of spirit" (*wqr rwḥ*) makes it evident that the proverb reflects an Egyptian character-type and that this phrase is really an Egyptianism.[2] However, when the root was no longer understood by the later tradents, the introductory ן was changed to a ' and the word was vocalized *yqr*, to mean "precious" of spirit. Apparently, this change had taken place as early as the time of Jerome, who translates the phrase *wyqr rwḥ* (*et pretiosi spiritus*).[3] That the reading "cool of spirit" (*wqr rwḥ*) is correct is attested not only by the parallel but also by the interpretation of the Septuagint (μακρόθυμος, "patient").[4] Since *qr* is used as an adjective elsewhere in the Old Testament and since it appears to be a Canaanite word, its close relation to the Egyptian parallel corroborates the written form.

In these two cases a confusion has arisen involving a ן and a '. In late Hasmonean script these two letters were not easily distinguished.[5] In fact, in some cases it would appear that a form midway between the two was used because the manuscripts that were copied did not preserve the distinction. Besides the confusion that arose in numbers, as well as the omission or use of the *wāw* consecutive on verbs, Gordis lists numerous examples of the interchangeable usage of these two consonants at the beginning of a word.[6] Whether this confusion was a result of the influence of the Hasmonean scripts or arose out of later textual corruption, it is clear that the tradents chose a meaning that incorporated a traditional interpretation and not the original foreign nuance.

Since it is apparent that the· later tradition misunderstood the precise use of the imagery in the characterization of this Egyptian type of man, it is not unusual that the Masoretic Text in Prov. 14:17, which deals with this same theme, is subject to suspicion. The verb "hate" (*śn'*) in the second half of the verse appears to have arisen as a result of a negative interpretation of the meaning of the phrase "a man of devices" (*'yš mzmwt*). Although there is no variant Hebrew reading, and this phrase is used elsewhere in a negative sense, the parallelism between the two parts of the verse is awkward both in structure and meaning.[7] The first three parts of the verse appear as the beginning of a parallel structure involving the negative stereotype "short-tempered" (*qṣr-'pym*), a description of his actions as foolish (*y'śh 'wlt*), then the characterization of the contrasting type of man (*'yš mzmwt*) by his clever actions. It might be expected that the last element in the verse (*śn'*, hate) would provide some contrast to the first, but it does not.

Evidence that a different reading from "hate" may have stood in the Hebrew text originally is provided by Origen's version of the Septuagint, which reads "he submits" (ὑποφέρει Heb., *nś'*).[8] The version of Symmachus also preserves a positive interpretation of the word "device" (*mzmwt*, συμβουλευτικός, "deliberative"), and this, of course, supports the view that the second half of the verse was meant to be a contrast. Therefore, the evidence of the Septuagint suggests that a different word stood at the end of the verse. Kittel has proposed the verb *š'n* (Prov. 1:33), which appears in the following version.

קצר־אפים יעשה אולת
ואיש מזמות ישאנן

A man of quick temper acts foolishly,
but a deliberate man rests securely.

The change from *śn'* to *š'n* involves a simple metathesis of the last two consonants, which could well have occurred in the case of this unusual verbal stem. Of course, the connection of folly with disaster in the preceding verses, the need for a direct object with the verb *nś'*, and the tendency of the tradition to interpret an *'yš mzmwt* as an evil man, are factors that support the change that Kittel has suggested.

In all three cases it is possible to see some connection between the interpretation that arose later and the original form. In a similar way the comparative form, which is fixed by its grammatical structure, can be identified. Although we cannot tell at which point it became a specifically Israelite *Weisheitsspruch*, we can trace a development in its usage. What is observed in the history of the tradition is a change in the content of this proverbial form and a widening of its usage. In Prov. 28:6, as in Ecclesiasticus, its content has been personalized.

טוב־רש הולך בתמו
מעקש דרכים והוא עשיר

Better is a poor man who walks in his integrity
than a rich man who is perverse in his ways.

The form of this proverb has been changed from a simple synonymous parallelism to a chiasmus. Also, the emphasis has been shifted with the use of the participles. The adjectival use of the participle with the poor man contrasts with the nominal use of it to identify "the one who is perverse." The contrast is no longer merely one of poverty and riches, but rather sharply focuses on the characterization of the types of men, the poor man who is honest and the rich man who is perverse.

Although it is difficult to date the collections of sayings in the book of Proverbs, the tendency to equate the poor with the righteous in the later period does corroborate my judgment about the place of Prov. 28:6 in the tradition. The collection of proverbs in Prov. 28-29 is more favorable toward the poor than the rich.[9] Whereas the poor are regarded as "wise," the rich man is wise only "in his own eyes" (Prov. 28:11). We have already observed the same tendency in the development of Egyptian wisdom. Moreover, the skeptical attitude toward kingship and the repeated emphasis upon the law, which in this collection could still refer to the priestly *tô-rāh*, are other indications that this group of proverbs belongs to a much later period.[10] This would confirm the suggestion that Prov. 28:6 represents the third stage in the history of tradition growing out of Prov. 16:8, which itself represents the assimilation of Prov. 15:16.

The wider use of the comparative form in wisdom literature is a creative development attesting a time when it had become thoroughly integrated into the tradition as an important literary tool. There is no way of demonstrating that it did not simply originate from the normal grammatical usage of the comparative in Israelite literature. However, as an artistic form this type of saying is usually found alone or at the most in pairs. It may have some ideological connection to its context, but because of its unique form it appears to stand somewhat in isolation. The similarity of this form in Ecclesiastes, and the use of it in contexts where the subject matter is the same, suggests that, as a proverbial form, it is related to the same group of forms that are found in Proverbs.[11] In Ecclesiastes, it is employed differently, however. Its use in a single context has been augmented, and it is subordinated to or supplemented by other statements. In Eccles. 7:1-10 "better" (*twb*) appears seven times in a longer composition, and the climax and conclusion of the whole section is achieved with its negation in v. 10:

אל־תאמר מה היה שהימים הראשנים היו טובים מאלה

Say not, "Why were the former days better than these?"

The simple repetition of this form, supplemented by explanation statements, creates a rhythmic movement that skillfully conveys the author's view of the nature of reality.[12] This tendency to take the form out of its isolation by fitting it into larger contexts shows that by this time it has become a highly polished literary tool in the hands of the Hebrew poets.

The comparative form in Ps. 37:6 embodies another aspect of the integrative stage of the tradition. Although it belongs to the same tradition as Prov. 15:16, 16:8, and 28:6, it appears here in a wisdom psalm.[13] Unlike the group of proverbs just discussed, with the exception of the passage of Ecclesiastes, it has not arisen directly out of the adaptive stage. It is a motif that has been developed from materials already assimilated into the Old Testament. Where such assimilated elements have been instrumental in the creation of the new proverbs, as in the instance cited from Ecclesiastes, or where they themselves have been reformulated, as in this case, one has moved one step further away from the original source. Thus, only by their association with themes that at one time were derived from Egypt can we identify them as part of the tradition.

The connection between the hymn and the wisdom literature can be attested throughout the ancient Near East. As literary categories they are not so sharply demarcated as would appear.[14] Wisdom motifs ofte'n appear in hymns, for apparently the wisdom literature offered a body of stock materials that the writers of hymns could use. Of course, this is particularly true of the preceptive hymn. The use of hymnic forms in the "instruction" of Sehetepibre to eulogize the king is an Egyptian example of a literary work that stands between the two. The Hymn to Shamash is a Babylonian example of a hymn that draws upon a common store of tradition both from hymnic and wisdom sources. In the Old Testament itself a number of compositions have been identified as unique because of their association with the wisdom movement.[15] Although the wisdom psalm and the hymn are somewhat distinct, Ps. 111, a hymn of thanksgiving, closes with a wisdom motif (v. 10). Thus, didactic poems were also included in the Psalter along with the hymnic materials.

Since the discovery of Amenemope it has been assumed that Ps. 1 has been derived from the poem concerning the "hot" man and the "silent" man in Amen. 6:1-12.[16] The subject of this poem, the two types of men, also found its way into Egyptian hymnology.[17] Since a connection has already been established between

Egyptian and Amarna hymns, it is not unreasonable to
suggest that the Israelite theme has also been influenced
by the Egyptian original.[18] However, the resemblances
between this psalm and the composition in Amenemope
are more thematic, so that connection between them has
been denied.

The correspondence between the two involves the contrast between two types of men, the image of the tree,
and the depiction of their fate. Only in a single verse,
Ps. 1:3, is the equivalence at all close to the passage in
Amen. 6:8-12:

sw mî š3 rd m tḥn·t
sw 3ḫ3ḫ ḳ3b·f šmw.f
sw n ḫft-ḥr n nb·f
dg3·f bnr h3îb·t·f ndm
in·tw pḥ·t·f m mnw[19]

He is like a tree growing in a plantation.
It is green, it doubles its yield.
It is before its lord.
Its fruit is sweet, its shade is pleasant.
Its end is reached in a plantation.

וְהָיָה כְּעֵץ שָׁתוּל עַל־פַּלְגֵי מָיִם
אֲשֶׁר פִּרְיוֹ יִתֵּן בְּעִתּוֹ
וְעָלֵהוּ לֹא־יִבּוֹל

He is like a tree
    planted by streams of water,
that yields its fruit in its season,
    and its leaf does not wither.

Considering the frequent use of the similitude of the
tree as a representation of a particular type of man, the

similarity between the psalm and Amenemope is not striking.[20]

Actually, the poem in Jer. 17:5-8 is in some ways more akin to the Egyptian composition. It preserves the characterization of the man "whose heart turns away from the Lord," the counterpart of the "hot man," as we observe in v. 6:

והיה כערער בערבה
ולא יראה כי־יבוא טוב
ושכן חררים במדבר
ארץ מלחה ולא תשב

He is like a shrub in the desert,
   and shall not see any good come.
He shall dwell in the parched places
   of the wilderness,
in an uninhabited salt land.

In this passage the essential point of the contrasts, the location of the tree in a favorable environment, is found. With it we may compare the characterization of the "hot man" in Amen. 6:2-6:

sw mî š3 rd m ḫnti-[š]
km [3]t p3y·f ḫ3' srdm
in·tw pḥ·t·f n mḫrm
sw mḥw w3w r st·f
t3 st3 t3y·f ḳrs·t

He is like a tree growing in the forest.[21]
A moment completes its loss of foliage.
Its end is reached in a port.
It is waterlogged far from its place.
The flame is his burial shroud.

A comparison of these two compositions shows that the imagery has not been adopted from the source but derives from the native geographical setting. Nevertheless, even though the imagery is different, the point of comparison is the same: both men are likened to trees that are growing in the wilderness.

Jeremiah also contains one statement that is more reminiscent of the poem concerning the righteous man than is the psalm. He states that the leaves of the tree remain "green," a parallel to the clause in Amen. 6:9 that says of the tree growing in the plantation, "it is green."[22] The statement in Ps. 1, that "its leaf does not wither," may be reminiscent of Amen. 6:3, which alludes to the loss of the foliage of the tree growing in the open. Moreover, the focus of the psalm upon the ultimate end of the two men captures a motif that seems to dominate the Egyptian poem. Of course, both of the Israelite compositions contain an allusion to the bearing of fruit, as does the Egyptian poem. However, given the different geographical settings, the version in Jeremiah more fully corresponds to the Egyptian original.

The general similarity between Jeremiah and Amenemope provides an earlier link and enables one to postulate a connection between Ps. 1 and Amenemope. However, the presence of a condensed version of the composition in Ps. 1 found within the same kind of literary framework as that in Jeremiah, the formula of blessing and cursing, makes it quite possible that the theme of the psalm is related to the poetic material in the prophetic book.[23] The inspiration for both compositions may ultimately have been the poem in Amenemope. Whether Jeremiah has assimilated it or derived it from a Canaanite source cannot be determined. If this is the case, Ps. 1 is an example of the integration of a literary motif into the Hebrew tradition, whose form, at least, may be traced back to its original source in Amenemope.

Ps. 37 is also a wisdom psalm, a didactic poem. Its form, based on an alphabetical series, was a favorite literary device of the wisdom school. In a way reminiscent of the introduction of the Egyptian wisdom book of Ptahhotep, its author speaks as an old man.[24] Its imagery and vocabulary, including the mention of wisdom, bespeak a wise man. Although the question of theodicy is implicit in it, the poem itself is a very positive affirmation of trust in Yahweh based on a consideration of the destinies of the righteous and the wicked.

More important than these general thematic similarities is the fact that it is possible to identify the sources of this psalm more specifically. The circle of tradition to which the comparative form in Ps. 37:16 belongs has already been mentioned.

טוב־מעט לצדיק
מהמון רשעים רבים

> Better is a little that the righteous has
> than the abundance of many wicked.

The key to the interpretation of this proverb is provided, not only by the context, but also by the use of the adjective *rbym*. This word is present in Prov. 15:16 and 16:8. In both cases it modifies the word for "riches" (*'wsr*, Prov. 15:16, *tbw'wt*, 16:8). It is not found in Prov. 28:6, where we observed a shift in emphasis from the question of riches to the characterization of the rich man as "perverse." However, the same emphasis that is found there appears here. The adjective "many" or "great" has been moved to the end of the proverb so that it now refers to the "many wicked," not the great wealth. The small portion that the righteous have is better than the abundance that the great number of wicked oppressors have. For even though the wicked prosper and even though the righteous suffer, the psalmist affirms the eventual triumph of Yahweh over the wicked and the exaltation of the righteous to the possession of the land.

There is also a clear connection between this psalm and the collection in Prov. 22:17-24:22.[25] Ps. 37 is an alphabetical psalm. It begins with א the first letter of the Hebrew alphabet, contained in the negative particle *'l*, continues with ב (*btḥ*, trust), and ג (*gwl*, delight in) continuing through the alphabet. Prov. 24:1-5 is also an alphabetical series, but it breaks off after the third letter. Prov. 24:1 commences in the same manner with א, the first letter of the negative particle *'l*, continues with ב (*bkḥmh*, "ɔy wisdom" v. 3), and breaks off after ג (*gbr*, "man" v. 5). With the exception of one phrase, the introductory clause of the admonition in the broken alphabetical series in Prov. 24:1 is identical with the second stichos of Ps. 37:1.[26]

אל־תקנא באנשי רעה
Do not be jealous of evil men.

אל־תקנא בעשי עולה
Do not be jealous of those who do injustice.

The main theme of the psalm, that Yahweh will deliver the righteous and punish the wicked, is mentioned frequently in "The Sayings of the Wise" (Prov. 22:23, 23:11, 24:12, 16, 20).[27] Although the collection of precepts in Proverbs involves a broader range of subject matter, careful observation confirms the fact that the two compositions are using a common stock of tradition.

However, there is an ideological shift in the psalm. Yahweh has become the sole agency of salvation. The righteous man is to play a passive role; he is to "be still" (*dwm*, v. 7), and to "wait" (*qwh*, v. 34). His active role is simply to depart from evil and do good (v. 27), that is, to keep the law of God (v. 31), including its exhortations to generosity (vv. 21, 26). Wisdom, which is equated with justice, is an external manifestation of the law of Yahweh in the heart (vv. 30-31). The relationship of the righteous man to Yahweh is quite direct. The intermediate agencies have disappeared. No longer is hope held out that a wise body of counselors will be able to overcome (Prov. 24:6) or that by obedience to the king disaster can be avoided (Prov. 24:22). Salvation is wholly from Yahweh (Ps. 37:39), a reward for pious obedience (Ps. 37:31), not a result of power realized in the application of wisdom (Prov. 24:5). The lack of any specific directions arising out of the context of man's historical life, combined with the stark sketch of the wicked, creates a sense of the threatening despair with which the psalmist struggles. The situation described in the psalm is so hopeless that help is not to be found in historical agencies. Thus the redemptive aspect is mediated by means of the moral intensity with which the psalmist relentlessly pursues his theme, trust in the vindication of Yahweh.

In Proverbs the note of pessimism is not so profound, nor is there an abandonment of the assessment of the role of wisdom in securing the future.[28] The mention of the future and hope in the wisdom collection (23:18; 24:14) leads on to the conclusion where the author foresees uncertain times. In the closing section of the book he mentions a "day of adversity" (24:10) and "dis-

aster" (24:22), which can arise suddenly. But he does not
fly from history in his hope. Wisdom is still able to provide a way of life that can establish security. By wisdom
even an enemy that is stronger can be defeated (Prov.
24:6). In the day of adversity a wise man may still be
able to rescue some from death (v. 11). Moreover, sudden disaster may come from the king, who is Yahweh's
agent, as well as from God (v. 22). Therefore, the task of
the wise man is twofold, to fear God and the king and to
seek wisdom. The wisdom book in Proverbs thus falls
short of the apocalyptic vision implicit in Ps. 37.

Of course, the comparison of the utilization of wisdom
materials in these two compositions does not itself establish any thesis concerning the integration of Egyptian
wisdom materials in the psalm. But it does show the context into which such materials have been woven. For in
two other places, elements assimilated from Egyptian
sources appear. Although it is not possible to grant them
any special connection to the Egyptian wisdom book, it
does seem that they represent remnants of this same
tradition.

In Ps. 37:10b a reminiscence of Amen. 9:19, which
has already been assimilated into Prov. 23:5, is found.

 והתבוננת על־מקומו ואיננו

You look well at his place, he will not be there.

Admittedly, the subject is different; it is the wicked that
is in view, not riches. But the parallel is strikingly similar
in word order to the clause in Amenemope. Moreover,
the appearance of the negative verb at the end of a
clause is found only a few times in the third person in
the Psalms and Proverbs, twice in this psalm and in Ps.

103:16. It is possible that this verb may have been derived from the usage in Ps. 103:16, since it appears there in connection with a similar theme, that of the transiency of human life. However, this would only explain the usage in Ps. 37:36 but not the strange coincidence of word order between 37:10 and Amen. 9:19. It is also rather peculiar that the context of v. 36 compares the wicked man to a tree, the same image that is common to the traditions of wisdom literature. It would appear, then, that the psalmist is using a common wisdom motif, known to us by its connection with riches, to describe the fate of the wicked.

A closer parallel to the collection in Proverbs is found in Ps. 37:8.

הרף מאף ועזב חמה

Refrain from anger, and forsake wrath!

If it were not for the numerous parallels to Proverbs in this section, it would not be possible to connect this passage with Prov. 22:24. Certainly it is not a direct parallel. Whereas the verse in Proverbs presents the stereotype of character, the psalm preserves only the two verbs for being angry. However, it is possible to maintain that this has been mediated in the Hebrew tradition through the collections in Proverbs, and that it has later lost its association with the particular types of men. Its appearance here with other motifs from the wisdom collection in Proverbs lends some support to this assertion.

If the author of Ps. 37 has not derived these motifs directly from the book of "The Sayings of the Wise" but from a common stock of wisdom traditions, he has skillfully reutilized them in a new setting. The injunction not

to be envious of the wicked, which may have been the
initial saying in another acrostic, from which Prov. 24:1
was also taken, is reinforced by the admonition not to be
angry (v. 8). Both of these are corroborated by the same
refrain, which reminds the righteous man that in a little
while he will look at the place of the wicked and he will
not be there (v. 9). This leads to the comparative proverb that asserts again that the lot of the poor man is
indeed better than that of the multitude of wicked men
(v. 16). Then, a traditional wisdom motif is used as an
introduction to support the theme of the psalm, that
even as an old man the author has never observed a
righteous man being forsaken (v. 25). Finally, by a skillful repetition of a motif used earlier, the psalmist reas-
serts his confidence in Yahweh. The wicked man is
compared to a towering cedar tree in Lebanon, but in a
matter of time this overbearing man was not to be found
(vv. 35-36). When the psalmist passed by the same place
where he once was, he was no more.

Several aspects of this psalm suggest that it belongs to
the apocalyptic vision that took rise in Israel in the later
period. The assertion of the psalmist that the righteous
will possess the land when the wicked are destroyed (v.
34) reflects an epoch of history when unjust and oppres-
sive rulers are in control. The lack of specific mention of
historical instrumentalities by which Yahweh will vindi-
cate his people implies one of two things. Either they are
absent so that they do not come into play in the consideration of the author, or, if present, they play no role in
the future redemption of the nation. The expectation of
the direct action of Yahweh on behalf of his people is a
mark of apocalyptic.[29] Also, the rigid separation of men
into two classes, the righteous who await redemption

from God and the wicked who are about to be destroyed, befits this vision of the future. A fully apocalyptic vision would, of course, involve something more, the mythologizing of the ancient wisdom motif, the belief that the wicked man will have his hour but will eventually be brought to justice. Here the righteous are simply asked to be patient because the "day" of the wicked is coming (v. 13). Counsel and advice that once dealt with personal and communal matters are now connected with the historical drama of redemption. At this point we have reached the final stage in the process of the adaptation and assimilation of wisdom motifs and the commencement of a religious vision similar to apocalyptic.

Finally, there is one other matter that must be discussed in connection with the explication of the integrative stage. It involves the thematic similarities that are found in Israelite and Egyptian wisdom.[30] As an example we may consider Prov. 25:21-22 in relation to Amen. 5:5-6. Although the form of the two commands is different, the advice that is given and the result that accrues from it appear to be the same. In a section that advises the Egyptian wise man concerning the treatment of the evil man, Amenemope asserts

> Mḥ ḥ·t·f m t m-dỉ·k
> s3·f mtw·f ṯm

> Fill his belly with bread of yours
> so that he shall be satisfied and ashamed.

Since the Hebrew version also enjoins the wise man to give bread and drink to the enemy, the two sayings are thematically the same in the first part. By interpreting the enigmatic Hebrew clause "for you will heap coals of

fire on his head" at the beginning of the second part of
v. 22 to signify shaming someone, the second half of
each saying also appears to be thematically similar.[31]
Thus, the question could be raised as to which of the
two sayings was original.

Actually, however, as observed earlier, this interpretation of Prov. 25:21-22 points out the danger of understanding Israelite wisdom purely in terms of ideological
parallels in the ancient Near East.[32] According to the
patterns of Hebrew parallelism, the third clause may be
given a quite different meaning, erasing the peculiar
idiom in v. 22, which finds no parallel in the Old Testament. Thus, Prov. 25:22a, the saying about coals of
fire, has been reinterpreted to complete the series about
giving bread to a hungry man and drink to a thirsty
man. Yahweh will reward such a generous man also, in
the direct address of the proverb,

kî gᵉḥālîm 'attā ḥōte ʿᵃlê-'iššô

If you yourself bring some coals for his fire.[33]

The natural parallel between bread, drink, and coals
brings this saying into line with the canons of Hebrew
parallelism, supplies a natural meaning to the third
clause, and eliminates the necessity of looking for contrived parallels outside of the Israelite literary traditions.

Since the traditions of wisdom were international, it is
not unusual to find many sayings in which the imagery
and thought are strikingly similar.[34] To trace these in
every case to external sources would reduce the quest
for closely associated parallels to a hopeless search.
Without any verbal or ideological control to identify
their source, the whole body of wisdom literature would

become an amorphous mass capable of producing connections in every direction. The individual sayings would lose their identity, and it would be impossible to trace any actual historical development grounded in a careful reutilisation of literary materials. This is not to deny, for instance, that the saying in Amen. 5:5-6 may have been the creative source for the coining of a saying such as is found in Prov. 25:21-22. There is simply no means available for establishing this except by contextual association.

The example I have chosen, however, does suggest this possibility. As already observed, the cluster of wisdom traditions surrounding those themes which have been created as a result of Egyptian influence involves two elements, the comparative form and the characterization of men in terms of their temperament. In Prov. 25:7, 24 the comparative form appears, and in v. 15 one hears echoes of Prov. 15:18. In addition to this, a series of phrases that are used here are reminiscent of the collection of the thirty sayings. The verb "stand" (*'md*, v. 6), used in relation to the king, reminds us of Prov. 22:29. Likewise, the phrase in 25:13 "to those who sent him" (*lšlhyw*) echoes Prov. 22:21. As in Prov. 16:32, the phrase "slow to anger" (*'rk 'pym*) in Prov. 25:15 has found a new parallel, which emphasizes persuasion, not silence. Where such clusters of material are present, some of which can be shown to trace directly to Egyptian wisdom, the case that other elements have been inspired by ideas originally found in Egyptian sources may be strengthened. At least, the case may be made that such collections derive from similar circles of tradition in Israel, circles in which Egyptian influence may have played a role.

This study of the integrative stage has disclosed three types of material, one of which can be related to Egyptian traditions only by a thematic study. The other two betray their relationship to Egyptian sources by their relatedness to materials that derived from this source, whether directly or indirectly. At this point in the tradition, it is not possible to show this connection except by an intermediate process, either textual emendation or similarity to other materials that have been assimilated into the Hebrew tradition. Where such a process of assimilation has taken place, the meaning has been changed or integrated into a context that is thoroughly Hebraic. We can only say that these two types come from a common stream of tradition and are now being utilized by the later tradents as part of a fund of wisdom materials available to the writers. Their original connection has been lost, and they are now serving the interests of traditional Hebrew-wisdom.

Up to this point we have observed a literary process at work, the adaptation, assimilation, and integration into Hebrew literature of proverbial materials that were originally native to Egypt. From this study the most immediate question that comes to attention is that of the original setting in which wisdom was formulated. How was it possible for Egyptian wisdom to pass into Israelite thought given the religious, social, and historical differences between these two peoples? Not unrelated to this question is the ancillary role that Egyptian wisdom can play in enlightening us as to the varieties of literary genre that may be included under the rubric "wisdom literature." As a fairly well-defined body of literature extending over two millennia, Egyptian wisdom does provide us with actual models of various types of compositions of wisdom. Thus, it gives us clues by which we may be guided in our study of Israelite wisdom. Likewise, if these Egyptian forms of wisdom originate in a definite context, they also offer comparative connections by which we can seek to understand the original context of some of the forms of Hebrew wisdom. It is to this aspect of the study, then, that we now turn, initially in connection with the collection of wisdom in Prov. 25 and subsequently in relation to political wisdom in Egypt and Israel.

6

The Wisdom of the Royal Court

The discovery of Amenemope and its subsequent use in the identification of the sources for the wisdom literature of the Old Testament has made scholars aware not only of the presence of Egyptian literary materials in Proverbs but also of the existence of small literary units that may be called wisdom "books."[1] In at least one case, the book of "The Sayings of the Wise" (Prov. 22:17-24:22), what was previously regarded as a loosely coordinated collection of sayings is now demonstrated to be an actual wisdom book, modeled upon a foreign literary type. Of course, this raises the possibility that there are other literary entities in the book of Proverbs that have not as yet been identified. If this is the case, Egyptian wisdom literature is able to play a further role in helping us to identify these small books by providing examples of other types of instruction that have their own unique content and structure and that enable the scholar to look for similar literary types in Hebrew proverbial literature.

The popularity of such small collections of wisdom is attested by their existence not only in Egypt but also in Syria, as well as in Palestine.[2] We have one example in Egyptian wisdom literature of such a collection. In reality the composition is an extract of a wisdom .book, adopted and utilized for a specific purpose. This text, which has a bearing upon our discussion, is the wisdom of Sehetepibre.[3] It is a literary work of the Middle Kingdom that is found principally in two forms: a larger work, the complete text of which is not available to us, and a smaller version, which is a condensation of the original. Although the smaller version is in the form of a panegyric, it is entitled "instruction" (*sb3y·t*), the typical word that is assigned to these wisdom books by the Egyptians and that often appears in the introduction. The editor has evidently taken it from a larger literary work to which the title "instruction" more properly belongs and has introduced elements into the text, including the name of the Egyptian king being eulogized, in order to create a hymn glorifying the reigning monarch.

The importance of this work for this study is related to its structure. The original instruction, which was apparently more general in scope than the abbreviated form, seeks to demonstrate the interdependence of the ruler and his subjects. It asserts that there is a reciprocal relationship between the ruler and the ruled. The people are at the mercy of Pharaoh, yet the monarch himself must have the support of his subjects if his rule is to continue. Thus, the people must fight for his name, and he must fight on behalf of the people. These two exhortations, which are much like "rubrics," summarize and thus form the two key clauses that represent the appropriate divisions of the text.[4] The first part, which contains the eulogy of the king, ends with the exhortation "fight for his name" (*ꜥḥꜣ ḥr rn·f*). The second half begins with instructions to the subject to be loyal, reminding its audience that the corpse of the rebel will have no burial place. After a series of injunctions urging support of the crown, another matter of wisdom is introduced, the duties of the king to his subjects. In this section typical agricultural matters concerning taxes, irrigation, and farm labor are treated. Then the book ends with a final exhortation to the king, "fight for the people" (*ꜥḥꜣ ḥr rmṯ*).

At this point one important observation about the instruction must be stressed. This text existed in at least two forms, one of which was a condensation of the original. It is quite evident that the latter is a piece of loyalist propaganda seeking to exalt the throne and urge the support of the monarchy.[5] Its popularity was, no doubt, due to its dissemination in the court, where it was subsequently adopted and utilized for a more specific purpose by Sehetepibre. This use of the original wisdom book appears to be part of a movement associated with one particular dynasty that was seeking to secure its claim to the Egyptian throne. Although the condensed version contains only one of the two rubrics marking its middle point and its end, the longer version contains both.

The propagandistic intention of the panegyric composed by Sehetepibre provides us with literary materials that also reflect a particular *Sitz im Leben* and that can therefore be helpful in determining the specific context in which Hebrew wisdom literature was written. Another important Egyptian composition of this type that may have a bearing upon this question is entitled the *Kemyt*, an Egyptian word meaning "complete."[6] By its apt title this model schoolbook implied that it contained the total material necessary for the training of a scribe who aspired to the court. Thus it has been suggested that this text was a kind of compendium, offering to the student the complete selection of material necessary for formal relations with officials of the government.

The remarkable thing about this composition is its size. It is very short, comprising only about two leaves. Its brief text is based upon a story similar to the tale of Sinuhe. A young man who has been absent from his family returns home. As in the story concerning Sinuhe, the contrast between the rough life experienced outside of the homeland and the oil and linen of Egypt is made explicit in an outburst of exclamatory exhortations that praise the life of the scribe and urge upon the reader the profits to be gained from the study of books. It is quite apparent that this text, which is similar in theme to the Satire on the Trades, extols the benefits of scribal and court life. Both Sehetepibre and the Kemyt encourage the support of the established government and the necessity of finding one's proper place in it.

These two texts may be compared with a literary composition in Proverbs that up to the present, has remained unidentified.[7] This work is another small collection of proverbs similar to "The Sayings of the Wise" in Prov. 22:17-24:22 but having its own unique structure and content. Although it has no direct relationship with

either of the Egyptian texts just discussed, these latter
serve as models that provide clues enabling one to look
for similar literary genres in Israel. Of course, this wisdom book has its own special structure, clearly demarcated by the presence of summary clauses as in the case
of Sehetepibre, and its own particular content, which at
one point is strikingly similar to the aforementioned
text. In its wide range of proverbial forms it also reminds us of the Kemyt. Certain phrases likewise reflect
the same cycle of tradition as that to which Prov. 22:17-
24:22 belongs.[8]

This small wisdom book is contained in Prov. 25:2-27.
It is found in a chapter that begins with a general heading and by all appearances contains a collection of approximately twenty-three sayings among its twenty-eight
verses.[9] The introduction to the chapter states that these
proverbs were transcribed by the men of Hezekiah. Apparently these scribes copied them from a collection of
sayings that was originally a unity within itself. Either
they or the tradents before them overlooked or misunderstood the precise relation of the last verse of the collection to the first verse. Thus, the important clauses
that serve as rubrics demarcating the structure of the
book were lost from view. Once this had happened, it
was a simple matter for another proverb, unrelated to
what preceded, to be added to the chapter. Just as the
corruption of the word "thirty" in Prov. 22:20 erased the
key word explaining the structure of the book called
"The Sayings of the Wise," so the misunderstanding of
the meaning and relationship of the last clause to the
rest of the book in Prov. 25 caused it to be treated simply as an uncoordinated collection of sayings.

The second reason why this collection of sayings has

not hitherto been regarded as a unity turns upon the interpretation of Prov. 25:27. Translators have resorted to various expedients to solve the apparent textual difficulties in this verse and clarify its meaning.[10] Although this cannot be achieved without at least one minor emendation, it is possible to establish the rest of the fixed elements in the verse on the basis of Hebrew usage and the evidence of the versions. The Hebrew text of the first clause, which finds support among the Greek versions and the Vulgate, employs a grammatical construction that is found elsewhere in the book of Proverbs.[11] The use of an introductory infinitive followed by the phrase "it is not good" (*l'-twb*) occurs in Prov. 17:26, 18:5, and 28:21. Following this usage, we may establish the principal fixed elements in the first stichos.

אכל דבש. . .לא־טוב

To eat honey . . . is not good.

A comparison of this clause with the same thought in v. 16 makes it quite clear that a qualifying word is required to complete its meaning. This is usually supplied by the interpretation of the enigmatic word *hrbwt* as "much," even though the adverbial rendering "excessively" is to be preferred.[12]

The second part of v. 27 has frequently been misinterpreted, leading to the loss of one rubric that is crucial to the structure of the book. It not only has the textual support of the Greek versions and the Vulgate, but also finds an ideological parallel in Job 12:11.[13] In the verse in Job, the examination of words through hearing is compared with the tasting of food by the palate. This parallel is similar to what we find in Prov. 25:27. Here

the physical activity of eating has as its parallel in the
second half of the verse the mental activity of investigation. The object of this research, which is the correspon-
dent to the honey that is eaten, are the "difficult things"
(*kbdm*) that require scrutiny. The antithetical parallelism
in the two parts of the verse is completed by the contrast
between that which is "not good" (*l'-ṭwb*), that is, eating
too much honey, and that which is "glorious" (*kbd*), the
investigation of difficult things. The same thought is
contained in the book of Tobit, which declares that the
revelation of the works of God is "glorious" (ἔνδοξον).[14]
By means of versional evidence, Hebrew usage, and the
parallelism of the two parts of the verse, the following
provisional interpretation of Prov. 25:27 is established:

אכל דבש הרבות לא־טוב
וחקר כבדם כבוד

To eat honey excessively is not good,
but to investigate difficult things is glorious.

Subsequently, the importance of this translation for the
structure of the book will be demonstrated.

Having determined what the fixed elements in Prov.
25:27 are, we may now examine the chapter to decide
whether or not it is indeed a wisdom book. Two criteria
are employed. The first involves the ideological structure
of the book and is concerned with content. The second
treats the subject of the formal structure and includes
whatever poetic and literary devices may have been used
to demarcate the outline of the book. Initially, we may
raise the following two questions concerning the conceptual development of the composition. Does Prov. 25:2-27
form a clear conceptual unity with a substructure of

thought that is integrally related? Moreover, apart from the formal structure, does it have a single theme to which each of the parts relates?

The composition in Prov. 25:2-27 has a clearly marked ideological structure. Its initial verse, which is easily recognized because it follows the chapter heading, commences an introductory group of sayings that contain the two principal themes of the two sections of the book (vv. 2-5). The introduction itself is in two parts, dealing with the two subjects of the book, the king (vv. 2-3) and the wicked (vv. 4-5). The first two verses are in the third person and are linked together by the use of the same word "search out" (*ḥqr*). Vv. 4-5 begin with the same verb in the imperative mood and conclude with a declarative statement. Thus, the introduction is clearly a separate unit both in form and content and presents the two main subjects of the book.

The two parts of the wisdom book begin and end with the mention of their principal subject. The first section includes vv. 6-15 and has as its main theme the ruler who is referred to in the first part of the introduction. The second part, extending from vv. 16-26, deals with the wicked, who are introduced in the second part of the introduction. As for the first section of the book, it commences in the first admonition with the mention of the king in v. 6. It ends by referring to the ruler in v. 15. As we shall presently observe, the first saying in the second half of the composition is actually v. 17, since v. 16 properly belongs to the rubrics demarcating the structure of the book. It presents as an exemplar of the wicked, who are the main subject of this part, the hateful neighbor. The last verse (26) brings this part to a close with the specific mention of the "wicked." Thus, both parts of the book are bracketed in the first and last sayings by their principal subjects, the king and the wicked.

A careful stylistic analysis of this composition not only establishes the number of units in each section but also strengthens the credibility of the notion that this composer was consciously employing catchwords and wordplays. The first section has six units, vv. 6-7, 8-9a, 9b-10, 11-12, 13-14, and 15. Each verse is linked to its partner within the unit by similar subject matter, by pronominal references, by rhyme or assonance, or even by means of the use of similar words or the same roots employed with different meanings. Although the individual units in this section are not related to each other in a direct way, they do have a common subject. This part of the book deals with the relation of the courtier to his superiors. References to the ruler and men superior in station occur five times, excluding the mention of the collective body in v. 8. In other verses this relationship is implied by the suggestion that such a person might be one to whom the courtier would lose a case at court or simply one who was a "reprover."

Employing the same criteria, the second section of the book may also be divided into six units, vv. 16-17, 18, 19-20, 21-22, 23-24, and 25-26. One clear example of the linkage between two apparently unrelated proverbs is found in vv. 19-20. One verse deals with the faithless man; the other concerns itself with a man who sings songs to one who is sad. But the connection between them is quite clear, as we may observe in the clever use of similar words that have different meanings in the underlined portion of our version.

ורגל מועדת מבטח בוגד ביום צרה

[Like . . .] and a foot that slips, so is one who trusts
a deceitful man in a day of distress (v. 19).

מעדה   בגד ביום קרה

He who removes a garment on a cold day . . . (v. 20).

This section also consists of six units that deal with a
series of wicked characters: the hateful friend, the false
witness, the faithless man, the tormentor, the enemy, the
backbiter, the contentious woman, and the wicked. As
Prov. 23:19-24:2 attests, the characterization of certain
types of people was a popular subject in wisdom literature.

Moreover, it is important to observe that neither v. 27
nor v. 28 finds any connection to its immediate context.
Vv. 25-26 are linked together by the contrasting imagery of similar metaphors ("cold water" and "muddied
spring"). V. 27 finds no connection with this or with the
verse that follows. In form and content it is quite different, bringing the matter of investigation into parallelism
with the eating of honey. It may be that v. 28, which
speaks of a man who lacks restraint, has been displaced
and ought to belong to the list of wicked characters
mentioned in the second part of the book. Regardless, it
does not recapitulate nor reflect on what has been
treated in the preceding verse but merely adds another
independent thought. The first half of v. 27, however,
does reflect the thought of v. 16, using some of the same
words. Since the first half of v. 27 reflects the same idea
that commences the second part of the book, the question must be raised concerning the relation of the sec-

ond half of v. 27 to what has preceded. Before we turn
to this matter, which has to do with the formal structure
of the book, one other aspect of the thematic treatment
ought to be considered.

A close inspection of the subject matter reveals that
there is a peculiar dialectic in the treatment of the material. Each statement is qualified by what follows. Although this is more apparent in the two main sections of
the book, it is present even in the introduction. The wisdom of the king, it is asserted, surpasses human understanding. At this point a qualification is inserted: a king
who is surrounded by wicked men will perish. Similarly,
the courtier is advised not to be "pushy" in striving for
position either in the presence of the ruler or in a court
of law. Then, positively, he is counseled to gain status by
persuading his superiors with a convincing report.
Again, he is warned not to become too familiar with his
associates, but in the same breath reminded to have
good associates who will help him in time of trouble.
Likewise, in his relationships with his opponents, he is
advised not to increase their enmity but to do good to
them, so that he can augment his store of good will at
court. The positive statements are qualified by negative
ones, and vice versa. In delicate matters the composer
shows himself to be a skillful counselor, suggesting
"enough" and cautioning "not too much."

On consideration of the formal structure of this small
collection of proverbs, one is immediately reminded of
the wisdom of Sehetepibre and the use of what appear
to be rubrics in this book. Here a similar phenomenon
can be observed. As already mentioned, the first clause
of the last verse of the composition (v. 27a) echoes the
first clauses of the first verse of the second section of the

book (v. 16a), as reflected in my translations that follow.

דבש מצאת אכל דיך
פן־תשבענו והקאתו

If you have found honey, eat only your sufficiency,
lest you become sated with it and vomit it (v. 16).

אכל דבש הרבות לא־טוב

To eat honey excessively is not good (v. 27a).

Since the first half of the verse relates to the clause at
the beginning of the second part of the book, logically
the second half of v. 27 ought to pick up something at
the beginning of the wisdom book. A comparison of v.
27b shows that it does.

כבד אלהים הסתר דבר
וכבד מלכים חקר דבר

It is the glory of God to hide a matter,
And it is the glory of kings to investigate a matter (v. 2).

וחקר כבדם כבוד

But to investigate difficult matters is glorious (v. 27b).

Like the Egyptian text, the rubrics in this composition
clearly demarcate the beginning, middle, and end of the
book.

It is interesting to observe the way in which the composer has used the last verse, if my tentative reconstruction of the fixed elements in it is accepted, to bring together in one statement all that has been said. Just as the
preceding proverbs often have qualifying companions,

so the first clause of the conclusion is qualified by the second one. To seek the honor of the court and to investigate difficult matters in such an enterprise is good only if it is undertaken correctly. Thus, the author has skillfully arranged the rubrics in the form of a chiasmus:

| Glory (v. 2) | Honey (v. 27a) |
| Honey (v. 16) | Glory (v. 27b) |

The book concludes on the very positive note with which it began, the glory involved in the quest to investigate what has been hidden.

The appearance of this literary work that has hitherto remained unidentified is another example of the similarity of forms as well as materials that were employed by authors and transmitted by scribes who were part of an international literary movement. Nor can the importance of this text for the education of courtiers be overlooked. In this respect the composition in Prov. 25 is similar in one respect to the Egyptian letter known as the Kemyt. Just as the Egyptian text contains a variety of forms and styles for the benefit of the student, so this Hebrew wisdom book offers a variety of proverbial types for study and consideration. Whereas Prov. 10:1-22:16 and 22:17-24:34 present proverbs grouped according to their form—the proverb and the admonition, respectively, Prov. 25:2-27 includes a mixture of forms, at least ten in all. This variety of forms may well have been occasioned by its composition as a model for students to copy and memorize. To acquaint the student with the ways of the court and the proper kind of behavior for success and promotion would have been one of the aims of the composer. The other could have been simply to provide the student with a variety of proverbial types, a fund of examples out of which he could commence his own literary activity.

Both Sehetepibre and the composition in Prov. 25 may be called "loyalist texts," and their intention to indoctrinate is not unusual. Both of them have a high regard for the king, placing him next to God in his capacity for revelation. The statement in Prov. 25:3 that "the heart of kings is unsearchable" reminds us of the affirmation of the Egyptian wisdom text concerning the king: "he is Sia who is in the hearts; his eyes search out everyone."[15] In the Egyptian panegyric the king is the personification of discernment; divine perception is personalized in him. The Egyptian word $d'r$ means "search out, investigate," a striking parallel to the Hebrew word $ḥqr$. Whereas the Hebrew text speaks of this in terms of its subjective meaning as an attribute of the king, the Egyptian equation of king and deity is more objective, focusing upon the action of the ruler. In both texts the relation between the king and his subjects is one of mutual support, even though the Egyptian composition spells out the responsibilities of the king to his people in more detail. Both texts urge upon the courtier the virtues of diligence and loyalty and promise him as a reward the opportunity to participate in an enterprise whose glory derives from God.

The wisdom book in Prov. 25 contains a clear and simple statement of the enterprise in which the wise men were involved and the sociological context in which this took place. The community to which the young courtier aspired consisted of wise men and counselors who constituted the administrative bodies of the royal court (vv.

5-6). His goal was to become an administrator of the government, ultimately, if possible, a member of the royal cabinet. If he conducted himself well and proved to be worthy, in due time he might be invited to stand in the place of the great (v. 6). Therefore, he was enjoined to be skillful in his work so that as a competent, as well as obedient servant, he might be honored to serve the king himself (Prov. 22:29; 24:21; 25:15, 27). The young man who came to be educated at the royal court ventured upon a political career. In most cases this would be quite natural for him because of the position and influence of his family. In other cases, however, young men of unusual talent would be recruited by the royal house to serve in various capacities (1 Sam. 16:18).[16]

It is true that in three of the older collections of wisdom (Prov. 16:1-25:28) the ruler is the subject of only twenty-four sayings out of more than three hundred.[17] However, in the two wisdom books that we have studied, the proverbial materials in these are organized and articulated with the royal service firmly in mind (Prov. 22-:29; 24:21; 25:6-7, 15). The central figure in them is the king, and the purpose for which they were written pertains to him. This is evident from the fact that references to the ruler occur in the introduction and conclusion of these compositions. If one adds to these two sources proverbs from the preceding collections that refer to the king (Prov. 16:1-22:16), approximately one-third of the total number of maxims and admonitions in these sources are related to the institution of kingship.[18] When it is also observed that almost every collection in the book of Proverbs has as its patron the royal figure, this forms an impressive witness in the tradition to the power and influence of the royalty in the development

of the wisdom literature of Israel. It accords well with
ancient Near Eastern traditions that associate this genre
of literature with kings, whether it is actually written by
them (Merikare, Ammenemes I), addressed to them
(Advice to a Prince), admonishing their support
(Sehetepibre), or advising royal personnel (Kagemni,
Ptahhotep, Khety, Amenemope, and Counsels of Wisdom).

The social background of this wisdom, represented in
Prov. 25 and the book of "The Sayings of the Wise", is
aristocratic. It is comprised of the rulers and the wealthy
and those associated with them by birth, profession, or
economic status. The specific exemplars of this society,
whom the persons addressed in these compositions serve
or aspire to serve, are kings, rulers, princes, lords, great
men, military counselors, wise judges, diplomats, righteous men, wise men, as well as fathers and mothers. Thus
the wise teachers, such as the author of the thirty sayings, are to be included among them. Their instructions
concern relations with rulers, elders, and skilled persons,
the three groups in the Old Testament that are characterized as possessing wisdom. The elders, who are considered wise because of their age and experience, were
directly involved in tribal and national affairs and were
associated with the king in the enterprise at the royal
court, whether they resided there, were advisors at administrative centers, or were the heads of great and in-
fluential houses.[19] Among the wise or skilled persons in
the employ of the king were craftsmen (1 Chron. 22:15),
military counselors (Prov. 24:5-6, 21:22; Eccles. 9:15),
and persons especially trained in esoteric lore and rites
(Eccles. 8:1, 5; Isa. 3:3). When the prophets use the attribute "wise" to designate this social group, they distin-

guish the wise men from the priests, prophets, and warriors. On the other hand, when they associate the wise men with others, it is the princes, scribes, and counselors to whom they refer. Thus, this designation has overtones of a professional class, a nuance that appears more emphatically when it is applied to foreign nations.

Numerous aspects of the wisdom literature of Israel are illuminated when the collections are placed in their proper social context. For instance, even though much of the imagery of proverbs derives from agrarian life, which reflects the close relationship between rural and urban settings in ancient times, terms such as "pleasant" (*n'ym*), "delicacies" (*mṭ'mwt*), "cocktail" (*mmsk*), "sweet" (*mtwq*), "ring" (*nzm*), and "ornament" (*ḥly*), as well as elegant imagery such as "apples of gold in a setting of silver" (*tpwḥy zhb bmśkywt ksp*), are to be associated with an affluent society.[20] In proverbial literature precious gems are frequently employed as an object of value and comparison. In fact, in many places the refined imagery of the book of Proverbs possesses a unique charm, especially evident when it is contrasted to the uncouth language of the prophets. For example, the announcement of judgment in Jer. 9:22, which is in a context appertaining to the wise and wealthy in Israel, is couched in repulsive imagery. The prophet declares that the corpses of men shall fall like dung. Such squalid imagery appears in the prophetic oracles. Often their vulgar rusticity stands in sharp contrast to the elegance and charm of proverbial imagery deriving from the royal court.

Moreover, the wise men go so far as to apply aesthetic language to the realm of morality. Where one might expect a moral or juridical term, words such as "pleasant" (Prov. 22:18) or "comely" (Prov. 17:7) appear. In this literature there is a tendency toward a fusion of that which is "right" with that which is "beautiful" or "becoming." Right is extended to include the realm of aesthetics, and goodness is manifested by its pleasantness. The good is that which contributes to harmony and order in human relationships and thereby fosters a life-style in accord with the best standards of social etiquette. At the royal court, then, the integration of life was total. Elegance in speech and grace in social relations were a mark of character as much as obedience to the canons of a moral code. The extension of the language of ˙aesthetics into the realm of piety and morality and the treating of etiquette with equal importance as matters of justice (Prov. 23:1-11) sets the wisdom literature off from the kind of instruction found in the Torah, particularly the book of Deuteronomy.[21] Of course, this can only be accounted for by assuming as its setting a social order that has developed a sophisticated value system through education and the development of the arts.

Although the ethics of the wisdom literature has been the subject of some discussion, this wisdom book in Proverbs also focuses upon an important distinction that must be made in dealing with this subject. In general, the ethics of the book of Proverbs has been characterized as "utilitarian," as a shrewd kind of morality.[22] Several scholars, however, have considered Prov. 25 to belong to what they have called the most "profane" or "worldly" collection of wisdom.[23] This lack of distinction between utilitarian and ethical good has been attributed to the conviction on the part of the ancients that the good is always the useful thing. However, to appeal to this or to the belief on the part of the ancients of the connection between a deed and its consequence may well overlook one thing, the difference in the ethical view-point of the several collections of proverbs. This raises the question concerning the degree to which scholars have simply treated the whole question too homogene-ously. Perhaps the distinction between utilitarian ethics and a morality deriving from religious injunction and experiential vision may be accounted for on the basis of the specific *Sitz im Leben* of a given collection of sayings. May this not be the case with reference to Prov. 25?

The reason that the wisdom book considered here may be characterized as utilitarian in its ethical vision is not hard to find. As a book instructing the young execu-tive how to succeed in the organization, it has a specific goal in mind. Although I have stated this too narrowly at this point, it does help in drawing attention to the specific rationale governing the material. The ethical viewpoint is tied into the specific enterprise in which the courtier is involved. The sociological setting in which the executive operates involves treating with enemies as well as friends as a constant factor. The various factions at court necessitate the implementation of the wisest possi-ble course. Part of this tactic is the favoring of the enemy, the political opponent, where possible, in order to build up a supply of goodwill should he or his politi-cal party ever assume control of the court.[24] To generalize the ethical perspective assumed here, whether as a characteristic of all wisdom literature or as a univer-sal morality, does not sufficiently take into account the specific context and setting of this individual collection.

Both the wisdom book in Prov. 25 and the composi-tion entitled "The Sayings of the Wise"(Prov. 22:17-24:22) have their *Sitz im Leben* in the royal service. Thus, the enterprise presupposed in each of these compositions is

similar. Their maxims engaged the courtier specifically
in terms of his role as a court functionary. Of course,
this does not mean that traditional themes deriving from
the instruction of wise men are completely ignored. But
the juncture at which this traditional wisdom receives a
new direction is in the intention of the composition to
provide the young man with advice that will guide him
in his new "way of life" at court. The aim of this discipline and training to which the courtier submits in the
fulfillment of his new responsibility is epitomized in
those sayings which set before him the reward of faithful
service, a station among the great, and audience with
kings.

The question may be raised whether this must be regarded as a secular or religious enterprise. Unfortunately, some scholars have sought to separate the two. Von
Rad has suggested that, beginning with the reign of Solomon, the ancient pansacralism of the pre-kingship
epoch was broken by an abrupt and incipient process of
secularization.[25] In the same vein he and other scholars
have regarded Prov. 25 as the most profane collection of
wisdom in the book of Proverbs. Yet it is precisely in the
composition in Prov. 25 that the whole enterprise involved in the pursuit of wisdom is given a religious
rationale. Von Rad himself has conceded this with reference to the work of Jolles and Herder, that wisdom does
deal with a hidden order of things.[26] This insight is
given specific formulation in Prov. 25:2: "It is the glory
of God to hide a matter." The same mysterious note
surrounding the work of God and king is sounded in
the "who knows?" of Prov. 24:22. Not only does this
theme enable us to explicate the relation between wisdom and kingship, but it also provides a fundamental

theological presupposition that links the wisdom of Israel with that of Egypt.

The wisdom book in Prov. 25 makes explicit a theme that has had a long history in the wisdom of the ancient Near East. It is first encountered in one of the most ancient and revered books of Egyptian wisdom, the instruction of Ptahhotep, the Egyptian vizier who lived in the twenty-fifty century B.C., Warning his disciples against greed and rapaciousness, the vizier urges them to live contentedly until the appointed time when the God would reward them. He reinforces his injunctions with a proverb that focuses sharply upon the antithesis between the human and divine.

> Nn p3 ḫr n rmṯ ḫpr
> wd·t nṯr pw ḫpr·t
>
> It is not the terror of men that happens;
> it is the command of God that comes to pass.[27]

The simple eudaemonism of this book is qualified by a paradoxical assertion. Reward is dependent upon the action of God and is not immediately guaranteed. Therefore, a man must wait patiently for God to act in rewarding him for his good conduct. Man cannot hope to predict the outworking of the decrees of God in history because they are hidden from him.

This proverb, which plays only an incidental role in the instruction of Ptahhotep, becomes paradigmatic of the antithesis of the divine and human in the wisdom of Amenemope and Ani. In Amenemope it appears as the midpoint in a cluster of sayings that sound out the enigmas of the divine-human relationship. This quasi-philosophical discourse, which is found in the eighteenth chapter (Amen. 19:10-20:6), commences with an admonition against anxiety and concludes with an assertion about the inability of man to control or predict the future.[28] At first, this appears to be merely a qualification of the human enterprise, a declaration that the future is controlled by God. The second proverb, however, extends the thought to a characterization of human nature itself. Whereas God is in his excellence, man exists in his deficiency.

This negation of human existence in the first part is contrasted with the positive affirmation concerning the power of God in the two proverbs that form the second part. It is useless for man to protest "innocence" or claim "success." On the one hand, it is God who determines iniquity, not man. On the other hand, there is no success, nor, for that matter, is there failure before God. Even if God were to lead a man to pursue excellence, in a brief space of time he would mar it. In the middle of this discourse the pivotal maxim (Amen. 19:16-17), which confirms the deficiency of man mentioned before it and introduces the sufficiency of God that follows in the second part, is strikingly similar to the proverb encountered in Ptahhotep.

> rwỉ3ty n3 md·t idd n3 rmt·w
> rwỉ3ty n3 ỉr·t p3 ntr
>
> The word that men say is one thing;
> that which the god does is another.

The ignorance and imperfection of man stand in stark contrast to the authority and power of God. This one maxim forms the nucleus of this cluster of proverbs that probe the mysterious relationship between God and man.

In the instruction of Ani a proverb of the same genre
forms the conclusion to a similar type of discourse (Ani
8:3-10).[29] In a passage that is strikingly Heraclitean in
tone, Ani draws attention to the flux of reality. The man
who was once rich is now a vagabond. The river bed of
the past season has disappeared and has become a different stream in the new year. What was once a great
lake is now a dry bed, and what was formerly a river
bank is now a deep pool. The flux and change in nature
and human history together point to the same truth
(8:9-10):

w' sḥr·w s
w['] wšby·t nb 'nḫ

The plans of a man are one thing;
the answer of the Lord of Life is another.[30]

The specific moral instruction deriving from this knowledge reminds us of Prov. 25:21-22, where the courtier is
advised to be kind to his enemy. In Ani the wise man is
to be kind to the beggar because one day he himself
might be fed by the surplus that comes from another
(8:7).

Undoubtedly this proverb in Ani provides the original
for the assimilated version that appears in Prov. 16:1.

לאדם מערכי־לב
ומיהוה מענה לשון

The plans of the mind belong to man,
but the answer of the tongue is from the LORD.

In each case the juxtaposition of the central elements in
the two lines is the same. The Hebrew version however,
has reversed the word order in the lines and added the

qualifying words "mind" and "tongue." Together with Prov. 16:8, which I have already shown to be an assimilated Egyptian proverb, this saying and its companion that follows develop themes that are found in late Egyptian wisdom. The contrast between man's evaluation of his moral standing and the right judgment of God in Prov. 16:2 is reminiscent of Amen. 19:18-21, where man's protest of innocence is also qualified by the just sentence of God. The close proximity of these sayings in Prov. 16:1-9 with those which relate to the king in 16:10-15 reinforce the suggestion that the parts of this chapter that were derived from an Egyptian source found their way into the book of Proverbs from collections preserved at the royal court.

Actually, proverbs concerning the transitoriness of life and the hiddenness of God, which are found in Ani and Amenemope, also appear in the royal wisdom of Egypt in the early Middle Kingdom period. In the wisdom of Merikare, the king asserts that God has hidden himself.

snn ẖ·t r ẖ·t m rmṯ
ỉmn n sw.nṯr rẖ·w ḳd·w

Among men generation after generation passes away;
God who knows characters has hidden himself.[31]

In spite of this, the author believes that the influence of God over the world is still pervasive and powerful. Quite mysteriously God's hidden power thwarts what is apparently coming to pass. The setting for this statement, like that in the book of Proverbs, is unusual. In the preceding discourse the king praises the institution of kingship and venerates the office of king because of its antiquity. Following his explicit confession of a crime, something remarkable in the royal literature of Egypt, the king makes the assertion that God had hidden himself, and then, in the face of his emphasis upon the withdrawal of the deity, proceeds to a celebration of him as creator. Though hidden, God's power is still visible in the world.

A similar cluster of themes appears in connection with kingship in Israelite wisdom. The collection of sayings in Prov. 16:1-9, which stresses the hiddenness of divine plans and purposes, is abruptly terminated with a maxim that makes reference to the inerrant judgment of the king (Prov. 16:10). The celebration of the oracular power of the king in this saying is reminiscent of the thought contained in the wisdom of King Merikare, that God has created rulers and given magical powers to man as a means of warding off evil.[32] It is significant, however, that following a series of proverbs that severely limit the possibility of man's discerning the purposes of God, a cluster of sayings appear that exalt kingship. Inerrancy, righteousness, death, and life are all manifestations of a sacral reality embodied in the king (Prov. 16:10-15). The mystery of God does not stand in contradiction to this epiphanic reality. Even though the divine plan is hidden from man, the power of God is revealed in the created order. Likewise, if God remains hidden in himself, he is manifest in the person and activity of the king.

This leads to the subject of creation, which though not specifically treated in Prov. 16 is implicit in the statement of Prov. 25:2 "it is the glory of God to hide a matter." This cryptic utterance stands in sharp antithesis to the repeated affirmations of the self-disclosure of God in the literature of the Old Testament. Paradoxically, it locates the glory of God in the concealment of meaning. Yet this divine action in concealing is not a momentary thing but a purposive act. The statement is all-encompassing and sets before man a mystery that is not confined to a specific time or situation. Were it not for the ballast provided in the second half of this verse, the theology of this composition would sink to the level of a practical agnosticism. No doubt, with the decline of kingship and the accompanying loss of a reliable source of revelation, the ground was prepared for the practical skepticism of the book of Ecclesiastes, which questions the reality of the divine disclosure in the world.[33]

In a sense, however, the first statement prepares for the upswing in the second part. The fact that the first part of the verse asserts that behind the apparent masquerade of the phenomenal order an intelligible divine plan lies hidden leads to the affirmation in the second half of the verse. In a simple and sweeping statement the writer ingeniously characterizes the whole enterprise involved in kingship. Just as the glory of God resides in the concealment of meaning, the glory of the king is lodged in his capacity and ability to disclose the truth hidden in the created order. The locus of revelation is not the person of God but that of the king. It is the king who has access to the divine secrets. By his special relation to the deity the king is privileged to inquire into that which is hidden from ordinary mortals. The discernment of the king is itself a matter for wonder and awe. It too is something mysterious and inscrutable. To stand in the presence of the king is celebrated as a unique blessing (1 Kings 10:8), and to share in the enterprise of kingship is regarded as a great honor (Prov. 25: 27).

Therefore, when we find the same theme appearing in connection with the two kings of the Old Testament who are most notably described as the wisest of all men, we cannot regard it as coincidental. In the legend of the visit of the queen of Sheba to the court of Solomon, the wisdom of Solomon is characterized by the use of the word "hidden." The queen is amazed at his wisdom because he is able to answer everything, for nothing was hidden from him (1 Kings 10:3). That this clause is not merely hyperbolic but actually does have a connection to the theme discussed is apparent from the description of the king of Tyre recorded in Ezek. 28.[34] The prophet concedes that he was the wisest of all the ancients, including the legendary wise man Dan'el. The extent of his wisdom is rehearsed in terms that are similar to those used of Solomon. The prophet asserts of the king, "No secret was hidden from you" (Ezek. 28:3). Because of their unique and special relation to the deity, these two kings are exemplars of that manifestation of sacral reality that is granted only to kings.

What is missing in each of these descriptions is the intermediate element, which is provided by the statement of Prov. 25:2. The institution of kingship involved an enterprise that was both active and investigative as well as passive and receptive. Amid the ever-changing temporal process, the divine revelation to the king did not take place in a vacuum but involved the employment of innate capacities and special skills that had been vouchsafed to the king by the deity. What is described passively in relation to Solomon and the king of Tyre is described actively in the characterization of the enterprise of kingship in this wisdom book. It was the glory of the king to search out what God had hidden. He stood not only as a visible manifestation of the presence of God, but as an agent through whom the secrets of God were disclosed.

It is unfortunate, then, that this wisdom book in Prov. 25 has been characterized as a "profane" collection of sayings and left outside of what might be called "theological" in the assessment of Israel's wisdom traditions. It is precisely in this composition that we have a specific unfolding of the basic enterprise involved in wisdom, one that seeks to ground the investigative enterprise in a specific religious rationale. As already observed from the study of Egyptian wisdom, this theme has had a long history in the ancient Near East. Although only a few texts reveal the indebtedness of Israel's wisdom traditions to Egyptian sources, they provide a background for understanding Israel's independent development of this theme.

The implementation of the quest to understand, to probe the secrets of nature and the life of man, and their interrelationships, was based upon Israel's belief that the glory of God was embodied in the hidden order of the world. To discover something about this order was in itself a revelation of the nature and purpose of God. For such a task the total resources of the nation were brought to bear—all of the skill and expertise of the royal court. At the head of this order was the king, who by his special endowment was peculiarly equipped to direct this operation. To encourage the young man at court aspiring to be an official of the government and to provide him with sound counsel in the development of his relationships at the court, this small wisdom book was written. The enjoyment of privilege and honor was a worthy quest for a young man. In this wisdom book in Prov. 25:2-27, he was invited to seek much, for to investigate the meaning of reality in the royal court was a sacred enterprise. At the same time he was given a warning, "not too much," because the quest brought with it its own inherent dangers. By seeking too much glory the courtier could easily fall from his position of honor. Only in seeking and enjoying that which was sufficient could he hope to continue his worthy service to both God and king.

7

Political Wisdom in Ancient Israel

As observed in the previous chapter, the relationship between Egyptian and Israelite wisdom literature extends
beyond the specific subject of the appropriation of literary materials on the part of the wise men of Israel. It
also concerns the similar sociopolitical context that was
the matrix for each, the established ruling order represented in the royal court and presided over by the
king. Since the connection between wisdom and kingship
is found in both Egypt and Israel, it is not surprising
that this is one of the principal themes in the treatment
of the reign of King Solomon in 1 Kings 3-11. In fact,
wisdom is mentioned by the narrator in connection with
the source from which he drew his sketch of the

dynasty, "The Book of the Acts of Solomon" (1 Kings 11:41). Whether this was actually the case, or whether the chronicle concerning the reign of Solomon was solely limited to an account of his economic and political achievements, the final version of the account of his reign conjoins the two. Moreover, wisdom itself is made the rationale for his other political and economic accomplishments (1 Kings 3:11-13).

Thus, the chauvinistic boast concerning the wisdom of Solomon contained in 1 Kings 4:29-34[1] and 10:23-24, that Solomon was wiser than all of the renowned sages of his time, has been taken seriously by most scholars.[2] The most comprehensive and far-reaching attempt to explain the circumstances that gave rise to these declarations was undertaken by Alt, who sought to link Israelite wisdom of this type with the onomastica of the ancient Near East.[3] As a key to understanding this genre of wisdom, which became the basis for the unique claim concerning Solomon, he selected the mention of natural phenomena in 1 Kings 4:33.[4]

> He spoke of trees, from the cedar that
> is in Lebanon to the hyssop that grows out
> of the wall; he spoke also of beasts, and
> of birds, and of reptiles, and of fish.

In the context of ancient oriental wisdom, this statement is reminiscent of the encyclopedic wisdom of Egypt contained in the compilations of natural phenemena called onomastica. Indeed, Alt suggested that the stimulus for the development of this kind of natural wisdom (*Natur-weisheit*) in Israel probably came from Egypt, where the development of such learning had long been a tradition of the wise. Influenced by this aspect of the cultural heritage of Egypt, Solomon became not merely the imitator of a type of wisdom already known, but the creator of a new form of poetic art in which prosaic explanations concerning natural relationships and the origin of things were transformed into sophisticated literary forms probing the interconnections of natural phenomena (Prov. 30:15-16, 18-20, 24-31). Since this new literary genre surpassed all the wisdom that was known previously, it engendered the praise echoed in the later tradition of the incomparability of the wisdom of Solomon.

A different alternative has been proposed by R. B. Y. Scott, who believes that the Deuteronomist does not unduly glorify Solomon, even in his use of source material.[5] He asserts that the extravagant boast concerning the wisdom of Solomon is not part of the original Deuteronomic edition of the account but stems from late insertions into the text on the part of editors who seek to glorify Solomon. Scott supports his contention by appealing to the different kinds of wisdom mentioned, the post-exilic linguistic affinities of the materials themselves, and the Septuagint version, which preserves a text quite different from the Hebrew of 1 Kings 5. According to Scott, the achievements of Solomon kept alive the memory of the splendor of his reign and led to the insertion of anecdotal and other folkloristic materials in the post-exilic period. The extravagant claims about Solomon's wisdom have no basis in real fact. The quest for the origins of Israelite wisdom and its international connections must be centered in the epoch associated with king Hezekiah, not Solomon.

There is a third possibility open to us by which to explain the apparent exaggerations in the narrative of 1 Kings regarding the wisdom of Solomon. It involves the connection between literature and politics, a relationship that has already been carefully studied in Egyptian literature.[6] Viewed from this perspective, the question is that of the function of wisdom literature within its social context. Of course, the fostering of the literary arts and the enrichment of the cultural heritage of a nation have always been part of the task undertaken by an established order that has tasted the fruits of civilization. Nevertheless, this should not dominate our understanding of the function of literature to the exclusion of other more sinister possibilities. Therefore, it is important to examine the relations between literature and politics in ancient Egypt, where the meaning of this relationship has been more fully explored, before considering this subject in the Old Testament.

In his study of the literature of Egypt during the period of the Middle Kingdom, Posener has demonstrated the close relation between the literary productions of this era and the political events that occurred during it. Taking his cue from earlier studies, he has expanded the subject to include a variety of literary types, suggesting that in each case there was a vital connection between the activity of the writers of the royal court and the necessities of the political situation.[7] The wisdom literature of this epoch, along with several other literary genres, was put into the service of the royal ideology as a means of strengthening the position of the newly emergent dynasty following a period of political turmoil. Thus, a series of Egyptian literary texts was adapted to serve as a medium of political propaganda. Of course, this led to the spontaneous production of other literary works favoring the special interests of the royal house. This politicization of literary works was particularly prevalent during the Twelfth Dynasty (1991-1786 B.C.).[8] Similar types of works are found earlier, during the reign of Merikare in the Tenth Dynasty (2130-2040 B.C.), and much later in the time of Rameses III (1198-1166 B.C.). Although various literary types are absorbed into this politicizing process, they are characterized by several persistent traits.[9] They are loyalist in tone, eulogizing the reigning monarch or his immediate predecessor and citing the accomplishments of the dynasty. They often include personal anecdotes or testimonies interpreting the historical and political situation. Usually these stories are not incidental but have some definite intention, explicating the political situation in relation to the person of the king in a manner that best serves the royal house. Although the educative and political functions are closely interwoven in these documents, they are consciously formulated in response to a particular political problem and seek to propagate a point of view that creates respect for and confidence in the royal administration.

I have already mentioned the wisdom of Sehetepibre, which is a wisdom book transformed into a panegyric dedicated to the reigning monarch, and have cited the passage in which the king is identified with the Egyptian god Sia.[10] That the equation of the king with various gods in this panegyric is not to be interpreted literally is shown by the fact that he is identified with male as well as female deities. However, the monarch is elevated to the divine sphere as the representative and embodiment of the awesome powers of the various gods. The king stands as a colossus casting his shadow over the whole land, a fact that is appealed to by the author when he connects national prosperity and even personal immortality with the loyalty due the king in all of the land.

Other texts express even stronger sentiments in regard to the person of the king. In the story of the journey of Sinuhe to Palestine, Sinuhe declares to Nenshi, the prince, his great esteem for the ruling monarch, Sesostris I, an assertion filled with awe, a fitting introduction to the hymn of praise to the king that follows.

> Nṯr pw gr·t nn snw·f, nn ky ḫpr ḥr ḫ3·t·f
> nb s3:t pw, iḳr sḫr·w, mnḫ wḏ·t-mdw[11]

> He is a god who has no equal; there does not exist another who is superior to him.
> He is the master of wisdom, skillful in counsels, effective with respect to command.

Not only is the king identified as the possessor or master of wisdom (*nb s3·t pw*), but he is also designated as a unique divine being.

> w' pw n dd nṯr[12]

> he is a unique being, a gift of God,

in the hymn that follows. In the Instruction of Ammenemes I an even more transcendent title is assigned to the Egyptian monarch Sesostris I. He is called "lord of the universe" (*nb-r-ḏr*), a title applied to the Sun God or to Osiris, but to other deities, only sparingly.[13] It emphasizes the total supremacy of the king over the land. The glorification of the king in Egyptian literature is extreme, almost without limits.

The Instruction of Ammenemes I may also be taken

to exemplify another trait of this genre of literature that is prominent in several other texts. The king, whether living or deceased, is lauded for his accomplishments. In the description of these, traditional formulae are used as well as references to specific historical events.

iw dỉ n·ỉ n šw3·w sḫpr·n·ỉ nmḥ

n ḥḳr·tw m rnp·wt·ỉ n ỉb·tw ỉm[14]

I gave to the poor; I nurtured the orphan.

No one has been hungry in my years; no one has been thirsty therein.

Among the exploits of Ammenemes I that are mentioned are his travels to the north and south of Egypt, his conquest of foreign peoples, and his personal triumphs in subjugating lions and crocodiles, the erection of great monuments, and the construction of a palace.[15] The rehearsal of these acts not only enhances the person and the office of the king but also serves as a proclamation of the greatness of the dynasty, thus assuring the successor, who relates the events, a share in the glory of his predecessor.

This is also effected by the introduction of personal anecdotes and testimonies on the part of the deceased king, who speaks through his son. The text presently under consideration contains a story of an assassination-attempt on the life of king Ammenemes I. The king tells how his enemies, who ate with him daily, sought to kill him during the night. The importance of this story does not revolve around the act of treachery alone, as though it were merely told for the sake of warning the reader concerning untrustworthy associates. This incident serves as a springboard to a much more important issue, the establishment of a clear line of succession to the throne. Thus, Sesostris I is introduced into the testimony as co-regent of the reigning king, Ammenemes I. The report also has another motivation, to castigate the rival party contending for the throne by showing their utter perfidy.

From an earlier period we have another example of this type of pseudonymous testimonial in the form of a wisdom book in the instruction of Merikare. Like the previous text, it too is ascribed to the father of Merikare, Khety III.[16] To his father the son attributes a confession of guilt for a crime that he had committed during his war with the Theban house. The conciliatory note in this text fits in with the political program of Merikare. He desires peaceful coexistence with the city of Thebes, which is becoming ever more powerful. Thus, the political stratagem of Khety III, which aims not only at the establishment of peaceful relations with the South but also the consolidation of local support, is adopted by Merikare. The issues discussed in the text and its mood reflect this political tendency.

The various literary types all share one thing in common, an element that relates less to the traditional form they espouse than to the function of the various themes in relation to the social and political context of the work. What we observe is the utilization of literature to serve as royal propaganda. Specific literary forms and traditional themes become tools in the hand of the government by which to create a loyal regime that will encourage the support of the subjects. If petty princes upon whom the crown is dependent are involved, or even rival states, as in the case of Merikare, concessions pertinent to current political developments may be made in order to foster amity. If enemies of the crown are represented by rival factions within the kingdom, an even more potentially dangerous situation, the party in power will employ every means possible to assure the continuance of their rule, including the development of literature that casts the crown into a favorable light. For this reason Sesostris I, upon his enthronement following the assassination of his father, issued a wisdom book in the name of the deceased monarch, asserting his own right to succession and discrediting his enemies. In each of these works, enclosed within an elegant literary setting, is an interpretation of the political situation from the perspective of the monarchy, which seeks not only to instruct and entertain, but also to convince its audience of the justice of its cause and elicit the support necessary to achieve its policies.

Among the variety of literary types involved a number of them are designated "instruction" (*sb3y·t*), the term usually used to describe an Egyptian book of wisdom. As applied to the type of wisdom discovered in the Middle Kingdom, however, this designation involves a change from the older style of literary instruction familiar to us in the books of wisdom written by Ptahhotep and Kagemni.[17] Although the chief theme of the older form is preserved, the writing of a book of wisdom by the father for the benefit of his son, with the introduction of a political motivation both the form and content change. Hybrid forms appear, such as the instruction of Sehetepibre, and the issues involved concern the whole nation, not just the relation of the individual to the social order. The instruction of Ammenemes I is really a kind of recriminative testimony in autobiographical form, written for an audience at court. Sehetepibre has plagiarized a book of wisdom to produce a panegyric made up of hymnic and instructional elements. However, I shall classify these varied texts under the rubric "political wisdom," a phrase that embraces their content and also, within limits, the variety of their forms.

In the literature of the Old Testament, there is one passage to which the description "political wisdom" can be applied, the narrative concerning the reign of king Solomon in 1 Kings 3-11. This section of 1 Kings contains a variety of materials, among which wisdom is prominent. In fact, the claims, reports, and anecdotes that it contains are together quite similar to the political wisdom of Egypt just described. The connection between wisdom literature and political history, however, is explicitly made in reference to the source of this account, "The Book of the Acts of Solomon" (1 Kings 11: 41). It is possible, of course, that this source was limited in its scope to annalistic records, the wisdom materials found here having been added by the Deuteronomic editor from other sources. Recently, scholars have tended to associate the wisdom literature in this narrative with the chronicle of the reign of Solomon, conceding that the source material has been reworked by the editor.[18] In spite of this, the presence of what appear to be authentic elements of wisdom that are in harmony with the standpoint of the Deuteronomist has been used to corroborate the thesis that the historical source used did contain wisdom literature or historical materials pertaining to this. Thus, wisdom and political history are interrelated in the Old Testament.

The Deuteronomist has interlarded historical materials and anecdotes concerning Solomon to show the achievements of his administration, to celebrate his eminence and riches, and to extol his wisdom and fame. Although the main concern of the narrator is religious, relating to the building of the temple and the revelation of the will of Yahweh to Solomon, his inclusion of matters of historical and political concern show that the political and religious history of Judah and Israel are organically related and cannot easily be dissociated. As is so often the case, religion is often simply an arm of politics used as a sanction, for political actions. For my purposes, then, I may use the description just given of political wisdom in Egypt as a foil to highlight the essential characteristics of similar elements that appear in 1 Kings and are relevant to the theme. Once these parallels are isolated, we can turn to the more important issue of the precise meaning of such political wisdom in the Old Testament.

In 1 Kings 4-10 the Deuteronomist presents a description of the various political and economic accomplishments of Solomon. Although this recitation of his exploits is primarily centered in the construction and dedication of the temple in Jerusalem (1 Kings 5-9), he does sketch a picture with sufficient scope to leave an indelible impression upon the reader of the magnitude and grandeur of the regime of Solomon. The fact that the various projects enumerated are described in the third person lifts them out of the category of administrative inscriptions, which usually employ the first person. The form, then, reminds of the speech of Sinuhe, in which he relates the deeds of the king in the third person.[19] Standing alone, this characteristic does not make

this account of the reign of an Israelite monarch too different from that of the reigns of other Israelite and
Judaean kings. Taken in connection with the other elements of political wisdom in the section, however, it
lends to the whole narrative a hyperbolic tone, making
one conscious of the efforts of the narrator to impress
his audience.

To gainsay the fictitious impression that this leaves,
scholars have worked diligently to corroborate the his-
toricity of the narrative.[20] Without denying that the Solomonic era was a period of colossal growth and development for the new nation, in the course of time it
would really matter little whether the great literary com-
plex here represented actual historical facts deriving
from the time of Solomon or whether it was merely an
association of legendary materials, folklore, and anecdotes with the person of Solomon. For example, the
speeches between Solomon and Hiram of Tyre in 1
Kings 5 do not appear to be authentic.[21] Regardless of
whether they are or not, they serve the purpose for
which the narrator introduces them, to show how Solomon's wisdom was called into play in the construction
of the temple and to connect this account with what precedes. In this sense, like many of the other descriptions
of the projects of Solomon, they reinforce and develop
the main theme of the narrative, the greatness and
splendor of the kingdom of Israel under Solomon.

In the account of the reign of Solomon there are also
three anecdotes concerning him, the story of the revelation to him in a dream, the tale of the two harlots, both
of these tied together in 1 Kings 3, and the account of
the visit of the queen of Sheba in 1 Kings 10. Unlike the
stories told in the political wisdom of Egypt, they are

narrated in the third person, not the first. Noth has
suggested that the editor has placed the first two stories
in a position of prominence, stressing them more than
the eulogy of Solomon for his wisdom in 1 Kings 4:29-
34.[22] Even if one draws attention to the fact that the
boast concerning Solomon's great wisdom is repeated
later, giving it greater emphasis, the structure of the
narrative, as we shall subsequently observe, confirms
Noth's judgment.

As a background for understanding the story of the
dream-revelation to Solomon, Hermann has suggested
the Egyptian *Königsnovelle*, an etiological story form that
crystallizes around the person of the king as an ideal figure.[23] It presents the king in his role as policy-maker
for the nation, from whose decisions great events are set
in progress. Integral to the story is the court setting in
which the king communicates his decisions to his follow-
ers. It is not in this, however, that Hermann finds a link
with the dream-revelation vouchsafed to Solomon and
the story built up around it, but in certain secondary
elements. The communication to Solomon through a
dream, Solomon's mention of his youth, his cultic activity
connected with the story, and the unusual fact that he
does not communicate with his courtiers but proceeds
directly to Jerusalem to sacrifice—these are elements
that appear in Egyptian variations of this type and are
singled out by Hermann as parallels.

The significance of Hermann's suggestion, however, is
not to be found in the adducing of parallels that show
that the Israelites have borrowed and modified this
form, but in the discovery of a literary vehicle, possibly
an Israelite type of *Königsnovelle*, which is utilized by the
Deuteronomist in 1 Kings.[24] The phrase "this day" in 1

Kings 3:6 (*kywm hzh*) which, as Hermann indicates, is associated with a series of terms regarding the enthronement of the king, lends credence to the conception that this form derives from the context of kingship, more particularly, the context in which the choice of the king by the deity is announced in connection with the dynastic succession. Since the latter element may be secondary in the account here, the emphasis in the original story is upon the choice of the deity. Solomon was made king before he was old enough to fully assume this responsibility. The religious ideology here is etiological; ·it associates the Solomonic accession with the decision of Yahweh and reveals the divine endowment he received. The Deuteronomist, on the other hand, places the dream-revelation at the beginning of the narrative, to show how Solomon received the gift of wisdom, and then immediately narrates an incident that corroborates his divine charisma, the necessity of making a decision about the child of the two harlots. The original context of the dream-revelation, however, leads me to believe that the question of accession to the throne was involved. If this is true, it is a type of story that would grow out of associated political events and their interpretation.[25]

The last element that is parallel to Egyptian political wisdom is the eulogy of Solomon in 1 Kings 4:29-34, which is repeated in 10:23-24. It has been regarded as problematical by several scholars. As already observed, Scott regards it as a later addition to the text, since it is not the habit of the Deuteronomist to unduly glorify the king. Noth finds it difficult to conceive that this type of assertion comes from the annals of Solomon because it has no identifiable connection with the historical processes from which such judgments come in a typical royal record.[26] Following a suggestion by Alt, he believes that it could well be the introduction to a collection of sayings and songs, ascribed to or even composed by Solomon himself. That this eulogy is part of the source used by the Deuteronomist is evident from its poetic structure, its unique vocabulary, and from the fact that the parallel in 10:23-24, which is derived from 4:29-34, is repeated in the later tradition in 2 Chron. 9:22-23. Of course, the general similarity of this eulogy to the boast of Sinuhe or the panegyric of Sehetepibre is quite evident. Nevertheless, since the idealization of Solomon here is paralleled by the idealization of Israel in the surrounding context, it will be more germane at this point to inquire into the reason for this.

In the framework of the narrative surrounding the eulogy of Solomon in 1 Kings 4:29-34, the Deuteronomist shows that the accession of Solomon to the throne and his judicial and administrative wisdom bring Israel to an epoch of great prosperity. Using the term "Israel" in an ideal sense (1 Kings 3:28; 4:1), he reveals the effect that the wisdom of Solomon has upon the nation, a nation that now extends to the limits of the kingdom promised to Abraham (Gen. 15:18; Jos. 1:4; 1 Kings 4:21; 8:65).[27] The fact that some of the phrases used, such as "Judah and Israel" (1 Kings 4:20, 25), appear to be post-exilic cannot be used to show that all of these references are secondary additions, especially if the narrative of the Deuteronomist has not taken final form until the exilic period.[28] Rather, these statements develop the motif of fulfillment introduced in the transitional verse, 1 Kings 2:46b, between the Succession Narrative and the story of Solomon's reign.

The establishment of the kingdom in the hand of Sol-

omon, including all of the territories promised to Abraham, shows the fulfillment of the promise of Yahweh
to Israel, a theme dealt with earlier by the
Deuteronomist in connection with the conquest of the
land (Jos. 23:15). It was not Yahweh who failed to keep
his promise; it was Solomon who failed to keep the covenant. In the early part of the career of Solomon, Israel experienced the blessings of the covenant, but when
Solomon became old and apostate, the nation was
punished (1 Kings 11:4, 11). Thus, without hesitation
the Deuteronomist can adopt the material that exalts
king Solomon and his reign in order to demonstrate the
fulfillment of the pledge that God had made to Israel.

Besides showing the fulfillment of the covenant on the
part of Yahweh, the Deuteronomist has another purpose, one more directly connected with political matters,
in introducing stories that exalt the kingdom of Solomon
and magnify his person. This is indicated by his use and
arrangement of his sources, particularly in the first and
final chapters describing the positive and negative aspects of Solomon's reign (1 Kings 3 and 11). Both of
these chapters bear the stamp of the Deuteronomist.[29]
Scholars have been uneasy about the preface to the
whole narrative in 1 Kings 3:1-3 which, as Noth comments, seems to lack unity and is clearly secondary. Although there appears to be a connection between the
order of events in the introduction and the sequence in
1 Kings 9:24-25, this parallel is much less significant
than the similarity between the structure of the introductory chapter and the last chapter. A comparison between
these two leaves us with the impression that the
Deuteronomist has arranged the first chapter with a
view to the last, or vice versa. Three of the four divisions

of the first chapter, 1 Kings 3, are parallel to the last chapter.

Pharaoh's daughter (3:1)	The daughter of Pharaoh (11:1-3a) (including other wives)
Sacrificing at high places (3:2-3)	Building a high place (11:7-8) (apostasy, vv. 3b-8)
Revelation of Yahweh (3:4-15)	Revelation of Yahweh (11:9-13) (mention of appearances earlier, 11:9)

The same order of themes in these two chapters, marriage to foreign women, cultic policy concerning high places, and the appearance of God is striking. That it is not coincidental is confirmed by the unusual introduction of the reign of Solomon with the mention of his connection with the royal house of Egypt through the daughter of Pharaoh.

There is also an irony in the mention of Solomon's marriage to the daughter of Pharaoh, for it is the turning-point in the narrative (1 Kings 11:1). If Solomon's wives enhance his court, and his women are blessed by his wisdom (10:8), he himself is strengthened by diplomatic ties but cursed by religious entanglements (11:3-4). Among his wives a prominent place is given to the daughter of Pharaoh, who is placed at the head of the list of princesses to whom Solomon was betrothed and who is singled out as the one woman for whom a house was built and a city reconstructed (9:16-17, 24).[30] Thus the stinging irony of the story about Hadad, one of Solomon's adversaries, how he fled to Egypt and was given in marriage the sister of Pharaoh's own wife (11:19), and how Jeroboam, whom Solomon sought to kill, also found refuge in Egypt (11:40). In this way the

Deuteronomist brings Solomon's political actions into tension with the religious heritage of Israel. In his arrangement of the materials, however, he also brings the fulfillment of the promise through Solomon in conflict with a particularism that cannot tolerate the political necessities that made such national prosperity possible.

The one section of 1 Kings 3 that does not appear at first to have a parallel in 1 Kings 11 is the story of the two harlots at the end of the chapter.[31] Upon closer inspection, however, it is quite similar in one respect to the prophetic tale at the close 1 Kings 11. In the story of the two harlots, two women appear before Solomon, each of them claiming to be the legitimate mother of the one child that is left to them. The real mother accuses her companion of having stolen the child when her own child died during the night. To settle the dispute Solomon does not appeal to the customary canons of jurisprudence. Instead, he offers to satisfy each woman by dividing the child in two and giving each of them half of it. The real mother, of course, protests this action, for to divide the child spells its death. Thus, the true mother of the child is manifested by a simple stratagem that revealed those sentiments which could only spring from the bond of motherhood.

In the prophetic tale of Ahijah, which brings 1 Kings 11 and the narrative concerning Solomon to a close, the encounter between Jeroboam and Ahijah, the prophet, takes place. According to the Deuteronomist, it occurs at an important time in the career of Jeroboam. He has just been appointed as an official overseeing the labor operation in the territory of the tribe of Joseph, the heartland of the north. Ahijah is wearing a new garment when he meets Jeroboam. Stripping it from himself, he proceeds to tear it into twelve pieces. To Jeroboam he offers ten of them, with the pronouncement that God is about to take the kingdom of Israel out of the hand of Solomon. The kingdom will be given to Jeroboam and will be represented by the ten northern tribes. Of course, the speech is not without its qualifications, which originate in the hindsight of the Deuteronomist. The Davidic house will be preserved (1 Kings 11:36), and the period of the affliction of Judah will be limited (11:39). Nevertheless, the kingdom will be divided, and with that division Jeroboam is given the opportunity to rule over Israel, which Yahweh promises he will build into a "sure house" like that of David, if the king obeys his commandments.

The speech of Ahijah, then, not only provides a link to what preceded in 1 Kings 3 but also prepares for what is about to occur in 1 Kings 14. In this chapter we read that the son of King Jeroboam has fallen ill. Concerned about the future of the dynasty, Jeroboam recalls the prophecy of Ahijah and sends his wife to him to discover what will happen to his son, who is the heir to the throne. The future of the kingdom is now embodied in the child, and his fate signifies to the king the destiny of Israel. Warned of the arrival of Jeroboam's wife, Ahijah is prepared, and upon her entry before him he delivers a prophetic oracle condemning Jeroboam for his disobedience and predicting the destruction of his household. The key to the prophecy, however, is his announcement that the child will die. His death signifies not just the destruction of the house of Jeroboam but proleptically embodies the fate of Israel. The death of the child signifies the forfeiture of the kingdom that Yahweh took from the house of David and gave to Jeroboam, the king of Israel.

When we compare the tale of the two harlots in 1

Kings 3 with the two prophetic stories in 1 Kings 11 and 14, this apparently innocuous story of the wisdom of the king takes on more significant dimensions. It is the symbolic dimension in this story that explains why this profane folktale, which was widely known, was used to introduce the reign of Solomon.[32] The key to its interpretation is provided in the symbol of the child. In 1 Kings 14 the child symbolizes the kingdom, in this case, the Northern Kingdom. Likewise, in 1 Kings 3 the child represents the ideal or legitimate kingdom. The two harlots are Judah and Israel. Together, they live in on "house," that is, a united kingdom. On the night of the third day, the very same day on which Israel rejected Rehoboam, the king of Judah, and initiated the division of the kingdom (1 Kings 12:12, 16), the harlot who was without child took the infant of her companion. For a brief time she possessed the child (1 Kings 11:35; 14:8), but in due time she showed that she was not the true mother of the kingdom. For when Solomon offered to divide the child in two so that each woman could have half of it, she agreed. Was it not Jeroboam who opted to divide the kingdom in two by establishing his own centers of worship in the North contrary to the command of Yahweh?[33] For this reason, the child was forfeited by the one woman and returned to its true mother.

These elements suggest that the story of the two harlots served as a subtle political commentary concerning the tragedy of Israel and Judah. Superficially, it appears to be a simple narrative demonstrating the judicial wisdom of Solomon. When correctly placed within the total structure of the narrative, however, it manifests a much deeper meaning. The riddle of the two harlots poses the question of the mystery of the kingdom. This political dimension in the story can only be observed in connection with the prophetic stories that follow and, of course, in relation to the ensuing events. In a similar way, the Deuteronomist uses the parable of Jotham in Judges 9 as a kind of commentary on the tragedy of kingship. Set in the total context of the narrative, these two stories proleptically symbolize the negative aspects of kingship and the tragic mystery of the kingdom. They also bring into sharp focus the deepest concerns of the narrator. In this case it is the fact that there is only one true kingdom of God and only one legitimate mother of that kingdom.

However, the two stories are not without tension when they are brought into connection with each other. Since the Deuteronomist frequently allows his sources to stand together without attempting to reconcile them, this is not unusual. The tension here is evident. According to the story of the two harlots, interpreted as a political type of commentary, the division of the kingdom means its death. According to the prophetic tale, on the other hand, the two kingdoms will dwell side by side for a time. However, if we do not press the interpretation of the first to cover every detail of the historical situation, the religiopolitical implications that emerge from it are quite in harmony with the Deuteronomic point of view. First, in the story of the two harlots there can be no doubt as to who the true mother was, in other words, the legitimate heir of the kingdom established by God. It is the dynasty of David, established in Judah in the city of Jerusalem, where the temple upon which Yahweh has placed his name is located. The temple in Jerusalem in association with the Davidic monarchy is the chosen center of God's kingdom and is the legitimate place through which he has revealed himself. Second, the division of the kingdom is a judgment upon it, one that in reality does bring its eventual death. Subsequently, there were attempts to unite the kingdom, but these were abortive. Retrospectively, then, this initial act of judgment was, for the Deuteronomist, not only an end to the reality of the kingdom as it was promised but a potential end that was to play itself out in the exile. The story of the two harlots reflects the judgment of the Deuteronomist relative to the meaning of the division for both Israel and Judah. The prophetic tale brings into sharper focus historical details related to this development.

If the story concerning the division of the kingdom as reflected in the tale of the two harlots is in reality a type of political commentary, a wisdom tale used allegorically, the question may be raised whether this is entirely the work of the Deuteronomist or whether this interpretation was already at hand in the sources he used. The appearance of a body of material in one section of the Old Testament with characteristics quite similar to those discussed in connection with the political wisdom of Egypt makes it quite probable that the Deuteronomist is not entirely responsible for this development but has taken over a type of political wisdom from his sources and utilized this in his narrative concerning the reign of Solomon for two purposes. On the one hand, he seeks to demonstrate how Yahweh fulfilled his promise to Israel, a promise brought to a climax in the building of the temple and the placing of an heir on the throne of David. On the other hand, ancillary to this but more vitally connected to sources of a more political nature, he attempts to demonstrate the legitimacy of the Davidic monarchy and the right of the Southern Kingdom to be

regarded as the true heir of the promise. Thus, the
Northern Kingdom, Israel, is regarded as a usurper,
permitted to exist for a time because of the judgment of
Yahweh upon the house of David.

It may be asserted, then, that the Deuteronomist derived some insights from his sources, which already represented a political genre of wisdom. With the division
of the two kingdoms, this type of literature would
emerge quite early in the struggle. In the realm of cult,
the Northern Kingdom very quickly opposed the
monopoly exercised by Judah through the Jerusalem
temple, or at least asserted in the context of the united
kingdom. Certainly, Rehoboam regarded himself as the
legitimate king over all Israel.[34] The wars between him
and Jeroboam may only have been border skirmishes,
but the issue at stake was much more serious than the
phrase "border warfare" would suggest.[35] The question
of which king Yahweh had legitimated and which kingdom was the true continuation of the united monarchy
had to be settled. The regnal formulas of the Northern
Kingdom that connect Jeroboam directly with David and
Solomon provide evidence of "the attempt to represent
the Northern Kingdom as the legitimate continuation of
all Israel."[36] Very early in the history of the two kingdoms, the Israelite and Judahite kings would have set
their scribes to the task of writing annals and reconstructing the materials of the royal archives to authen-
ticate their claims and bring them into connection with
the two great rulers of the United Kingdom.

If the period of political turmoil immediately following the dissolution of the united kingdom provided a
stimulus for the kind of activity, there were also other
periods when this process would be intensified. Certainly

the reign of King Hezekiah is one such period, an era of reconstruction modeled upon the kingship of Solomon.[37] The epoch of Josiah, which is noted because of its connection with the Deuteronomic movement and the reforms associated with this group, also attests a type of political activity that would have been reinforced by the efforts of the royal court to convince the North to join in the prospect of a revival of a united kingdom.[38] Some of the materials in the present Deuteronomic corpus, especially the political wisdom, may well trace back to this period when the captivity of Israel could have been used to legitimate the Judahite claim and to project its vision of the unified kingdom through a prism shaped by the ideal of the Solomonic era. Such a prospect would intensify efforts to recapture the past, rewrite it in terms of the political realities of the present, and promote the desires and hopes that it would rekindle. Thus, an impetus may have been given at this time to the collection of materials from the royal archives and the association of them with the reign of King Solomon.

We may conclude, then, that the Deuteronomist has brought together from his sources a group of disparate materials, some of which belonged to the category of political wisdom, and has used them in his own way both for political and religious purposes. No doubt, some of these had already been used to show that the kingdom of Judah was the rightful successor of the United Kingdom. Since this kingdom centered in Judah, glorification of David and Solomon and the exaltation of the place of the temple in the reign of Solomon would only serve to substantiate the claims of the Judahite monarchy and bring the greatest epoch in the history of Israel into association with it. Records kept in the royal archives and reports that filtered down through the annals that selected and recorded events and transactions would become a rich source for this activity, some of it circulating orally, and other portions giving rise to various anecdotes and legends. The fall of the Northern Kingdom did not stifle hopes for a return to the United Kingdom but apparently led to the hope in propitious times that the kingdom could once again be restored. Thus, the reign of Josiah revived old political aspirations and produced new efforts, primarily on the part of the Deuteronomic school, to bring the religiopolitical traditions of the nation into line with the purposes of Yahweh. Either at this time or later, elements of political wisdom were incorporated into the account of the reign of King Solomon by scribes of this school, or simply transcribed and passed on so that they came into the hand of the Deuteronomist who wrote from them and other sources his account of the reign of King Solomon and used it to show the glory and tragedy of the history of Israel and Judah.

Although I have not attempted to establish any definite connection between Egyptian sources and the literature of the Old Testament in this respect, it is in the political wisdom of Egypt that the clue is found for understanding some of the unusual elements in the record of the dynasty of Solomon. The boast of the greatness of his kingdom, the eulogies to him for his wisdom, the account of his great deeds—these were not rehearsed by the Deuteronomist simply because they were historical curiosities. Rather, they grew out of, and were brought into relation to the political events that occurred in the subsequent history of Israel and in the era of the narrator in order to recover a history, one that embodied the will of Yahweh for his people, a past from which lessons for the political and religious future of the nation could be learned.

8

Wisdom and Kingship in the
Religion of Israel

Thus far this study of Israelite and Egyptian wisdom has concentrated on two facets of their interrelationship: the process by which Egyptian wisdom was assimilated into the Old Testament and the sociopolitical conditions in which each developed. The latter has also become a means by which literary types in the Old Testament, occasioned by the similar social setting, could be identified. To be fully understood, however, these phenomena cannot be considered in isolation from the religious context in which they were fostered. This does not necessarily mean the introduction of something alien to the main

189

structure of this study, the process of adaptation, assimilation, and integration. As a matter of fact, this very process, which, as I have shown, was at work in Israel's appropriation of literary materials not originally a part of her own heritage, has also played a role in the development of the religion of Israel. Thus, when we turn more specifically to the question of how the tradents of the faith of Israel dealt with aspects of religion that bore witness to its ancient heritage, a similar development can be traced. In this final chapter, therefore, I will focus upon the relationship between wisdom and the religion of Israel, leaving aside very general comparisons between Israelite and Egyptian religion, which cannot really contribute decisively to the important question of the relation between wisdom and kingship in the Old Testament.

Previous attempts to place wisdom literature in the context of the faith of Israel have been too onesided. On the one hand, the characterization of the wisdom of Israel as "profane" or "secular" has persisted.[1] Such an interpretation regards it as something alien to the best insights of Israelite religion, a somewhat humanistic phenomenon that must first be domesticated before it can become an integral part of the faith of Israel. On the other hand, it has been connected too closely to aspects of the religious heritage of Israel, such as law and prophecy, or derived too directly from the religious experience of the nation as recorded in the historical traditions of the Pentateuch.[2] Yet these two interpretations are quite antithetical. The latter point of view looks upon the older wisdom, at least, as a descendant of the same lineage of faith; the former characterizes it as an alien element tinged by a humanism that is not fully at

home with the religious perspective of the rest of the
Old Testament.

The characterization of wisdom literature as a more
secular phenomenon is reflected in the rubric applied to
it by Rankin some years ago, "The Documents of Hebrew Humanism."³ Unfortunately, this way of viewing
wisdom has persisted even in more recent literature. In
his summary of the thought of the book of Proverbs,
Weiser speaks of "ethical rationalism" as one of the important strains of thought characterizing the book.⁴ Although scholars have admitted that the older wisdom of
Israel was pietistic, it was the rationalistic impulse that
was regarded as important, the fact that the wise man
was not to be governed by the authority of law but was
free to consider moral choices and weigh them against
his own self-interest. This mood is reflected in the following statement by von Rad, which sums up one side of
his own interpretation:

> The wisdom teacher wanted to help the young man to
> preserve his strength and fortune and to safeguard his
> manhood. But he did so not with divine commandments:
> these he had no authority to give, for his counsels were
> of course derived essentially from experience. . . . Such
> counsel does not demand obedience.⁵

The older wisdom of Israel is thus humanistic, an-
thropocentric, and eudaemonistic, experimental, not
doctrinaire, and autonomous, not legalistic.

In his study of the wisdom of Solomon, Noth has
suggested that there is something peculiarly secular
about the Hebrew word "wisdom" (*ḥkmh*).⁶ Therefore, it
has only a restricted use with reference to God in the

Old Testament. Only in the book of Daniel is it attributed to God as his possession in a generalized sense (2:20). It is described as a gift of God only in passages that are late, being ascribed, not to God, but only to divine agents in earlier passages (1 Kings 4:29; cf. 2 Sam. 14:20). The ironic statement of Isaiah in which wisdom is attributed to Pharaoh, triggering the response that God too is wise, is unusual (31:2). No doubt, this sparing use of wisdom in relation to God is due to the fact that the term "wisdom" can be morally ambiguous, "cleverness intensified into roguishness."[7] According to Noth the secular connotations of the term "wisdom" in ancient Israel are evidence that the assertion about the wisdom of Solomon in I Kings 4:29-34 is not a late addition but genuinely reflects the spirit of his time.

As already observed, in the ancient Near East wisdom is attributed to the king.[8] This is true not only of Egyptian and Babylonian sources but also Phoenician and Canaanite texts. The inscription of king Azitawadda contains the assertion that

ואף באבח פעלן כל מלך בצדקי ובחכמתי

Also every king dealt with me as father because of my righteousness and my wisdom.[9]

From Ugarit the legend of king Keret contains the following assertion about his wisdom:

kil . ḥkmt . kṯr . lṭpn

Like El, wisdom like Bull, the Kindly One.[10]

In Ezek. 28:3 the wisdom of the king of Tyre is compared with that of Dan'el.[11] Scholars have perceived in this name a reference to the legendary king mentioned in the Ugaritic texts. The Hebrew consonants correspond exactly with those of the Ugaritic name. If this is the case, Dan'el must also be associated with the legendary hierophants who were especially renowed for their wisdom (1 Kings 4:31; Prov. 30:1; 31:1; Ezek. 14:14, 20).

In the Old Testament wisdom is attributed to a number of kings and is associated with their judicial function in several cases.[12] The connection between wisdom and kingship is strengthened by the association of wisdom with the royal court of Egypt (Isa. 19:11b), with hierophants such as Dan'el (Ezek. 28:3), and with the future king-messiah (Isa. 11:2). The request of king Solomon for understanding "to judge the people" (1 Kings 3:9) accurately reflects the old tradition of the association of wisdom with the judicial function of the king (Prov. 20:8, 26; 29:4). In the legendary story of King Keret from Ugarit, his son Yassib lays claim to the throne because the sick king is unable to judge the widow and the oppressed,[13] reminding us of Prov. 29:14:

מלך שופט באמת דלים
כסאו לעד יכון

If a king judges the poor with equity,
his throne will be established forever.

The wise woman whom Joab appoints to intercede on behalf of Absalom pleads for a favorable judgment because she is a widow with only one remaining son. When David perceives the ruse, that it is really Joab who is behind her request, the woman lauds him for his wisdom, which is like that of an emissary of God who knows all things (2 Sam. 14:20). Both David and Solomon make judicial decisions that are based on their own prerogatives as leaders of the people and not on customary law or jurisprudence (1 Sam. 30:25; 1 Kings 2:6; 3:28).

That this particular aspect of the juridical function of the king is not an entirely profane matter, totally dependent upon his human skill, is suggested by several facts. In the Ugaritic literature, as well as the Old Testament, the place of judgment is also a cult-place. The king, Dan'el, judges the widow and the orphan in front of the gate of the town at a threshing floor.[14] It is at precisely the same place that the kings of Israel and Judah take counsel with their prophets who are performing ritual acts to ensure victory in war (1 Kings 22: 10). During the seige of Samaria by the Syrian King, Ben Hadad, a starving woman appealed to king Jehoram for help. In his reply the king designated the place of help from which he could not assist her if Yahweh did not come to their aid, the threshing floor and the wine press (2 Kings 6:27). Both of these places are connected with cultic activities which sought to ensure fruitfulness for the coming year.[15] Because Israel had served Baal at these sites, Hosea declared that the threshing floor and the winevat would not feed Israel (9:1-2). At such a Jebusite cult center David erected an altar to avert a plague (2 Sam. 24:18, 25). Thus, the kings and leaders of Israel take counsel with their priest-prophets, carry out cultic instructions given by their religious advisors and receive divine instruction from God at these centers of worship (Judges 6:11).

If such cult places contained local sanctuaries and were permanently inhabited, they became towns re-

nowned for their counsel and wisdom. Such a place was
Abel, where a wise woman pleaded with Joab not to de-
stroy the city because it was a "mother in Israel." This
epithet, which is applied to counsellors such as Deborah
and used in connection with the process of the consultation of lots by the king of Babylon, shows that Abel was
a famous oracle place.[16] Thus, a popular proverb grew
up about it, "Let them but ask counsel at Abel" (2 Sam.
20:18). The use of the phrase "ask counsel," which often
refers to oracular consultation, reveals that this city was
inhabited by people who were renowned for their di-
vinatory powers.[17] No doubt, other cultic centers, such
as Shiloh, where petitions were brought (1 Sam. 1:17)
and where the word of the Lord was revealed (1 Sam.
3:21), became famous for their wisdom. At such centers
not only were inquiries made of local seers, but ecstatic
phenomena involving artistic skills such as music-making
occurred. In ancient Israel legal and religious judgments
were integrated more fully, and justice was a matter of
divine as well as human judgment.

Therefore, when the Deuteronomist conjoins the
dream-revelation of Solomon and his judicial function,
he reflects a pattern of thought that is older, connecting
regal decisions with cultic activity. In the case of king
Saul, the dream, the prophet, and the Urim, a type of
lot to determine the will of the deity, are all used as a
means of assistance in the process of making decisions (1
Sam. 28:6). The ephod, which was worn by David during official religious ceremonies, was also used by him
on two occasions for the reception of an oracle that
would determine his course of action (1 Sam. 23:6-12;
30:7-8). It is true, as Noth asserts, that we are not told
how the decision is mediated.[18] But more significant

than this is the fact that both David and Saul take these oracular instruments and use them themselves. The decisions are given directly to them. Of course, the use of this nonrational means of determining the will of the deity, particularly visions and dreams, is common in the ancient Near East.[19] In the case of Saul and David, however, even if a process of intellectualization is at work in the composition of the chronicles concerning them, it has not completely suppressed the religious factors involved in the formulation of their political and military decisions.

The close association of wisdom with cultic instrumentalities and personnel is found in the Old Testament as well as in Babylon and Egypt. In Babylon the lots used to determine the destiny for the coming year were called "the tablets of wisdom."[20] Of course, the connection between wisdom and cult in Egypt in the late period does not make Isaiah's disclosure at all surprising, that Egyptian wisdom derives from counsel given by idols and diviners, as well as by Pharaoh and the ancient kings (Isa. 19:3, 11).[21] But the situation is little different in Jerusalem, according to the prophet, where diviners, elders, counselors, wise magicians, and charmers all work together in the service of the king (Isa. 3:2-3). In Isa. 3:3 and Hos. 3:4, when these two prophets are enumerating the various offices and instrumentalities that are essential to the life of a people but that Yahweh will take away when he punishes them, Isaiah includes diviners and elders, the counselor and the wise magician, and Hosea mentions the ephod and teraphim. It is also clear from Micah 3:5-7 that divination and visions were also a recognized means of securing divine response to particular questions.[22] The negative judgment directed against these kinds of activity is not leveled at the activity itself but at its false and deceptive results. During the monarchical period the king and his counselors employed such cultic means in the hope that through them the deity would communicate his will.

The presence of a special genre of sayings in the book of Proverbs that is strikingly similar in content to the omen-wisdom of Babylonia shows the remnants of a priestly tradition still present in the wisdom literature. Babylonian diviners not only used lots to predict the future, a practice also employed by Israelite priests and alluded to in proverbial utterances, but they also developed a specific lore interpreting the movements of the body. This lore, found in the omen collections of Babylonia, is strikingly similar to a small cluster of sayings in the book of Proverbs (16:30; 10:10; 6:12-15, 4:25; 9:12).

[š]umma ī[nē]šu ukattam sartam itammu[23]
If (a man) closes his eyes, he will speak falsehood.

עצה עיניו לחשב תהפכות
If (a man) shuts his eyes, he will plan perversity.

The presence of a series of such allusions in Proverbs, with a similar development in the tradition to this genre in Babylonian literature, reveals the existence of esoteric proverbial traditions in Israel that derived from the priests and were developed by them into a type of Israelite omen-wisdom. Along with the many general references to personnel, places, and observances related to cultus, as well as a series of priestly terms appearing in Proverbs, this tradition attests the participation of the priests of Israel in the formulation and development of wisdom.[24] In these traditions a sharp distinction is not made between human insight and divine revelation.

Thus, skillfulness in counsel is not measured by an abstract standard divorced from the process by which the will of the deity is mediated. It is compared to those decisions which are achieved by cultic means. The wisdom of Ahitophel is likened to the counsel that was given when a person consulted an oracle of God (2 Sam. 16:23). If the wisdom of Ahitophel was esteemed, the counsel of the priest-prophet Samuel was also valued because what he said came true (1 Sam. 9:6). Although the actual way in which Samuel reached his decisions is not described, like Eli and the priests before him, he too wore the ephod, a garment associated with oracle-giving (1 Sam. 2:18, 28). Similarly, the associates to whom Hushai, a counselor of King David, disclosed his decision in opposition to Ahitophel, were priests (2 Sam. 17:15). The allusion to divination in Prov. 16:10a is also striking, particularly when interpreted in this context.

קסם על־שפתי־מלך

Divined oracles are upon the lips of the king.

"In other words, the king's ruling upon any matter is as trustworthy as one secured by means of קֶסֶם or 'divination'. . . ."[25] The ultimate standard for judging skillfulness in counsel is one that relied upon the direct decision of the deity (Prov. 18:18).

The mystery and infallibility of the determination of the will of God by lot, a means used by both king and priest, is etched in one proverb (Prov. 16:33):

בחיק יוטל את־הגורל
ומיהוה כל־משפטו

The lot is cast into the lap,
but the decision is wholly from the LORD.

What this proverb asserts is the control of the cultic instrumentalities by Yahweh.[26] Both divination and the lot are inerrant because they give the decision of the deity. In Prov. 21:31 this divine determination is extended to historical events. Finally, it is brought into relation to the activity of men in planning the future. At this point the mystery is even more intensified, and the will of God is realized in spite of human intentions (Prov. 16:1, 9). In the final analysis Yahweh controls all of reality, even the falling of the lot.

Having sketched this background, it can now be asserted that the later tradition, which regarded wisdom as a divine endowment, harks back to an ancient theme, that God is wise, and that he bestows his wisdom upon his servants. One of the oldest direct statements that God is wise is found in Isa. 31:2. For Isaiah, God is the counselor *par excellence*. In one passage the prophet adopts a small wisdom book, modeled upon the genre of wisdom similar to the Sumerian "Farmer's Almanac," and with it eulogizes him for his wisdom, concluding with the epithets

הפליא עצה
הגדיל תושיה

wonderful in counsel,
excellent in wisdom.[27]

De Boer has also directed our attention to the hymn in Isa. 40:12-26 that declares that Yahweh was counseled by El.[28] As in Ugarit, El was the wise one; in Israel he bestowed his wisdom upon Yahweh, just as it was El Elyon who allotted to Yahweh the people of Jacob (Deut. 32:8-9). When the people forsook El and Yahweh, they became void of counsel and without understanding (v.

28). Although wisdom is said to have been created by Yahweh, this probably represents an assimilation of this attribute to him. It is first brought forth in the council of God, whence it is shared among the gods (Job. 15:8; Ps. 89:7).[29]

Thus, the ascription of wisdom to the king in the Old Testament cannot be divorced from a sacral context. The ideology of kingship, which affirmed that the king was the son of the deity (Ps. 2:7) and therefore divine (Ps. 45:6-7), represents him as the wisest of all men on earth, even wiser than the legendary hierophants of old (1 Kings 4:31; Ezek. 28:3).[30] The indictment of the prophets against foreign monarchs manifests the reality behind this sacral ideology. For such self-exaltation, even of the type found in the royal inscriptions, Isaiah asserts that Yahweh will punish the king of Assyria (Isa. 37:24; 10:13) and also the king of Egypt (19:11). In Ezek. 28:6 the prophet charges that the king conceived that his "heart" (= wisdom) was like the heart of El.[31] Ezekiel proceeds to remind him that he is only "Adam" (*'dm*), and he will die at the hand of his enemies. The play on the word, however, indicates that the prophet is not reducing the king to the level of a man. For he was "Adam," who dwelt in Eden as the first man, full of wisdom and perfect in beauty (vv. 12-13). He is associated with the cherub, a guardian appointed of God (v. 14). The king dwelt with the deity on the holy mountain, until sin was found in him. The mythological imagery applied to the king by Ezekiel describes a semi-divine being, not a man.

Since the king is the son of God and the representative of the deity on earth, the sacral imagery surrounding him transcends human dimensions. He is described in terms used elsewhere only of God. In Prov. 25:3 his heart is called "unsearchable," a phrase applied only to God in the Old Testament. His throne is the throne of God (Ps. 45:6). He exercises divine prerogatives in his judicial function so that he is to be feared as God (Prov. 14:35; 16:10, 14; 19:12; 20:2, 8; 24:21). In Prov. 16:15, a verse that contains a motif similar to those found in the Amarna letters, with the sun god, his life-giving power is described.

באור־פני־מלך חיים

In the light of a king's face there is life.[32]

Even if we accept the fact that there were certain linguistic conventions appropriate to the royal court, the sacral imagery of kingship goes beyond this. It involves the extension of the reality of divine rule into both the political and the religious spheres. Divine kingship is ultimately a matter of religious sanction and right; therefore, sacral ideology is found in the service of human pretensions and materialistic interests. From a royalist point of view, however, it is divine reality.

The king was enthroned in Jerusalem as monarch and as leader of the royal cult embodied in him.[33] Yet the peculiarities of the political situation in Israel at the time of the development of the monarchy left it isolated so that the sacral traditions that developed in connection with it were never fully integrated into the older theocratic heritage of the tribes. The geographical and religious center of the nation, Jerusalem, belonged to neither Judah nor Israel. It was a city-state ruled over by David. Even with the bringing of the national religious symbol, the ark of the covenant, to Jerusalem, the worship center was constituted as a royal shrine and was presided over by the king. Surrounded by his officials and mercenary soldiers, David was enthroned in a Jebusite city. Thus, the religious policy of David, which was syncretistic, became the legacy of his successor, Solomon. Similarly, the cultic center of the nation remained under the domination of the king. Solomon administered the temple, conducted worship, and appointed new religious personnel. As high priest, he appointed a Jebusite, Zadok, thus furthering the Jebusite contribution to the religion of Israel. Finally, his internationalism led to religiopolitical alliances that opened the door of Jerusalem to all kinds of cultic traffic, foreign as well as domestic.

Thus, with the development of the monarchy, not only was a new political institution with a different geographical center thrust upon Israel but also a novel religious ideology, which stood over and against the religious traditions of the theocracy. In sacral kingship the religious and political ideology became one. Mediation of the will of the deity was conceived of through the established religious structures of kingship, through the religious personnel who were organized under the leadership of the king. True revelation from the deity involved the disclosure of knowledge that contributed to the strengthening of the divine order embodied in the royal government. In the prophetic period it is quite evident that this religiopolitical order formulated national policy as it related to the international developments on the basis of diplomatic skill as well as religious insight.[34] In the best interests of the nation its religious policy was syncretistic and pragmatic, rejecting religious particularism in favor of sacral alliances that would further its political aims. Technical skill, based on a kind of primitive empiricism, combined with accumulated lore of a quasi-religious kind, led to the extension of the frontiers of knowledge and included the exchange of scientific and cultural knowledge with other kingdoms.

For a time the royal court in Jerusalem, including the temple with the priest-king at its head, became the center of the religious and intellectual life of Israel. The clearest model for understanding the social context in which the wisdom literature of Israel was fostered is found in Prov. 25.[35] In this ideal social order structured around the king and his court, including the factions that support the monarchy and those that do not (righteous and wicked), a bureaucracy was developed in order to carry out the functions of government. Besides the appointment of officials to carry out the more mundane politicoeconomic functions, the aggrandizement of the royal house necessitated the development of an elite corps of officials, priests, scribes, and diplomats, architects of the religious, cultural, and economic life of the nation.[36] Since the utilization of the resources of the kingdom involved scientific technique as well as legal and religious insight, it would be natural to assume that a process of intellectualization would begin in which the development of a high culture and the arts would play a role. Also, in the political context of sacral kingship religious ideology would develop hand in hand with the political policy of the royal house. The basis of this whole order, however, was the inspired rule of the king, which drew its certainties from divine resources and invited the courtier to serve with promise of great honor.

On the literary side, scribes of the royal court were employed not only to record transactions of the government that were vital to its existence but also to enrich the cultural and artistic heritage of the nation. As already observed, this went hand in hand with the glorification of the reigning dynasty. Propagandistic literature, exalting the king and seeking to strengthen the kingdom by encouraging the loyalty of its officials, needed development. Books for the education of the courtier and materials for use in royal schools were produced. The task of studying and arranging proverbs was also undertaken for educational purposes. The development of Israelite onomastica, compendia of natural and religious phenomena, was also a part of this quasi-scientific operation.

More practical projects such as treatises on customary and royal law, the compilation of chronicles of the reigns of the different kings from various kinds of annals and journals, the production of liturgical and hymnic materials for the royal cult, added to the administrative burden. Moreover, the collection and absorption of other scientific and literary materials relating to commerce, medicine, architecture, and sculpture from other centers of civilization would be pursued by foreign scribes who were in the service of the king. Since the court of Israel was a rather late arrival in the ancient Near East, other cultural centers, including Egypt, apparently provided not only a stimulus but also a means by which Israelite culture and wisdom could associate itself with ancient lore and thus enhance its place among the literature of the nations. Thus a body of literature arose that had no special relation to the old sacral traditions of the nation preserved by the tribes and found in the archives of local sanctuaries.

On the religious side, the theology of kingship involved a sacralization of the divine order embodied in the royal government. Unlike the theocratic traditions of Israel's faith, which asserted the direct revelation of the will of Yahweh by redemptive action in history, it embraced a sacral structure in which the revelation of the will of the deity was mediated more obliquely. Divine power was bestowed by the deity upon his servants in accordance to their relationship in the sacred hierarchical order. As the son of the deity, the divine king was not only endowed with superhuman ability but also given a claim to divine prerogatives through his heirship. Thus, rank and title, not just charisma, were prerequisites to a greater share in the divine blessing. Of course, the possession of unusual skills also indicated that one was specially endowed by the deity. Therefore, a person who revealed that he had special gifts that could be used in the service of the king could hope to be elevated to a position nearer to the ultimate source of revelation.

At the level of meaning, revelation is even more oblique. The glory of God was not located just in his self-disclosure. It was manifest in His ability to baffle men, to set before them things whose place in reality and therefore whose ultimate meaning was hidden (Prov. 25:2). Such things are too deep for ordinary men. Only the king, whose divine endowment bestowed upon him the capacity of spirit to search out the meaning of the divine secrets, is able to reveal the counsels of God. Like the mind of a god, the king's mind is unsearchable, open to visions and dreams from the divine realm, able to penetrate the purposes of God by using oracles, sufficient to discern from his prophets what is false and what is true. As an inspired being, the king possessed intellectual and artistic skills to create proverbs, compose songs, and write poetry. There is no divorce here between religious and profane reality. The king may use both rational and nonrational means by which to formulate his policies, and from the reports he receives from diplomats and seers he sifts reality, separating that which is true from that which is false. At his disposal are all of the resources of the court and the kingdom, both empirical and magico-religious. Because of his relation to the deity, his divine endowment, and the various means available to him, the king could search out meaning that has been hidden from mortal eyes. The king ruled by wisdom (Prov. 8:15).

It is no wonder then, that in the literature deriving from the royal court, we move in a realm alien to the kind of divine self-disclosure that is found in the sacral traditions of Israel's theocracy. Likewise, it is not altogether surprising that the older wisdom literature is never fully integrated into the mainstream of Israel's historical heritage found in the Pentateuch.[37] Of the Law revealed at Mount Sinai, of the covenant made between Yahweh and Israel, of the great miracle of the Exodus we hear not even a whisper in the book of Proverbs. The attempt to treat wisdom as an outgrowth of law and prophecy is vitiated by the total lack of religious premises necessary for such literature. Proverbs appeals to the authority of experience as well as tradition, the sanction of observation as well as retribution, the compulsion of discipline as well as punishment, the paternal example as well as the legal precedent, and the enlightenment of knowledge as well as the threat of divine judgment. Proverbial counsel stands midway between the demand of the Law and the freedom of conscience, something more than sage advice but something less than direct divine decree. Its patron is the king, who is the mediator of divine revelation, and its authority is based on a religious way of life that combines experience and insight with prudential piety.

If the *Deus Absconditus* of wisdom literature has as its counterpart the *Deus Revelatus* of the law and the prophets, the tension between these two perspectives appears in the Old Testament.[38] Political resistance to the institution of kingship emerges in the person of Samuel, who embodies the anti-kingship forces in a religious form. The selection of a king was regarded as a rejection of the old theocratic ideal in which Yahweh was king over the people. Later, the prophetic movement that appealed to the direct action of Yahweh in history in his self-revelation set the counsel of God against the diplomacy of the royal court. The wisdom of Yahweh will thus confound the insights of the wise counselors and even the wisdom of kings when he reveals himself by acting in judgment in history. Thus, the Deuteronomist qualifies the claims of the king by the demands of the covenant and writes the history of kingship in Israel and Judah from this perspective. Conversely, the themes of the older wisdom of Proverbs concerning the hiddenness of God and the mystery of His self-disclosure in creation are developed in discourses that place divine wisdom beyond human grasp. In a more radical form these are turned into full-scale discussions of the question of theodicy, such as in the book of Ecclesiastes.

It is possible, however, to distinguish two stages in the complicated interplay of these two traditions in the Old Testament. With the decline of kingship and its final denouement in the exile, wisdom found a new home in

Judaism. By the inter-biblical period it is being equated with the Torah.[39] Gradually the old traditions of the wise men of the royal courts of Israel and Judah are integrated into the faith of Judaism. Wisdom and Torah are fused. Even the skeptical literature that sprang from the ancient belief in the hiddenness of God was domesticated as a part of the legal heritage of Israel. The proper reverence for the mysterious yet all-powerful divine being enjoined by the wise men, "the fear of God" as the beginning of wisdom, became the necessary prerequisite and the true attitude of the pious man who knew Torah and was instructed in the keeping of its commandments. For Judaism, wisdom and law came to their proper end in the injunction: "Fear God and keep His commandments."

However, we can also distinguish an earlier stage in this process. It appears in the narrative concerning King Solomon in 1 Kings 3-11. Here the Deuteronomic editor has taken over elements of royal wisdom and has used them in the structure of the narrative to show how Yahweh fulfilled his promise to Israel. Although a few verses appear to be insertions or stand somewhat in isolation from the rest of the Deuteronomic narrative, the editor has incorporated enough wisdom into the literary structure to assert that he has actually subordinated the themes of the wisdom materials to his overarching purpose, which is to show the realization of the promises related to the historical traditions of Israel's faith found in the Pentateuch. At this stage wisdom is not equated with the Torah revealed at Sinai, nor is it fully integrated into the Deuteronomic themes, such as the dedication of the temple. But it has been assimilated into the thematic structure of promise and fulfillment found in the Pentateuch. In this way it became serviceable to the historical traditions of Israel's faith, which declared the self-disclosure of Yahweh through the great events that had founded the nation, the promise to Abraham, the Exodus, and the Conquest of the land of Palestine. Similarly, Ps. 37 represents a later stage of the same assimilative process that we find in 1 Kings 3-11.

In a sense, then, the history of the literary traditions of Israel as I have sketched them in the earlier portion of this study is a paradigm reflecting a process that also appertains to Israel's religious heritage. Novel elements in religion were likewise only gradually assimilated and integrated into the faith of Israel as it developed. As this occurred, the kaleidoscopic historical scene brought new elements into play that fostered the growth of the tradition in unexpected directions. The development of some aspects of literature and religion was thus halted, left dwarfed and truncated. Others were reinterpreted and absorbed into larger perspectives that gave them new meaning. Some were left behind as puzzles still unsolved. With the termination of Israel's manifest destiny as proclaimed by the forces behind the monarchy of Israel, the old royal themes and the instruction that they enjoined found new meaning in the later tradition as they were personalized for individual instruction, institutionalized for the life of the family, or transcendentalized for the aspirations of the people of Israel. Fortunately, the original context and meaning of some have also been rediscovered, helping us to understand their role in the formulation of the religion of Israel.

The assimilative capacity of the faith of Israel thus kept alive an ancient heritage for Western culture and the Church. In this it also attested a process, the ever-

constant interaction of two religious traditions, the
theocracy with its heritage of law, and the institution of
kingship, the patron of wisdom. When the particularism
of the Jewish faith eventually conquered, it did not entirely violate the spirit and form of the wisdom literature
that came from its older and more universal traditions.
Fortunately, from these Israel was able to assimilate
some of the wisdom that belonged to its more ancient
and revered neighbors in the Near East. Thus, a few
remnants of the forms and content of Egyptian wisdom,
as well as the genius and spirit of its wise ancestors,
passed into Israel. For almost two millennia the Old Testament has been a unique witness to this ancient legacy
of Oriental wisdom, a witness that also attests a remarkable assimilative capacity, one by which Israel was able to
incline her ear, hear the words of the wise, and apply
her mind to knowledge.

Notes

Chapter 1

1. E. A. Wallis Budge, *Facsimiles of Egyptian Hieratic Papyri in the British Museum with Descriptions, Summaries of Contents, Etc.*, p. 12, n2; p. 13, n1. References to the text of Amenemope (abbreviated Amen.) will follow the numerical division found in H. O. Lange, *Das Weisheitsbuch des Amenemope*. A translation of the text of Amenemope was recently made by W. K. Simpson, trans., "The Instruction of Amenemope," in *The Literature of Ancient Egypt*, pp. 241-65, also earlier by F. Ll. Griffith, "The Teaching of Amenophis the Son of Kanakht. Papyrus B. M. 10474," JEA 12 (1926): 191-231, as well as the partial one by John A. Wilson, "Proverbs and Precepts," ANET, pp. 421-24. A transliteration and translation, as well as a complete textual study of Amenemope, was recently completed by Irene Grumach, *Untersuchungen zur Lebenslehre des Amenope*, pp. 7-185 and *Anhang*. (The reader is referred to the list of abbreviations for references.)

2. Budge, *Facsimiles of Egyptian Hieratic Papyri*, p. 13.

3. The translation is that of Budge (*ibid.*, n1).

212   A LEGACY OF WISDOM

4. E. A. Wallis Budge, *The Teaching of Amen-em-Apt, Son of Kanekht,* pp. 103, 130-31.

5. Adolf Erman, "Eine ägyptische Quelle der 'Sprüche Salomos'," SAB 15 (1924): 86-93.

6. *Ibid.*

7. *Ibid.,* p. 87. Indented quotations from the Bible and Apocrypha are from the Revised Standard Version unless otherwise noted. In this case I have provided a translation of Erman's German text.

8. *Ibid.,* p. 88. The following interpreters and translators accept the emendation: Hubert Grimme, "Wieteres zu Amen-em-ope und Proverbien," OLZ 28 (1925): 57; H. Wiesmann, "Eine ägyptische Quelle der Sprüche Salomos?" BZ 17 (1926): 47; Josef Linder, "Das Weisheitsbuch des Amen-em-ope und die 'Sprüche von Weisen' (Prov. 22,17-23,11)," ZKT 49 (1925): 142; Johannes Theis, "Die Lehre des Amen-em-ope, eine ägyptische Quelle des biblischen Spruchbuches," PB 36 (1925): 261; H. J. Heyes, "Das Buch der Sprüche und das altägyptische Weisheitsbuch des Amen-em-ope," BZTS 3 (1926): 3; Joh. Döller, "Das Buch der Sprüche und die Lehre des Amen-em-ope," TPQ 79 (1926): 312; D. C. Simpson, "The Hebrew Book of Proverbs and the Teaching of Amenophis," JEA 12 (1926): 236; Alex R. Gordon, trans., "Proverbs," *The Complete Bible,* p. 601; Paul Humbert, *Recherches sur les sources égyptiennes de la littérature sapientiale d'Israël,* p. 18; H. J. Cadbury, "Egyptian Influence in the Book of Proverbs," JRel 9 (1929): 105; B. Gemser, *Sprüche Salomos,* p. 64; Achille Brunet, "Proverbes (XXII, 17-XXIV, 22) et la possibilité d'une source égyptienne," ScEccl 1 (1948): 28, nl; Charles T. Fritsch, "The Book of Proverbs," in *The Interpreter's Bible,* 4: 909; Vinzenz Hamp, *Das Buch der Sprüche* p. 59; Heinrich Schneider, *Die Heilige Schrift für das Leben erklärt,* 7 (pt. 1):123; Helmer Ringgren and Walther Zimmerli, *Sprüche, Prediger,* p. 88; J. C. Rylaarsdam, "The Proverbs," in *Peake's Commentary on the Bible,* p. 454; R. B. Y. Scott, *Proverbs, Ecclesiastes,* p. 135; André Barucq, *Le Livre des Proverbes,* p. 170; William McKane, *Proverbs,* p. 369; JB; NEB. Detailed considerations of the emendations from a different point of view may be found in the work of John Ruffle, "The Teaching of Amenemope," pp. 388-449, cited in the following notes.

9. Similarly, Hugo Gressmann, "Ägypten im Alten Testament," *Vossische Zeitung,* 22 June 1924, p. 2; not, however, repeated in "Die neugefundene Lehre des Amen-em-ope und die vorexilische Spruchdichtung Israels," ZAW 42 (1924): 274; Ernst Sellin, Review of "Eine ägyptische Quelle der 'Sprüche Salomos,'" by Adolf Erman, DLZ 45 (1924): 1326; Wiesmann "Eine ägyptische Quelle," p. 47; Linder, "Das Weisheitsbuch," p. 143; Theis, "Die Lehre des Amen-em-ope," p. 261; Marion Hiller Dunsmore, "An Egyptian Contribution to the Book of Proverbs," JRel 5 (1925): 302; Heyes, "Das Buch der Sprüche," pp. 2-3; Humbert, *Recherches sur les sources égyptiennes,* p. 18; Fritsch,

Notes

"The Book of Proverbs," p. 909; D. C. Simpson, "The Hebrew Book," p. 236; William Henry Sassaman, "The Influence of the Wisdom of Amenemopet on the Book of Proverbs," pp. 19-20; Döller, "Das Buch der Sprüche," p. 307; Rylaarsdam, "The Proverbs," p. 454; Ludwig Keimer, "The Wisdom of Amen-em-ope and the Proverbs of Solomon," AJSL 43 (1926-27):14, n1; JB. 10. Erman, "Eine ägyptische Quelle," p. 89. Also the following, though not always for the same reason: Theis, "Die Lehre des Amen-em-ope," p. 262; Sassaman, "The Influence of the Wisdom," p. 23; Simpson, "The Hebrew Book," p. 236; Keimer, "The Wisdom of Amen-em-ope," p. 14, n3; Humbert, *Recherches sur les sources égyptiennes*, p. 20; Gemser, *Sprüche Salomos*, p. 66; Brunet, "Proverbes," p. 29; Fritsch, "The Book of Proverbs," p. 910; Ringgren and Zimmerli, *Sprüche*, p. 89, n1; Wolfgang Richter, *Recht und Ethos*, p. 29. Crawford H. Toy's earlier proposal that qšṭ be deleted from the first half of the verse was also accepted by many interpreters *(A Critical and Exegetical Commentary on the Book of Proverbs*, p. 425).

11. Erman, "Eine ägyptische Quelle," pp. 88-90; Gressmann, "Ägypten im Alten Testament," p. 2; Grimme, "Wieteres zu Amen-em-ope," p. 58; Max Löhr, Review of "Eine ägyptische Quelle der Sprüche Salomos," by Adolf Erman, OLZ 28 (1925): 73; Wiesman, "Eine ägyptische Quelle," p. 49; Alan H. Gardiner, "Writing and Literature," in *The Legacy of Egypt*, pp. 68-69. Brunet takes note of the fact that another scholar by the name of Vaccari had already proposed the number "thirty" even before its discovery by Erman in 1925 ("Proverbes," pp. 28-29); Wiesman ("Eine ägyptische Quelle," p. 49), followed by Ringgren and Simmerli (*Sprüche*, p. 88), suggested the deletion of hywm in Prov. 22:19 since it was added as a parallel to the adverb ʾlšwm in v. 20. Other interpreters proposed the reading drky ḥyym in its place: Samuel A. B. Mercer, "A New Found Book of Proverbs," AnglTR 8 (1926): 241, n7; Simpson, "The Hebrew Book," p. 236; Humbert, *Recherches sur les sources égyptiennes*, p. 19; J. M. Plumley, "The Teaching of Amenemope," in *Documents from Old Testament Times*, p. 175.

12. Erman, "Eine ägyptische Quelle," pp. 92-93. Like Erman, Richter agrees that the Hebrew text is dependent upon the Egyptian book but does not believe that the number "thirty" plays any role in the present form of the Hebrew wisdom book. The editor of "The Sayings of the Wise" has merely adopted some materials from Amenemope that were originally reproduced and used by the Hebrew translator of the Egyptian text *(Recht und Ethos*, pp. 36-37).

13. Gressmann, "Ägypten im Alten Testament," p. 2.

14. Most interpreters followed the additional emendation proposed by Grimme ("Wieteres zu Amen-em-ope," p. 58) and Sellin (Review of "Eine ägyptische Quelle," p. 1326) reading "like a peg" *(kytd)* in correspondence with the text of Amenemope: Gressmann, "Ägypten im Alten Testament," p. 2

(but not in "Die neugefundene Lehre," p. 274); Heyes, "Das Buch der Sprüche," pp. 2-3; Mercer, "A New Found Book," p. 241, n6; Simpson, "The Hebrew Book," p. 236; Keimer, "The Wisdom of Amen-em-ope," p. 14, n1; Plumley, "The Teaching of Amenemope," p. 176; Ringgren and Zimmerli, *Sprüche*, p. 88; Hamp, *Das Buch der Sprüche*, p. 60; Rylaarsdam, "The Proverbs," p. 454; *idem, The Proverbs, Ecclesiastes, The Song of Solomon*, p. 76; Scott, *Proverbs*, p. 135; Richter, *Recht und Ethos*, p. 30.

15. Likewise, Grimme, "Wieteres zu Amen-em-ope," p. 60; Heyes, "Das Buch der Sprüche," p. 7; Keimer, "The Wisdom of Amen-em-ope," p. 16, n4, 17; Alexis Mallon, "La 'sagesse' de l'Egyptien Amen-em-opé et les 'Proverbes de Salomon,' " Bib 8 (1927): 12; Humbert, *Recherches sur les sources égyptiennes*, p. 24; Gottfried Kuhn, *Beiträge zur Erklärung des Salomonischen Spruchbuches*, p. 57; Gemser, *Sprüche Salomos*, p. 66; Hamp, *Das Buch der Sprüche*, p. 62; Ringgren and Zimmerli, *Sprüche*, p. 89; Gordon, "Proverbs," p. 601; Rylaarsdam, "The Proverbs," p. 454. Linder interpreted *š'r bnpšw* as avarice ("Das Weisheitsbuch," p. 144; Toy, *A Critical and Exegetical Commentary*, p. 430).

16. Gressmann, "Ägypten im Alten Testament," p. 2; idem, "Die neugefundene Lehre," pp. 273, 285. The following accept Gressmann's interpretation of the significance of the number "thirty": Sassaman, "The Influence of the Wisdom," pp. 20-21; Dunsmore, "An Egyptian Contribution," p. 302-3; Friedrich Zimmermann, "Altägyptische Spruchweisheit in der Bibel," TGl 17 (1925): 211; Keimer, "The Wisdom of Amen-em-ope," p. 14, n3; Linder, "Das Weisheitsbuch," p. 143; Theis, "Die Lehre des Amen-em-ope," p. 261; Heyes, "Das Buch der Sprüche," p. 4; D. C. Simpson, "The Hebrew Book," p. 236; Gordon, "Proverbs," p. 601; Mallon, "La 'sagesse,' " pp. 11-12; Cadbury, "Egyptian Influence," p. 106; Humbert, *Recherches sur les sources égyptiennes*, p. 28; Kuhn, *Beiträge zur Erklärung des Salomonischen Spruchbuches*, p. 54; Albrecht Alt, "Zur literarischen Analyse der Weisheit des Amenemope," in *Wisdom in Israel and in the Ancient Near East*, p. 25; Fritsch, "The Book of Proverbs," p. 910; Plumley, "The Teaching of Amenemope," p. 173; Hamp, *Das Buch der Sprüche*, p. 60; Edgar Jones, *Proverbs and Ecclesiastes*, p. 188; Ringgren and Zimmerli, *Sprüche*, pp. 88, 91; Rylaarsdam, "The Proverbs," p. 454; *idem, The Proverbs*, p. 75; Scott, *Proverbs*, p. 135; Ernst Sellin and Georg Fohrer, *Introduction to the Old Testament*, p. 321; McKane, *Proverbs*, p. 372; JB; NEB.

17. Gressmann, "Die neugefundene Lehre," p. 285; idem, "Ägypten im Alten Testament," p. 11.

18. Gressmann, "Ägypten im Alten Testament," p. 2; idem, "Die neugefundene Lehre," p. 275; Ernst Sellin, "Die neugefundene 'Lehre des Amen-em ope' in ihrer Bedeutung für die jüdische Literatur- und Religionsgeschichte," DLZ 45 (1924): 1876.

19. Gressmann, "Die neugefundene Lehre," pp. 281, 293-96.

20. Sellin, Review of "Eine ägyptische Quelle," p. 1327. Likewise

Gressmann, "Die neugefundene Lehre," p. 277; Theis, "Die Lehre des Amen-em-ope," p. 260; Linder, "Das Weisheitsbuch," p. 142; D. C. Simpson, "The Hebrew Book," p. 238; Keimer, "The Wisdom of Amen-em-ope," p. 17; Humbert, *Recherches sur les sources égyptiennes,* pp. 25, 29; Ringgren and Zimmerli, *Sprüche,* p. 93; Scott, *Proverbs,* p. 143.

21. Sellin, Review of "Eine ägyptische Quelle," p. 1326; also, Simpson, "The Hebrew Book," p. 236; Humbert, *Recherches sur les sources égyptiennes,* p. 19.

22. Sellin, Review of "Eine ägyptische Quelle," p. 1326; likewise, Gressmann, "Die neugefundene Lehre," p. 278; Zimmermann, "Altägyptische Spruchweisheit," p. 213; Theis, "Die Lehre des Amen-em-ope," p. 260; Linder, "Das Weisheitsbuch," pp. 142, 144; Keimer, "The Wisdom of Amen-em-ope," p. 17; Gemser, *Sprüche Salomos,* p. 66; Gordon, "Proverbs," p. 601; Ruffle, "The Teaching of Amenemope," pp. 415-16; Richter, *Recht und Ethos,* p. 17; Erman preferred the reading "die alte Grenze" ("Eine ägyptische Quelle," pp. 90-91).

23. Sellin, Review of "Eine ägyptische Quelle," p. 1326; also, Gressmann, "Die neugefundene Lehre," p. 276n; Linder, "Das Weisheitsbuch," pp. 141, 143; Theis, "Die Lehre des Amen-em-ope," p. 264; Keimer, "The Wisdom of Amen-em-ope," p. 16; Jones, *Proverbs,* p. 191; Ruffle, "The Teaching of Amenemope," pp. 417-18; JB.

24. Sellin, Review of "Eine ägyptische Quelle," p. 1326; Linder, "Das Weisheitsbuch," pp. 141, 143; Heyes, "Das Buch der Sprüche," p. 7; Keimer, "The Wisdom of Amen-em-ope," pp. 15-16; Ruffle, "The Teaching of Amenemope," pp. 414-15.

25. Sellin, Review of "Eine ägyptische Quelle," pp. 1327-29.

26. Hugo Gressmann, *Israel's Spruchweisheit im Zusammenhang der Weltliteratur,* pp. 36-46; *idem,* "Die neugefundene Lehre," p. 281.

27. Gressmann, "Die neugefundene Lehre," p. 274.

28. *Ibid.,* p. 276n. Likewise, Linder, "Das Weisheitsbuch," pp. 141, 143; Humbert, *Recherches sur les sources égyptiennes,* p. 23.

29. Gressmann, "Die neugefundene Lehre," p. 275n; Richter, *Recht und Ethos,* p. 29. Barucq considered the whole phrase *'mry 'mt* ("words of truth") to be a gloss (*Le Livre,* p. 172).

30. Gressmann, "Die neugefundene Lehre," p. 276; also, Theis, "Die Lehre des Amen-em-ope," p. 263; Zimmermann, "Altägyptische Spruchweisheit," p. 214, n16; Keimer, "The Wisdom of Amen-em-ope," p. 15; Kuhn, *Beiträge zur Erklärung des Salomonischen Spruchbuches,* p. 55.

31. Gressmann, "Die neugefundene Lehre," p. 276n; also, Kuhn, *Beiträge zur Erklärung des Salomonischen Spruchbuches,* p. 55; Theis, "Die Lehre des Amen-em-ope," p. 263.

32. Gressmann, "Die neugefundene Lehre," p. 276n.

33. *Ibid.,* p. 277.

34. *Ibid.*

35. *Ibid.*, p. 278n.; McKane, *Proverbs*, pp. 379, 246; RSV; JB; NEB.

36. Gressmann, "Die neugefundene Lehre," p. 275n.

37. Grimme, "Wieteres zu Amen-em-ope," p. 58. I have freely translated the Greek cited by Grimme and also have given his German rendition of Amenemope.

38. *Ibid.*, pp. 58-60. Likewise, Theis, "Die Lehre des Amen-em-ope," p. 261; Keimer, "The Wisdom of Amen-em-ope," pp. 14-15.

39. Grimme, "Wieteres zu Amen-em-ope," p. 60.

40. *Ibid.*, pp. 57, 60, 62.

41. Humbert, *Recherches sur les sources égyptiennes*, pp. 177-79, 26-28.

42. *Ibid.*, pp. 19-21.

43. *Ibid.*, pp. 24-25.

44. The following dates were proposed by scholars: Budge—1200-950 B.C. (*The Teaching of Amen-em-apt*, p. 94); Erman—1000-600 ("Eine ägyptische Quelle," p. 86); Wilhelm Spiegelberg—950-750 or earlier (*Review of Facsimiles of Egyptian Hieratic Papyri in the British Museum*, by E. A. Wallis Budge, OLZ 27 (1924): 185); Gressmann—ca. 900 ("Ägypten im Alten Testament," p. 2); Griffith—750-500 ("The Teaching of Amenophis," p. 226); Lange—1100 *(terminus a quo)*—300, probably Persian or Greek period (*Das Weisheitsbuch*, pp. 13-14). The dates supplied in place of references to Egyptian dynasties are from Sir Alan Gardiner's *Egypt of the Pharaohs* (Appendix, pp. 446-51).

45. Erman, "Eine ägyptische Quelle," pp. 92-93.

46. Gressmann, "Die neugefundene Lehre," pp. 282-84; 293-96; *idem, Israel's Spruchweisheit, passim.*

47. Gressmann, "Die neugefundene Lehre," pp. 294, 285-86.

48. Sellin, "Die neugefundene 'Lehre des Amen-em-ope'," p. 1877.

49. Humbert, *Recherches sur les sources égyptiennes*, pp. 180-83.

50. *Ibid.*, p. 29.

51. Rudolf Kittel, *Geschichte des Volkes Israel*, 3 (pt. 2): 721-25.

52. *Ibid.*, pp. 715-17, 722.

53. Georges Posener, Review of *Recherches sur les sources égyptiennes de la littérature sapientiale d'Israël* by Paul Humbert, REJ 88 (1929): 97-101.

54. D. Herzog, "Die Sprüche des Amen-em-ope und Proverbien Kapp. 22,17-24,35," ZSG 7 (1929): 124-60.

55. *Ibid.*, pp. 138, 159-60.

56. *Ibid.*, pp. 134-35.

57. *Ibid.*, pp. 135, 138, 146-47, 151, respectively.

58. *Ibid.*, pp. 140-42, 148.

59. *Ibid.*, pp. 136-37, 158.

60. Ruffle, "The Teaching of Amenemope," p. 107.

Chapter 2

1. W. O. E. Oesterley, *The Wisdom of Egypt and the Old Testament in the Light of the Newly Discovered 'Teaching of Amen-em-ope,'* pp. 60-106; Robert O. Kevin, *The Wisdom of Amen-em-apt and its Possible Dependence upon the Hebrew Book of Proverbs*, pp. 115-57.

2. Oesterley, *The Wisdom of Egypt*, pp. 105, 95-97.

3. *Ibid.*, pp. 98-102, 24.

4. *Ibid.*, pp. 64-65, 104. At one point, however, Oesterley was less certain about the exact nature of dependence (*The Book of Proverbs with Introduction and Notes*, pp. liv, 190).

5. Kevin, *The Wisdom of Amen-em-apt*, pp. 125-30.

6. The five Semitisms were "grasping" (*mš'f* from Heb. ̌s'f, Amen. 7:4), "trap" (*m'km'rt=mkmrt* from Heb. *mkmwrt*, Amen. 7:6), "fine gold" (*k3tm=ktm·t* from Heb. *ktm*, Amen. 18:12), "cheat" (*š̌g=š̌k* from Heb. *'š̌q*, Amen 6:14), and "where" (*iwt3=it* from Heb. *'y zh*, Amen. 15:3). Kevin's identification of these Semitisms is the basis of Gleason Archer's case for Egyptian borrowing (*A Survey of Old Testament Introduction*, pp. 467-68). This study laid the foundation for Kevin's introduction of a large number of other Semitic roots as evidence of Egyptian dependence (*The Wisdom of Amen-em-apt*, pp. 131-37).

7. Adolf Erman and Hermann Grapow, eds., *Wörterbuch der aegyptischen Sprache im Auftrage der Deutschen Akademien*, vol. 6, *Deutsch-aegyptisches Wörterverzeichnis im alphabetischer und sachlicher Ordnung nebst Verzeichnissen der koptischen, semitischen und griechischen Wörter*, pp. 243-44; idem, *Aegyptisches Handwörterbuch*, pp. 226-28; Aaron Ember, *Egypto-Semitic-Studies*, pp. 6-118; W. F. Albright, "Notes on Egypto-Semitic Etymology," and "Notes on Egypto-Semitic Etymology, II," *AJSL* 34 (1917-18): 81-98, 215-55; idem, "Notes on Egypto-Semitic Etymology, III," *JAOS* 47 (1927): 198-237.

8. Kevin, *The Wisdom of Amen-em-Apt*, pp. 140-43.

9. *Ibid.*, pp. 143-44, 141, 147-48, respectively.

10. *Ibid.*, p. 149.

11. Georges Posener, "Quatre tablettes scolaires de basse époque (Aménémopé et Hardjédef)," *RE* 18 (1966): 61, 62, n6.

12. James McGlinchey, "The Teaching of Amen-em-ope and the Book of Proverbs," pp. 76, 104, 131-32.

13. *Ibid.*, pp. 111-12, 59, 99-100.

14. *Ibid.*, pp. 56-58, 102.

15. *Ibid.*, pp. 120-22, 130.

16. Edward J. Young uses the same line of reasoning to show Egyptian dependence (*An Introduction to the Old Testament*, p. 304).

17. Humbert, *Recherches sur les sources égyptiennes de la littérature sapientiale d'Israël*, pp. 31, 34; Ernst Sellin, *Geschichte des israelitisch-jüdischen Volkes*, 2: 179; Hilaire Duesberg, *Les Scribes inspirés*, vol. 1, *Le Livre des Proverbes*, p. 469; Al-

brecht Alt, "Zur Literarischen Analyse der Weisheit des Amenemope," in *Wisdom in Israel and in the Ancient Near East*, p. 17; Pierre Montet, *L'Egypte et la Bible*, pp. 112-13.

18. Etienne Drioton, "Le Livre des Proverbes et la sagesse d'Aménémopé," in *Sacra Pagina*, p. 230.

19. *Ibid.*, pp. 231-36; *idem*, "Sur la sagesse d'Aménémopé," in *Mélanges bibliques redigés en l'honneur de André Robert, passim; idem*, "Une colonie israélite en Moyenne Egypte à la fin de VIIe siècle av. J.-C.," in *A la rencontre de Dieu*, pp. 182-83.

20. In the following examples, which will suffice to demonstrate Drioton's method, the Egyptian word with its alleged Hebrew meaning is listed first, followed by the reference to the passage where it appears in Amenemope and the Hebrew word to which it corresponds: *mtr·w* préceptes" (1:2), *'dwt; wḏ3*, "salut" (1:2), *šlwm; s'k3*, "diriger" (1:7), *hkyn; h3y*, "entrer" (1:9), *yrd*. He did not distinguish between syntactical constructions that were Semitic, combinations of Hebrew words embodying Hebrew idiom, and actual Egyptian words that were allegedly used with a secondary (i.e., Semitic) meaning. Etienne Drioton, "Sur la sagesse," pp. 257-60; "Un livre hébreu sur couverture égyptienne," *La Table ronde* (Oct. 1960), p. 87.

21. Drioton, "Sur la sagesse," p. 257; F. Ll. Griffith, "The Teaching of Amenophis the Son of Kanakht, Papyrus B. M. 10474," JEA 12 (1926): 193.

22. Drioton, "Une colonie israélite," p. 184.

23. Drioton, "Sur la sagesse," pp. 259-61.

24. Drioton, "Le Livre des Proverbes," p. 231-32; *idem*, "Sur la sagesse," pp. 257-61.

25. Drioton, "Sur la sagesse," pp. 261-62, 265, 272; *idem*, "Le Livre des Proverbes," p. 235.

26. Drioton, "Sur la sagesse," pp. 263, 275, 277, 258 respectively; *idem*, "Le Livre des Proverbs," pp. 238-39.

27. Drioton, "Une colonie israélite," pp. 186-90; *idem*, "Sur la sagesse," pp. 278-79.

28. Drioton, "Une colonie israélite," pp. 185-86.

29. *Ibid.*, pp. 188-89; *idem*, "Sur la sagesse," pp. 279-80; *idem*, "Le Livre des Proverbes," p. 240.

30. Drioton, "Une colonie israélite," p. 190.

31. Ronald J. Williams, "The Alleged Semitic Original of the 'Wisdom of Amenemope,'" JEA 47 (1961): 102-3; B. Couroyer, "L'origine égyptienne de la sagesse d'Amenemopé," RB 70 (1963): 214-21; John Ruffle, "The Teaching of Amenemope," pp. 136-37, 149, 151; B. Couroyer was actually the first to challenge Drioton's contention that the two phrases "put his hand on his mouth" and the "way of life" were Semitisms ("Mettre sa main sur sa bouche en Egypte et dans la Bible," RB 67 (1960): 205-9).

32. Williams, "The Alleged Semitic Original," pp. 101, 104; Adolf Erman, *Neuägyptische Grammatik*, pp. 353-54; Sarah Israelit Groll, *Non-Verbal Sentence Patterns in Late Egyptian*, p. 15.

33. Adolf Erman, *The Ancient Egyptians*, pp. 88, 309; Raymond O. Faulkner, *A Concise Dictionary of Middle Egyptian*, p. 114 *(mḥyt);* Ruffle, "The Teaching of Amenemope," pp. 156-57.

34. Williams, "The Alleged Semitic Original," p. 106; Bengt Julius Peterson, "A New Fragment of *The Wisdom of Amenemope*," JEA 52 (1966): 121; Posener, "Quatre tablettes scolaires," pp. 46-62; "Une nouvelle tablette d'Aménémopé," RE 25 (1973): 251-52.

35. Ruffle has suggested the twelfth century because of the appearance of words and grammatical constructions, titles, and names from the Middle Kingdom in Amenemope ("The Teaching of Amenemope," pp. 21-24). On the basis of a study of the religious terminology relating to the personnel of the deity Min, Henri Gauthier suggested that the persons mentioned in Amenemope probably lived in the eighteenth dynasty (1600-1300 B.C.) *(Le personnel du dieu Min,* p. 56). Professor Edward F. Wente of the Oriental Institute of the University of Chicago related to me in private conversation that on the basis of thematic considerations he believes that Amenemope properly belongs to the Rameside era. For a discussion of this matter as regards the religion of the Egyptian text, see Hellmut Brunner's article "Der freie Wille Gottes in der ägyptischen Weisheit," in *Les sagesses du Proche-Orient ancien,* pp. 103-17.

36. "Quatre tablettes scolaires," p. 59.

Chapter 3

1. Hugo Gressmann, "Die neugefundene Lehre des Amen-em-ope und die vorexilische Spruchdichtung Israels," ZAW 42 (1924): 291-93; *idem, Israel's Spruchweisheit im Zusammenhang der Weltliteratur, passim;* Walter Baumgartner, *Israelitische und altorientalische Weisheit,* pp. 23-30; Johannes Fichtner, *Die altorientalische Weisheit in ihrer israelitisch-jüdischen Ausprägung, passim.*

2. In the report of the journey of Wenamon to Phoenicia, the prince of Byblos admits the indebtedness of his city to Egypt for wisdom and education (John A. Wilson, "Egyptian Historical Texts," ANET, p. 27). The connection between Wenamon and Amenemope was made by H. J. Heyes, "Das Buch der Sprüche und das altägyptische Weisheitsbuch des Amen-em-ope," BZTS 3 (1926): 10. For discussion of the translation and significance of the passage concerning Wenamon and the prince of Byblos, see Charles F. Nims, "Second Tenses in Wenamūn," JEA 54 (1968): 163; E. F. Wente, "The Report of Wenamon," in *The Literature of Ancient Egypt,* pp. 142, 148, n15; 149, n19;

152, n29, and W. F. Albright, "Some Canaanite-Phoenician Sources of Hebrew Wisdom," in *Wisdom in Israel and in the Ancient Near East,* pp. 2-3.

3. With respect to the development of the tradition of Israelite wisdom, various theories have been proposed. Most of them have followed the line of development from a more secular, eudaemonistic type of wisdom characteristic of the early period to a more religious or pietistic kind of wisdom found later, as originally suggested by Rudolph Kittel (*Geschichte des Volkes Israel,* 3 (pt. 2):721-25). Recent theories have proposed a development from secular *(weltlich)* to theological wisdom (Hans Heinrich Schmid, *Wesen und Geschichte der Weisheit,* pp. 144-56), from the Egyptian through the Yahwistic and finally to the theological stage (Michael V. Fox, "Aspects of the Religion of the Book of Proverbs," HUCA 39 (1968): 55-69), and from the training of the individual for a successful life in the more ancient wisdom through the developing communal concern for proper social behaviour and finally to the moralism of Yahwistic piety (William McKane, *Proverbs,* pp. 10-11).

4. J. A. Knudtzon, ed., *Die El-Amarna-Tafeln mit Einleitung und Erlaüterungen,* 1: 608-12; 2: 1246; Hugo Gressmann, "Hadad und Baal nach den Amarnabriefen und nach ägyptischen Texten," in *Abhandlungen zur semitischen Religionskunde und Sprachwissenschaft,* pp. 208-9; Albrecht Alt, "Hic murus aheneus esto," ZDMG 86 (1933): 39-48; W. F. Albright, "The Egyptian Correspondence of Abimilki, Prince of Tyre," JEA 23 (1937): 196-200.

5. Alt, "Hic murus," pp. 39-41. For other references see Adolf Erman and Hermann Grapow, eds., *Wörterbuch der aegyptischen Sprache im Auftrage der Deutschen Akademien,* 1:436 (no. 11); 1:437 (no. 16). The reference to the bronze wall in the Gilgamesh Epic may not be correct (E. A. Speiser, "The Epic of Gilgamesh," ANET, p. 73 (Tablet 1, 1:11); Leo Oppenheim has suggested a different translation ("Mesopotamian Mythology II," Or 17 (19-48):19). The reference in the letter to the city or house or even the name of someone perishing and the phrase "the entire country" (11. 11, 46-47), previously regarded as Egyptianisms, are not foreign to Akkadian idiom (Ignace J. Gelb *et al.,* eds., *The Assyrian Dictionary of the Oriental Institute of the University of Chicago,* 1 (pt. 1): 384; 6: 38, 39; 5: 4). For further discussion of the question including other examples of Canaanite expressions in the letter see Stanley Gevirtz, "On Canaanite Rhetoric: The Evidence of the Amarna Letters from Tyre," Or n. s. 42 (1973): 176-77.

6. C. Bezold and E. A. Wallis Budge, eds., *The Tell El-Amarna Tablets in the British Museum with Autotype Facsimiles,* p. 62 (no. 29); Knudtzon, *Die El-Amarna-Tafeln,* 1: 608. In the transliteration I have left several Canaanite words in the syllabic orthography. The word *it-ta-ṣa-ab* need not be an incorrect usage as Albright suggests, but simply a past tense of *naṣābum,* used actively as in the Ugaritic texts (no. 125:52; 2 Aqht 1:27); Albright, "The Egyptian Correspondence," p. 198, n9.). As a perfect tense it would stress the temporal aspect as I have translated it.

7. My own reconstruction of the Egyptian differs considerably from the one given by Albright with the assistance of B. Gunn. Some of the idiom in his translation is too literal, not representing contextual Egyptian usages, and matters such as tenses and transcription are not entirely correct. Albright, "The Egyptian Correspondence," p. 198, n12. For example, see Jan Assmann, *Liturgische Lieder an den Sonnengott*, p. 119, n.22. I am indebted to Professor George R. Hughes for numerous suggestions on my own rendition.

8. Franz M. Th. Böhl, "Die Sprache der Amarnabriefe mit besonderer Berücksichtigung der Kanaanismen," *Leipziger semitistische Studien*, 5 (pt. 2): 82; Albright, "The Egyptian Correspondence," p. 197. The proposal of a Canaanite root for this word was suggested by Gevirtz, "On Canaanite Rhetoric," p. 176.

9. For the evidence on the transliteration of this letter into Akkadian, see H. Ranke, "Keilschriftliches Material zur altägyptischen Vokalisation," *Abhandlungen der Königlich Preussischen Akademie der Wissenschaften: Philosophisch-historische Klasse*, 1910, Anhang 2: 23-24, 91; Th. O. Lambdin, "Egyptian Words in Tell Amarna Letter No. 14," Or 22 (1953): 364 (no. 9), 365 (nos. 10-11), 367 (no. 27); W. F. Albright, "Cuneiform Material for Egyptian Prosopography," JNES 5 (1946): 11; Daniel Haigh, "Assyro-Aegyptiaca," ZÄS 9 (1871): 113; Max Burchardt, *Die altkanaanäischen Fremdworte und Eigennamen im Aegyptischen*, pt. 2, nos. 417, 657, 661, 664. The word represents a verb beginning either with "*r*" or an initial weak letter followed by "*r*" in the first person singular. The Canaanite gloss *yr'*, "fear," suggested by Hugo Winckler, does not fit the context (*The Tell-el-Amarna Letters*, p. 149; Böhl, "Die Sprache," p. 86). The proposal "I drink (my fill?)" from the root *rwh* does not make sense (Samuel A. B. Mercer, *The Tell El-Amarna Tablets*, 2: 844). Since the Hebrew root *rw'*, "shout," is used once in the noun form in parallelism with joyful laughter (Job 8:21), possibly it offers another option for the interpretation of line 28: "I shout in joy day by day."

10. The combination of these words in Egyptian literature leaves no doubt that this has been borrowed, even though Knudtzon, citing Grapow, gives only one example of the phrase "sweet breath of life" (*Die El-Amarna-Tafeln*, 2:1606). For an exact parallel from the late period see Erman and Grapow, *Wörterbuch der aegyptischen Sprache im Auftrage der deutschen Akademien, Die Belegstellen*, 4:12 (citations 46,6). A perusal of hundreds of epithets in the hymns to Shamash confirms the fact that this clause, and also the reference to the sun being "hidden," are Egyptianisms. P. Anastasius Schollmeyer, *Sumerisch-babylonische Hymnen und Gebete an Šamaš*, pp. 29-137.

11. Erman and Grapow, *Wörterbuch*, 1: 83; John Wilson, "Egyptian Hymns and Prayers," ANET, pp. 366, 368, n6; Assmann, *Liturgische Lieder*, pp. 83-87, 310; Albright, "The Egyptian Correspondence," p. 198.

12. The paradoxical idea that the sun god "becomes youthful" when he sets, is discussed by Assmann, who cites numerous texts and literature (*Liturgische*

Lieder, p. 241), a meaning that the Akkadian verb has in one instance in reference to the significance of the name of a plant (Gelb, *et al., The Assyrian Dictionary,* 16:122).

13. Sélim Hassan, *Hymnes religieux du Moyen Empire,* p. 162 (also *ḥwn nfr nṯr imn,* "beautiful young man, hidden god" in reference to Re, p. 161). Erman and Grapow, *Wörterbuch: Belegstellen,* 2 (pt. 1): 40 (nos. 15-16); 2(pt. 2):648 (nos. 16-17).

14. The examples are found in Alan H. Gardiner, *Late-Egyptian Stories,* pp. 60, 68, and *The Later Historical Records of Ramses III by Epigraphic Survey,* 2, Plate 87 (11. 2-3), 79 (1. 22). Translations may be found in Edward F. Wente Jr., trans., "The Contendings of Horus and Seth," and "The Report of Wenamon," in *The Literature of Ancient Egypt,* pp. 125, 149; John A. Wilson "Egyptian Historical Text," ANET, p. 249.

15. Cyrus H. Gordon, *Ugaritic Textbook: Texts,* p. 171 (51 V 70; VII 29); *idem, Ugaritic Literature,* pp. 32, 36.

16. For references see Gressmann, "Hadad and Baal," p. 205; Rainer Stadelmann, *Syrisch-palästinenische Gottheiten in Ägypten,* p. 27; G. A. Wainwright, "Some Aspects of Amūn," JEA 20 (1934): 150-51; *idem,* "Some Celestial Associations of Min," JEA 21 (1935): 154, 168-69; *idem, The Sky Religion in Egypt,* pp. 99-100; *idem,* "The Origin of Storm-Gods in Egypt," JEA 49 (1963): 13-20; J. Zandee, "Seth als Sturmgott," ZÄS 90 (1963): 144-66; Arvin S. Kapelrud, *Baal in the Ras Shamra Texts,* p. 63.

17. Prov. 22:24. The Hebrew citations are from *Biblia Hebraica,* ed. Rudolph Kittel. The Septuagint translates the two phrases *b'l 'p* and *'ys ḥmwt* with ἀνδρὶ θυμώδει and φίλῳ.. ὀργίλῳ. The Hebrew idiom *bw' 't* could be rendered literally like tne Egyptian phrase "go into the presence of," although the translators have usually translated it in relation to its parallel *ḥlk 't* "associate with" (LXX: συναυλίζου, "have dealings with"). References to the Septuagint are found in the *Septuaginta,* ed. Alfred Rahlfs.

18. H. O. Lange, *Das Weisheitsbuch des Amenemope,* p. 62. Unless otherwise indicated the translations of the Egyptian texts are my own.

19. Francis Brown, S. R. Driver, and Charles A. Briggs, *A Hebrew and English Lexicon of the Old Testament,* p. 945.

20. References to the hot-headed man occur in the oldest Egyptian wisdom literature beginning with Ptahhotep as well as in Amen.4:17; 5:15; 6:1; 11:13; 13:11; 15:13. For references, see Ronald J. Williams's study, "Some Egyptianisms in the Old Testament," in *Studies in Honor of John A. Wilson,* pp. 97-98, also Gunter Lanczkowski, "Reden und Schweigen im ägyptischen, Verständnis, vornehmlich des Mittleren Reiches," in *Ägyptologische Studien,* pp. 195-96.

The Hebrew phrase *b'l ḥmh* occurs only once elsewhere in the Old Testament (Nah. 1:2). D. Herzog's objection that *ḥmh* was heavier than *'p* ignores the frequent equation of these two words in parallelism (Pss. 6:1; 37:8; 78:38;

90:7; Isa. 63: 3, 6; "Die Sprüche des Amen-em-ope und Proverbien Kapp. 22:17-24:35," ZSG 7 (1929): 141). Ruffle's denial of the equivalence of the two words because of the plural form of *ḥmh* disregards Ps. 76:10, which uses the plural form, possibly an emphatic plural as we find in other texts according to Carl Brockelmann (*Hebräische Syntax*, p. 16) and this syntactical possibility (John Ruffle, "The Teaching of Amenemope," p. 407).

21. Amen. 13:1; Lange, *Das Weisheitsbuch*, p. 63.

22. Amen. 5:10; Lange, *ibid.*, p. 39.

23. Of course, the figurative use of "fire" or "flame" with reference to disputes is universal. In Sumerian wisdom we read counsels such as "When [a spirit of] fighting consumes someone like a fire, put it out" (J. J. A. van Dijk, *La sagesse suméro-akkadienne*, p. 106, 1.18) and in Babylonian wisdom as follows: "Should it be a dispute involving you, extinguish the blaze" (*na-pi-iḫ-ta;* W. G. Lambert, *Babylonian Wisdom Literature*, p. 100, 1. 37).

24. References to the "silent man" are widespread, found in biographical literature, religious texts, and instructional materials. For these and similar references see Otto, *Die biographischen Inschriften der ägyptischen Spätzeit*, pp. 66-67, 132, 138; Wilson, "Egyptian Hymns and Prayers," p. 379; E. A. Wallis Budge, *The Book of the Dead*, p. 211; Ricardo A. Caminos, *Late-Egyptian Miscellanies*, pp. 30, 321, 323, 463; Lanczkowski, "Reden und Schweigen," pp. 192-96; Williams, "Some Egyptianisms," pp. 97-98.

25. *'rk 'pym*, Prov. 14:29; *ḥwšk 'mryw // wqr rwh*, Prov. *17:27; mšl brwḥw*, Prov. 16:32.

26. Erman and Grapow, *Wörterbuch, Belegstellen*, 5:5 (citations: 23,4); also "silent, patient, calm of speech, subduing passion," cited by Williams ("Some Egyptianisms," p. 98) from the same source (23, 12).

27. Lange, *Das Weisheitsbuch*, p. 42. A similar idea is found in Amen. 4:14 where the cooling north wind descends on a sultry day to bring to an end the hour of the "hot" man.

28. Amen. 6:6; Lange, *Das Weisheitsbuch*, p. 42.

29. Georges Posener, *Catalogue des ostraca hiératiques littéraires de Deir el Médineh*, 2, Plate 16.

39. Lange, *Das Weisheitsbuch*, p. 52.

31. For a survey of the use and development of this literary form in Egypt and Israel see my own study, " 'Better'-Proverbs: An Historical and Structural Study," *The Society of Biblical Literature One Hundred Eighth Annual Meeting: Book of Seminar Papers*, 2: 343-54. Examples of this form are not found in Assyro-Babylonian literature since it employs the prepositional form (*eli,* "over") to express the comparative. It does appear in Aramaic wisdom (*ṭb kbš . . .*, Ahiqar 152; A. Cowley, *Aramaic Papyri of the Fifth Century* B.C., pp. 217, 225; F. Stummer, *Der kritische Wert der altaramäischen Aḫiḳartexte aus Elephantine*, p. 61).

32. Zbyněk Žába, *Les Maximes de Ptahhotep*, p. 45 (1. 365). My translation,

somewhat free, is based upon the comments of Žába (p. 150).

33. Aksel Volten, *Zwei altägyptische politische Schriften*, p. 68 (P. 128-29).

34. Adolf Erman was the first to discuss the parallels in this section ("Eine ägyptische Quelle der 'Sprüche Salomos,' " SAB 15 [1924]: 87-88). Interpreters were not sure whether Amen. 9:7-8 was parallel to Prov. 15:16 or 15:17. Gressmann made Amen. 9:5-6 parallel to Prov. 15:16 (Hugo Gressmann, "Die neugefundene Lehre des Amen-em-ope und die vorexilische Spruchdichtung Israels," ZAW 42 (1924): p. 278; D. C. Simpson, "The Hebrew Book of Proverbs and the Teaching of Amenophis," JEA 12 (1926): 2). Grumach discusses the Egyptian sayings but makes no reference to the Hebrew connection (*Untersuchungen zur Lebenslehre des Amenope*, pp. 60-61).

35. Amen. 9:5-6; 16:11-12.

36. 1 Sam. 5:9, 11.

37. *ṭwb* or *yṭb* with *lb* appears in Prov. 17:22; 15:15; Judges 16:25; 1 Sam. 25:36; 2 Sam. 13:28; Esther 1:10.

38. Amen. 9:5-6; Lange, *Das Weisheitsbuch*, p. 52.

39. Amen. 8:19-20; 9:5-6, 7-8; 16:11-12, 13-14 (22:15-16). For a discussion of the Demotic example see Helmut Brunner, "Die religiöse Wertung der Armut im Alten Aegypten," Saec 12 (1961): 328. For Old Testament references see Prov. 15:16; 16:8; 19:1; 28:6 and Ps. 37:16, also Ecclus. 30:14. Other examples of the *ṭwbspruch* in Proverbs are found in 12:9; 15:17; 16:19, 32; 17:1; 19:22b; 21:9 // 25:24; 22:1; 25:7; 27:5, 10b.

40. Hans-Jürgen Hermisson, *Studien zur israelitischen Spruchweisheit*, p. 84; Wolfgang Richter, *Recht und Ethos*, pp. 67, 141, 189-92.

41. Hermisson, *Studien*, p. 85.

42. Gordon, *Ugaritic Textbook: Text*, p. 248; *Ugaritic Literature*, p. 90.

43. Hugo Gressmann, "Ägypten im Alten Testament," *Vossische Zeitung*, 22 June 1924, p. 11; B. Gemser, *Sprüche Salomos*, p. 54.

44. Prov. 19:18; 20:13; 20:22 (vetitive); 20:16 (*ky* following imperative), 16: 26; 21:7, 25 (*ky* with declaration). Walther Zimmerli, "Zur Struktur der alttestamentlichen Weisheit," ZAW 51 (1933): 185.

45. In Ugaritic literature parallels to Prov. 23:13 ('*l* with following *ky* clause) and Prov. 23:6-7 (double negation followed by a *ky* at the beginning of two parallel clauses, also in Prov. 23:10-11; 24:1-2, 15-16; 19-20) are found in 2 Aqht 6:34-35 and Keret 133-136, although the causal connection must be inferred from the meaning in the latter example (G. R. Driver, *Canaanite Myths and Legends*, p. 31). Also, it must be observed that Hermisson admitted that the Egyptian origin of the vetitive form may not have been a case of direct literary influence but merely the appropriation of the admonitory form by the wisdom school as a result of Egyptian influence (*Studien*, p. 85). Of course, virtual causal clauses such as the one cited from Keret are common in the literature of the ancient Near East being represented in Egyptian by the old perfective tense (Gustave Lefebvre, *Grammaire de l'Egyptien classique*, p. 362). In

Egyptian wisdom literature examples may be found in Merikare (P. 49, 71; Volten, *Zwei ältagyptischen politische Schriften*, pp. 22, 36). Similarly, in Babylonian wisdom literature no conjunction will be found in cases where a causal clause is implied (Lambert, *Babylonian Wisdom*, pp. 104-5; 11. 132-3).

46. Wilson, "Proverbs and Precepts," ANET, pp. 412, 418, 431. For a discussion of the significance of these texts in Egyptian wisdom literature see Georges Posener, *Littérature et politique dans l'Egypte de la XIIe, dynastie*, pp. 4-20, 61-86, 117-40.

47. Lange, *Das Weisheitsbuch*, p. 134. For a discussion of the origin and use of the tradition of the "thirty" in Egyptian literature see Kurt Sethe, *Von Zahlen und Zahlworten bei den alten Ägyptern und was für andere Völker und Sprachen daraus zu lernen ist*, p. 40; Alan H. Gardiner, *The Admonitions of an Egyptian Sage from a Hieratic Papyrus in Leiden (Pap. Leiden 344 Recto)*, p. 50. The reference in Amenemope to the "amusement" provided by the thirty chapters may be an allusion to draft boards of thirty squares upon which a game was played. The object of this game was to reach the hall of the "thirty" judges, though in Egyptian religious stories the playing of it involved the use of magic (Günther Roeder, *Altägyptische Erzählungen und Märchen*, p. 149; *Die ägyptische Religion in Text und Bildern*, vol. 4, *Der Ausklang der ägyptischen Religion mit Reformation, Zauberei und Jenseitsglauben*, pp. 254-61. Game boards, some of which have thirty squares, have also been discovered in Palestine at the beginning of the Late Bronze Age (W. F. Albright, "A Set of Egyptian Playing Pieces and Dice from Palestine," Miz 1 (1933): 130-34).

48. Van Dijk, *La sagesse*, p. 101.

49. Jean Nougayrol, *et al.*, eds. *Ugaritica V*, pp. 273-90; Lambert, *Babylonian Wisdom*, pp. 92-93.

50. John Ruffle, who does not accept the emendation of the text to the number "thirty," presents a thorough statement of the problem from this perspective ("The Teaching of Amenemope," pp. 393-401; also Herzog, "Die Sprüche," pp. 136-37).

Irene Grumach has proposed that both Proverbs and Amenemope have used older sources. One of these consists of a series of sayings from old Egyptian wisdom that can be isolated in Amenemope but that does not appear in Proverbs. The other, which is more important, is called the *Alte Lehre* and was used by both Proverbs and Amenemope. However, Proverbs retains the original order of the source so that it can be reconstructed. Composed during the reign of Haremheb in the fourteenth century, it was an admonitory instruction seeking to check bureaucratic corruption and containing teachings directed to officials. This *"Alte Lehre"* may well have employed a thirtyfold division to express in symbolic form its relation to the judicial office, thus explaining the origin of the number thirty in both Amenemope and Proverbs. It was mediated to the Old Testament through Canaanite sources.

The hypothesis of Grumach is vitiated by several factors, not the least of which is its inutility in actually enabling us to trace the history of the tradition. For example, one would expect that Amenemope, being closer to the *Alte Lehre*, would have preserved its consecution of sayings, yet the haphazard arrangement of these is simply transferred by Grumach from Proverbs to Amenemope. If the element of amusement mentioned in Amen. 27:8 at the conclusion of this instruction did not belong to the introduction originally, one would expect that the Hebrew rendition, which preserves the old source, would be closely parallel to it. But the clause "they cause the ignorant to know" in the introduction of the *Alte Lehre* (Amen. 27:8, 10) is scarcely reproduced in the Hebrew phrase, which refers to thirty sayings "of counsel and knowledge," especially when Hebrew has an idiom to render the word "ignorant" (Job 35:16; Prov. 19:2). Of course, since the original was mediated through a Canaanite source, this complicates the problem. Nevertheless, the selective and organizational technique of the Hebrew composer of "The Sayings of the Wise" is quite original, as the presence of purely Hebrew materials shows (22:26-27). Does this not rather suggest that the cluster of Egyptian elements in Proverbs is the work of the Hebrew writer and is original at this point, not at all providing a source for the reconstruction of a common source, mediated through Canaanite traditions to the Old Testament?

Moreover, with respect to the number "thirty," why is it necessary to posit an original to explain this in Amenemope and Proverbs? As far as Amenemope is concerned, it was a concept quite current, as numerous references to it show. With respect to Proverbs, the widespread use of Amenemope in the schools of Egypt is strong evidence of the fact that, as far as wisdom literature is concerned, Amenemope is the source for the number that appears in Proverbs.

Unfortunately, concern about an Egyptian *Vorlage* shifts our attention away from the more significant aspect of the relationship suggested by Grumach, the way in which traditions from Egypt have been adapted in the Canaanite-Hebrew milieu. It is this phase of the study that is most important from the point of view of the relationship between Israelite and Egyptian wisdom literature. For a discussion and reconstruction of the text of the sources, see Irene Grumach, *Untersuchungen,* pp. 4-6, 183-85, and "Anhang: Rekonstruktion der Alten Lehre," "Rekonstruktion der Alten Quelle."

51. S. R. Driver, *Notes on the Hebrew Text and the Topography of the Books of Samuel with an Introduction on Hebrew Palaeography and the Ancient Versions and Facsimiles of Inscriptions and Maps,* pp. 364-67.

52. In the two passages just discussed, the Septuagint has τρία, the translator interpreting šlš to mean "three things."

53. The Septuagint has τρισσῶς; the Vulgate reads *tripliciter* (*Biblia Sacra juxta Vulgatam Clementinam,* p. 704). The Sahidic Coptic has *enšᵉmtsōp* (*sic! Z 24: nšomnt;* William H. Worrell, ed., *The Proverbs of Solomon in Sahidic Coptic according to the Chicago Manuscript,* p. 72), and the Syriac Peshitta translates the word

with the phrase *'al t^elāt zabnīn* ("three times"; Trinitarian Bible Society ed., London, 1954). For these two readings, respectively, I am indebted to Professor Bruce M. Metzger and Professor Joseph A. Fitzmyer, S. J.

54. Exod. 23:14, 17; Num. 22:28, 32, 33; Judges 16:15; 1 Sam. 20:41; 1 Kings 17:21; 2 Kings 13:18, 19, 25.

55. The only occurrence of τρίσσως elsewhere is in reference to tiers of windows in 1 Kings 7:4-5 (*šlš p^cmym*, 3 Kings 7: 41; Edwin Hatch and Henry A. Redpath, *A Concordance to the Septuagint and Other Greek Versions of the Old Testament (Including Apocryphal Books)*, 2: 1373.

56. Lists of the "thirty" sayings as isolated by various scholars may be found in the following studies: Gressmann, "Die neugefundene Lehre," p. 285; Paul Humbert, *Recherches sur les sources égyptiennes de la littérature sapientiale d'Israël*, p. 28; W. M. W. Roth, *Numerical Sayings in the Old Testament*, pp. 88-89; R. B. Y. Scott, *Proverbs, Ecclesiastes*, pp. 137-46; William McKane, *Proverbs*, pp. 374-406.

57. Some Greek versions omit Prov. 23:23. Prov. 22:28 and 23:10 are a doublet, and Prov. 23:15 and 23:19 are very similar.

58. Prior to the discovery of Amenemope, Crawford H. Toy regarded the *Qere* text as improbable. More recently Robert Gordis refers to it as "meaningless" (Crawford H. Toy, *A Critical and Exegetical Commentary on the Book of Proverbs*, p. 423; Robert Gordis, *The Biblical Text in the Making*, pp. 150, 198, n507).

59. Most scholars divided the collection of sayings into three parts with the beginning of the second part at 23:12, although no unanimity has been reached on this subject.

60. Gottfried Kuhn, *Beiträge zur Erklärung des Salomonischen Spruchbuches*, p. 53; James M. McGlinchey, "The Teaching of Amen-em-ope and the Book of Proverbs," p. 107.

Chapter 4

1. Cullen I. K. Story, "The Book of Proverbs and Northwest Semitic Literature," *JBL* 64 (1945): 319-37; W. F. Albright, "Some Canaanite-Phoenician Sources of Hebrew Wisdom," in *Wisdom in Israel and in the Ancient Near East*, pp. 1-15; Mitchell Dahood, *Proverbs and Northwest Semitic Philology*, pp. 3-63; *idem*, "The Phoenician Contribution to Biblical Wisdom Literature," in *The Role of the Phoenicians in the Interaction of Mediterranean Civilizations*, pp. 123-48.

2. Where there is an ideological correspondence between Hebrew and Egyptian thought, rendered by Hebrew idiom that is equivalent in thought but not a word-for-word rendition, we may speak of a "semiticization" of Egyptian ideas.

3. The phrase "slow to anger" (*'rk 'pym*) is used nine times in the Old Testament in a liturgical formula appertaining to God (Exod. 34:6; Num. 14:18; Joel 2:13; Jon. 4:2; Nahum 1:3; Pss. 86:15, 103:8, 145:8, and Neh. 9:17). The uses of this idiom with reference to man are found in Prov. 14:29; 15:18; 16: 32; 25:15; and Eccles. 7:8. The phrase rendered "impatient" with *qṣr* appears twice in Proverbs (14:17, 29). In Prov. 17:27 the two expressions "one who holds his words in check" (*ḥsk 'mryw*) and "one who is cool of spirit" (*qr rwḥ*) give the precise attributes of the Egyptian characterization of a man who is both silent and calm.

4. Stanley Gevirtz has demonstrated the existence of fixed pairs of words in parallelism in the Old Testament (*Patterns in the Early Poetry of Israel, passim*). With regard to parallelism in Egyptian literature, it was the opinion of Adolf Erman that "parallelism was never consolidated into an established form of poetry" (*The Ancient Egyptians*, p. lxi). On the other hand Pierre Lacau has adduced examples of the systematic use of parallel words in Egyptian literature ("Sur le parallélisme dans les textes des pyramides et ailleurs," in *The Pyramid Texts*, vol. 4, *Excurses*, pp. 140-57). In Amenemope parallelism does not appear to be employed as regards fixed words and pairs of terms, but it is used as a stylistic device in general. For an exhaustive study of this subject, see Loren R. Fisher, ed., *Ras Shamra Parallels: The Texts from Ugarit and the Hebrew Bible*, Analecta Orientalia, no. 49 (Rome: Pontificium Institutum Biblicum, 1972), vol. 1.

5. Prov. 8:20; Pss. 36:6; 72:1; 103:6; 106:3; associated in Ps. 89:14; Job 37: 23. William McKane's view, that Prov. 15:16 represents a later Yahwistic reinterpretation of the tradition integrating the saying more fully into Israelite piety, is clearly contrary to the history of the tradition as reflected in Prov. 16:8 (*Proverbs*, pp. 11, 486-87). This verse shows that the addition of specifically Israelite religious concerns occurs at the very beginning of the process, something not unnatural in view of the fact that the source of the proverb was non-Israelite. In the subsequent development, as the proverb was reinterpreted, it lost this distinctively Israelite trait (Prov. 19:1; 28:6). Of course, references to "fear of the Lord" need not be a sign of later Israelite piety. This expression occurs frequently in Babylonian religious and wisdom literature (*palāḫ ili, palāḫum*; W. G. Lambert, *Babylonian Wisdom Literature*, pp. 104 (1. 146), 229 (1. 24); 136 (1. 165); Wolfram von Soden, *Akkadisches Handwörterbuch unter Benutzung des lexikalischen Nachlasses von BRUNO MEISSNER (1868-1947)*, 1:375; 2:813).

6. *twb'h* may refer to revenue in general, even to one's possessions. In Proverbs it is parallel to *p'lh*, "wage" (10:16), *br*, "grain" (14:4), *ḥsn*, "wealth" (15:6).

7. It was Budge who suggested that the strong emphasis upon morality in Amenemope was due to "some Asiatic influence." According to Erman, both cultures shared a particular "*seelische Stimmung*" that was the prerequisite for the enjoyment of riches. In general, however, scholars did seek to emphasize

the superior ethical quality of Hebrew proverbial thought in contrast to Egyptian literature. For these and other studies upon this subject see E. A. Wallis Budge, *The Teaching of Amen-em-Apt, Son of Kanekht*, pp. 103-4; Adolf Erman, "Eine ägyptische Quelle der 'Sprüche Salomos,'" SAB 15 (1924): 88; D. Herzog, "Die Sprüche des Amen-em-ope und Proverbien Kapp. 22,17-24,35," ZSG 7 (1929): 129; Hilaire Duesberg, *Les Scribes inspirés*, vol. 1, *Le Livre des Proverbes*, pp. 492-93; Walther Zimmerli, "Ort und Grenze der Weisheit im Rahmen der alttestamentlichen Theologie," in *Les sagesses du Proche-Orient ancien*, p. 129.

8. Hans-Jürgen Hermisson, *Studien zur israelitischen Spruchweisheit*, pp. 181-82.

9. Amen. 8:19-20; H. O. Lange, *Das Weisheitsbuch des Amenemope*, p. 51.

10. The Hebrew version of the Cairo Genizah manuscripts shows that this is a *ṭwbspruch:*

$$\text{ṭwb mskn wḥy b'ṣmw m'šyr wng' bbśrw}$$

(S. Schechter and C. Taylor, eds., *The Wisdom of Ben Sira*, p. 11).

11. "Il vaut mieux mourir dans la sollicitude que vivre sans pudeur" (Francois Lexa, *Papyrus Insinger*, 1:86 (text); 2:66 (trans.).

12. Hellmut Brunner, "Die religiöse Wertung der Armut im Alten Aegypten," Saec 12 (1961): 327-29, 344.

13. S. R. K. Glanville, *Catalogue of Demotic Papyri in the British Museum*, vol. 2, *The Instructions of 'Onchsheshonqy (British Museum Papyrus 10508)*, 1:48,49 (21: 22). The transcription and translations of the Demotic proverbs, cited respectively, are those of the author.

14. *Ibid.*, 1:44,45 (19:17).

15. *Ibid.*, 1:54,55 (24:13).

16. See the discussion at the end of chapter 3.

17. With regard to the significance of this number John Ruffle states, "It is upon this point alone that the whole question of a close link between *Proverbs* and *Amenemope* may stand or fall. . . .If *Proverbs* 22:20 really does refer to 30 maxims, the connection could not reasonably be denied ("The Teaching of Amenemope," p. 400).

18. With reference to Ruffle *(ibid.)* and Paul Humbert *(Recherches sur les sources égyptiennes de la littérature sapientiale d'Israël*, pp. 19-28, 57-62, 177-79), who represent the two extremes of complete denial of relationship and assertion of almost total dependence.

19. Lange, *Das Weisheitsbuch*, p. 32.

20. Prov. 5:13; Pss. 17:6, 45:10; Jer. 7:24, 26; 11:8; 25:4; 34:14; 35:15; 2 Kings 19:16; Dan. 9:18.

21. Herzog, "Die Sprüche," pp. 134-35; Ruffle, "The Teaching of Amenemope," pp. 389-92.

22. "Écoutez le conseil de Šube'awilum" (J. Nougayrol, *et al.*, eds., *Ugaritica V*, pp. 277, 280.

23. Cyrus H. Gordon, *Ugaritic Textbook: Texts*, p. 194 (127:41-42); also cf. p. 161 (6:22-23).

24. 2 Kings 19:16; Isa. 37:17; Pss. 17:6, 31:2, 71:2, 86:1, 88:2, 102:2; Dan. 9:18; Prov. 4:20, 5:1. In Hebrew the normal parallel to *šm'* is *h'zn* (Gevirtz, *Patterns*, p. 27). The Egyptian language also has several expressions such as *imi msḏr* or *ḫ3' msḏr* (Ricardo A. Caminos, *Late-Egyptian Miscellanies*, p. 555; Ronald J. Williams, "The Alleged Semitic Original of the 'Wisdom of Amenemope,' " JEA 47 (1961): 103).

25. Exod. 7:23; 2 Sam. 13:20; Pss. 48:13, 62:10; Prov. 24:32, 27:23 and, respectively, Anastasi V 8, 6; III 4, 3 (Caminos, *Late-Egyptian Miscellanies*, pp. 231-32; Adolf Erman and Hermann Grapow, eds., *Wörterbuch der aegyptischen Sprache im Auftrage der Deutschen Akademien: Die Belegstellen*, 1: 13 (references; 76,14).

26. The comment of Ruffle on this passage entirely misses the point: "An injunction to 'Listen because what I have to say to you is good for you' is what any writer of any wisdom book might be expected to say, and there is no reason why two writers with roughly the same conventions of poetic style should not express themselves in poetic terms" ("The Teaching of Amenemope," p. 443). What strikes one about these so-called stereotyped introductions is their variety, indicating the use of various stylistic devices on the part of the authors and reflecting their remarkable literary skill. This enables one to discover unusual similarities, which may be a sign of dependence.

27. Of course, this is connected to the proposal that the two words form the title of the collection, "The Sayings of the Wise." On the other hand, R. N. Whybray has suggested that this translation of the title is incorrect, also the traditional rendering of the title in Prov. 24:23. Both titles should be translated without the definite article. Since there was no class of professional persons in Israel known as "the wise," the title of the collection beginning in Prov. 22:17 lacks the definite article. It really belongs to the prose section, not the poetic material, and translators are incorrect when they refer to sayings of "the wise" instead of "Sayings of Wise Men." In his study of the contexts in which this designation is used, he tries to demonstrate "that there is no evidence in the Old Testament for a class of writers known as 'the wise men,' or indeed of *any* class of men so designated" (*The Intellectual Tradition in the Old Testament*, p. 50; see also p. 53).

Yet the position that Whybray adopts with respect to the titles may be used as evidence that there was a group in Israel known as "*the* wise men." In general it may be said that the same titles, whether in prose or poetry, may have the definite article or may be without it (1 Sam. 17:55; 2 Sam. 2:8; Gen. 37: 36; 2 Kings 25:8). Titles that refer to books, or specific literary genres, or that serve as rubrics or headings of collections, almost always have the definite article, unless, of course, they contain proper names that make them definite (Ps. 120:1; Cant. 1:1;1Kings 14:19; Prov. 25:1). The title in Prov. 24:23 is unusual and according to the Masoretic text can be translated with or without the article, either "These also are (sayings) of *the* wise men" or simply "of wise men." The Greek translators thought that it referred to a specific group and translated it with the definite article. One parallel in the Old Testament to this particular grammatical construction, found in Deut. 33:7, a heading or introduction to the blessing of Judah, is also definite, employing a proper name. Therefore, it would appear that the evidence favors the translation of Prov. 24:23 as definite, referring to a specific group of writers or collectors of tradition.

Nevertheless, the evidence is not conclusive for several reasons. First, since titles and rubrics may often have been late additions, they cannot inform us about the titles of poetic collections in the earlier period. Second, titles may be ambiguous, as a comparison of Prov. 30:1 and 31:1 show. Third, with respect to Prov. 22:17, since the title is conjectural, it is even more difficult. The fact that the phrase used as the original title could be placed in quite a specific context, indicates that it may have referred to a definite tradition of sayings, deemed to have been gleaned from Israelite teachers who are designated "the wise." It is also possible that the title, if late, did have the definite article in it, but that it was omitted when the title was placed within the collection. Finally, it should also be noted that, with respect to the infinitive construction at the end of Prov. 22:17, it is possible for the pronominal suffix of the first person to be attached directly, contrary to the view of Herzog (E. Kautzsch and A. E. Cowley, eds., *Genesius' Hebrew Grammar as Edited and Enlarged by the Late E. Kautzsch,* pp. 353-54).

28. Prov. 1:8; 2:1; 3:1; 4:1-2, 4-5, 20; 5:1, 7; 7:1-3, 24; 8:32. Dahood's proposal, to consider *ḥakāmi-m* to be in the genitive case and *leda'ṯ* to be third person singular, as in Phoenician, really represents the interpretation of the Hebrew language on the basis of Phoenician grammar, a procedure that sets aside Hebrew usage and tradition ("The Phoenician Contribution," p. 132).

29. This pair is found in parallelism in Job 36:11; Pss. 135:3; 147:1; as verbs in Gen. 49:15; Prov. 24:25. In this wisdom book *n'm* appears three times (Prov. 22:18; 23:8; 24:4).

30. Where a material object occurs the preposition *b* is used with *šph* (Isa. 37:29; 2 Kings 19:28).

31. Judges 4:21, 22; Ezra 9:8; Isa. 22:23. As for the verb *yknw* (*kwn,* "be firm," Prov. 22:18), Aquila, Symmachus, and Theodotion have preserved the meaning "be ready" in their rendering of it as ἑτοιμασθήσονται as against the Septuagint's translation "cheer" or "gladden" (εὐφραίνω) (Fridericus Field, *Origenis Hexaplorum quae Supersunt,* 2:356).

32. The former is preserved by Aquila and Symmachus, and the latter is found in important manuscripts of the Septuagint, though some render the phrase τὰς ὁδοὺς αὐτοῦ (Field, *ibid*).

33. *Ecce* (Vulgate), καί (LXX). The agreement of these versions with the prepositional phrases at the end of the verse indicates a fairly stable textual tradition here.

34. The translation "to report back to those who sent him" (Hebrew "you") fits both passages.

35. *Recherches sur les sources égyptiennes,* pp. 18-25.

36. James M. McGlinchey, "The Teaching of Amen-em-ope and the Book of Proverbs," p. 108.

37. In my translation of these phrases I have sought a correspondence of meaning that renders the original rather literally.

38. For references see Erman and Grapow, *Wörterbuch: Belegstellen,* 2 (pt. 1): 299-300 (citations: 290:12-22); (pt.) 2:504-5 (citations: 348:6-14). Irene Grumach proposes *nš* (verdrängen; *Untersuchungen zur Lebenslehre des Amenope,* p. 31).

39. Hugo Gressmann, "Die neugefundene Lehre des Amen-em-ope und die vorexilische Spruchdichtung Israels," ZAW 42 (1924): 295; A. F. Rainey, "The Soldier-Scribe in 'Papyrus Anastasi I,'" JNES 26 (1967): 58-59; William A. Ward, "Comparative Studies in Egyptian and Ugaritic," JNES 20 (1961): 39.

40. The description of the *Maher* in Papyrus Anastasi I as the possessor of horses, chariot, and attendant fits that of the *snny,* the chariot-warrior of Papyrus Anastasi III. The description of the lot of the *Maher* is similar to that of the soldier whose attendant has run away and whose clothes have been stolen (Anastasi III 6, 1-2). Although the two professions, scribe and *Maher,* appear at times to be treated as one and the same, the descriptions of the unfortunate condition of the soldier following the use of this title corroborate the conclusions of Rainey ("The Soldier Scribe," pp. 58-59; A. H. Gardiner, *Egyptian Hieratic Texts, Transcribed, Translated, and Annotated,* ser. 1, pt. 1, p. 60 (Text 18:4); Caminos, *Late-Egyptian Miscellanies,* pp. 91-96, 396-402; Max Burchardt, *Die altkanaanäischen Fremdworte und Eigennamen in Aegyptischen,* pt. 2, p. 26 (no. 486).

41. A variety of expressions are used of the scribe in Egyptian, Aramaic, and Hebrew, respectively: *ṭpr yd'* (Anastasi I 17, 7-8); ₃š.. .š₃ (Amen. 27:16); [s]pr' *ḥkym',* *y't* (Ahiqar 1:12), *spr ḥkym* (3:35); *yw'ṣ,* *'yš-mbyn, swpr* (1 Chron. 27-32), *swpr mhyr* (Ps. 45:1). The last example is remarkably similar to Egyptian metaphors in which some part of the body is likened to an object related to the work of a scribe: "My tongue is like the pen of a ready scribe" (Ps. 45:1), "As for the beak of Ibis, it is the finger of the scribe" (Amen. 17:7), "Your tongue is the weight of the balance" (The Complaints of the Peasant, B 1, 166), "The scales of men is their tongue" (B 2, 92), "You pen, papyrus, and palette of Thoth. . ." (B 1, 305).

42. Ptahhotep 120 refers to "one greater than you" *(wr r·k;* Zbyněk Žába, *Les Maximes de Ptahhotep,* p. 25 (1.120). Amenemope mentions a "prince" *(sr;* Lange, *Das Weisheitsbuch,* p. 115). The Greek text of Ecclus. 31:12 has "a great

table" (τραπέζης μεγάλης), but the Hebrew text may be read "the table of the great 'man' " (*'yš;* Israel Levi, ed., *The Hebrew Text of the Book of Ecclesiasticus,* p. 31).

43. Žába, *Les Maximes de Ptahhotep,* p. 26 (1. 123). L2, a manuscript of the Eighteenth Dynasty, reads *dgg,* possibly emphasizing the adverbial element at the end of the assertion: "It is at that which is before you that you ought to look."

44. Amen. 23:17; Lange, *Das Weisheitsbuch,* p. 115.

45. Prov. 23:1. The translation is my own. Even if according to Job 6:30 the verb were interpreted to mean "taste," the meaning would not be greatly divergent from the tradition, as Ecclus. 31:16 shows.

46. Ecclus. 31:16.

47. Kagemni 9-10.

48. Ruffle suggests the translation "pretend to chew," according to d'Orbiney 4:8 ("The Teaching of Amenemope," pp. 130, 218).

49. Amen. 9:19; Lange, *Das Weisheitsbuch,* p. 55.

50. Prov. 23:5. (The translation is my own.)

51. Lange, *Das Weisheitsbuch,* pp. 71-72.

52. Lor. Dürr, "Hebrew נֶפֶשׁ =akk. *napištu*=Gurgel, Kehle," ZAW 43 (1925): 262-69; Ruffle, "The Teaching of Amenemope," pp. 421-23; Herzog, "Die Sprüche," pp. 149-51. The simple emendation of *š'r* to *'šyr* "rich man," ignores the fact that the passage concerns a miser: (Melville Scott, *Textual Discoveries in Proverbs, Psalms, and Isaiah,* p. 69). The rendering of the Septuagint, "Swallow a hair," is not convincing because it provides no connection with the context.

53. John Gray, *The Legacy of Canaan,* p. 266; Dahood, *Proverbs,* p. 47. Gray's proposal "as one purposes in his mind" is too general.

54. The verb *šḥt* in Prov. 23:8 is also found with reference to water that is polluted (Prov. 25:26). Herzog drew attention to the meaning "spoiled" for the root *š'r* but rejected this interpretation in favor of the rendering "a split in his soul" (!) ("Die Sprüche," p. 150).

Chapter 5

1. In all of its other uses in the Old Testament the adverbial *šlšwm* appears with the root *tmwl.* Therefore, scholars who suggest reading the phrase adverbially assume that *'tmwl* dropped out in the process of transmission (Crawford H. Toy, *A Critical and Exegetical Commentary on the Book of Proverbs,* p. 423; Robert Gordis, *The Biblical Text in the Making,* p. 198, n507). John Ruffle simply regards it as an ellipsis ("The Teaching of Amenemope," pp. 398-400).

2. Ronald H. Williams, "Some Egyptianisms in the Old Testament," in *Studies in Honor of John A. Wilson,* pp. 97-98.

3. *Biblia Sacra juxta Vulgatam Clementinam*, p. 698.

4. This renders '*rk pym* in Prov. 14:29; 15:18; 16:32.

5. Frank Moore Cross, "The Development of Jewish Scripts," in *The Bible and the Ancient Near East*, pp. 168-69.

6. Gordis, *The Biblical Text*, pp. 149 (Zech. 14:6; Ps. 10:10), 150 (Prov. 23:5; Job 10:20; 2 Chron. 24:27), and 152 (1 Chron. 22:7).

7. With a negative connotation it appears in Prov. 12:2 and 24:8 but positively in Prov. 1:4.

8. Fridericus Field, *Origenis Hexaplorum quae Supersunt*, 2:339.

9. Udo Skladny, *Die ältesten Spruchsammlungen in Israel*, p. 61. Prov. 19:1 cannot be precisely located, having developed from 28:6 or independently in its own context.

10. In favor of the association of *twrh* with law-code or the Law is the use of the phrase *šmr twrh* (Prov. 28:4; 29:18), which in its uses elsewhere is associated with a written law (1 Chron. 22:12; Ps. 119: 44, 55, 136; Deut. 17: 19).

11. Glendon E. Bryce, " 'Better'—Proverbs: An Historical and Structural Study," *The Society of Biblical Literature One Hundred Eighth Annual Meeting: Book of Seminar Papers*, 2:351.

12. Robert Gordis, *Koheleth—The Man and His World*, pp. 265, 207.

13. Hermann Gunkel and Joachim Begrich, *Einleitung in die Psalmen*, p. 386; Sigmund Mowinckel, *The Psalms in Israel's Worship*, 2: 112-13; *idem*, "Psalms and Wisdom," in *Wisdom in Israel and in the Ancient Near East*, p. 213.

14. W. G. Lambert, *Babylonian Wisdom Literature*, pp. 121-23; Hellmut Brunner, "Die Weisheitsliteratur," in *Handbuch der Orientalisk*, 1 (pt. 2): 109-10.

15. Gunkel and Begrich, *Einleitung*, pp. 381-97; Mowinckel, *The Psalms*, 2: 104-25.

16. H. O. Lange, *Das Weisheitsbuch des Amenemope*, pp. 42-43. E. A. Wallis Budge, who first drew attention to this connection, related the Egyptian passage to Ps. 1 *(The Teaching of Amen-em-Apt, Son of Kanekht*, p. 107). Hugo Gressman suggested a relation to Jer. 17 ("Die neugefundene Lehre des Amen-em-ope und die vorexilische Spruchdichtung Israels," ZAW 42 (1924): 280).

17. Adolf Erman, *The Ancient Egyptians*, pp. 306, 311.

18. Egyptian singers are found in Palestine in the second millennium B.C. as we know from the story of Wenamon and the Megiddo ivories (John A. Wilson, "Egyptian Historical Texts," ANET, p. 263; *idem*, "Egyptian Myths, Tales, and Mortuary Texts," ANET, p. 28, n39; Jean Leclant, "Les relations entre l'Egypte et la Phénicie du voyage d'Ounamon à l'expédition d'Alexandre," in *The Role of the Phoenicians in the Interaction of the Mediterranean Civilizations*, pp. 11, 23, n16).

19. Lange, *Das Weisheitsbuch*, p. 42.

20. Jer. 17:5-8; Ps. 37:35; Job 8:16-18. Ani 10:13-15 (Aksel Volten, *Studien zum Weisheitsbuch des Anii*, pp. 171-72).

21. The precise meaning of the two words *ḫntï-š* and *mḫrm*, translated respectively as "forest" and "port," are difficult. Adolf Erman first suggested these two meanings (*"Wald," "Hafenplatz"*, "Das Weisheitsbuch des Amen-em-ope," OLZ 27 (1924): 243). Other proposals for *ḫntï-š* include "fore-court" or "abroad" (F. Ll. Griffith, "The Teaching of Amenophis the Son of Kanakht. Papyrus B. M. 10474," JEA 12 (1926): 202; Ruffle, "The Teaching of Amenope," pp. 110, 163; John A. Wilson, "Proverbs and Precepts," ANET, p. 422). *Mḫrm* also means "swamp" (Griffith, "The Teaching of Amenophis," p. 202, n2), even "carpentry shop" has been suggested (W. K. Simpson, "The Instruction of Amenemope," in *The Literature of Ancient Egypt*, p. 246). Irene Grumach translates the first as "orchard" according to the parallelism of 6:2 to 6:8 and the second simply as "water." Discussion, including Drioton's proposals, is found in *Untersuchungen zur Lebenslehre des Amenope*, pp. 42-43.

22. The Egyptian word *3ḫ3ḫ* means "grow green." The Hebrew word *r'n* may mean "luxuriant" as well as "green."

23. Mowinckel, *The Psalms*, 2: 52.

24. Žába, *Les Maximes de Ptahhotep*, p. 15 (1. 8); Ps. 37:25.

25. Most scholars agree that this psalm is to be dated quite late (Moses Buttenweiser, *The Psalms*, pp. 853-58; Artur Weiser, *The Psalms*, pp. 312-23; Mowinckel, "Psalms and Wisdom," pp. 213-17; *idem, The Psalms*, 2: 113; Charles Augustus Briggs and Emilie Grace Briggs, *A Critical and Exegetical Commentary on the Book of Psalms*, 1: 324-25).

26. Gottfried Kuhn, *Beiträge zur Erklärung des Salomonischen Spruchbuches*, p. 53. (The following translations are my own.)

27. James M. McGlinchey, "The Teaching of Amen-em-ope and the Book of Proverbs," p. 106.

28. This is particularly true of the third section of the book, which begins with the statement about the wicked (Prov. 24:1) as does Ps. 37.

29. H. H. Rowley, *The Relevance of Apocalyptic*, pp. 141-42; Stanley Brice Frost, *Old Testament Apocalyptic*, pp. 48-56; D. S. Russell, *The Method and Message of Jewish Apocalyptic 200* BC—AD *100*, p. 269.

30. As Ruffle persuasively shows, in many cases similarities between Egyptian writings and the Old Testament are often more apparent than real, reducing themselves simply to similar subject matter ("The Teaching of Amenemope," pp. 377-87, 427-31, 448-53).

31. John A. Wilson, "Proverbs and Precepts," ANET, p. 422, n9. For a history of the interpretation of this verse see Siegfried Morenz, "Feurige Kohlen auf dem Haupt," TLZ 78 (1953): 187-92.

32. *Ibid.*, pp. 189-90. Morenz interprets the verse in the light of an alleged

Egyptian rite of atonement in which the penitent carries a brazier of coals on his head.

33. Léonard Ramoroson, " 'Charbons ardents': 'sur la tête' ou 'pour le feu'?" Bib 51 (1970): 234. I have provided a translation of his French version, omitting the metric accents in the transliteration.

34. Ruffle provides lists of alleged parallels between Amenemope and other Egyptian wisdom literature, and Mesopotamian wisdom as well as the Old Testament. In most cases the resemblances are merely thematic ("The Teaching of Amenemope," pp. 250ff.).

Chapter 6

1. I am using the word "book" in the sense of our English word "composition," as in the case of the book of "The Sayings of the Wise," implying something more than an uncoordinated collection of sayings but something less than is meant by our word "discourse."

2. Although no corpus of Canaanite wisdom literature is extant, an extract of the wisdom book discovered at Ugarit, "The Wisdom of Shube'awilum," appearing at Boghazköy, is evidence of the international character of wisdom and also the popularity of such small collections (J. Nougayrol, *et al.*, eds., *Ugaritica V*, pp. 276-77).

3. I am indebted to Professor Edward Wente of the Oriental Institute of the University of Chicago for a copy of the text, which is entitled "The Instruction of [Ptaḥ-em-Djeḥuty?] adapted by Seḥetepibrēʿ," transcribed from the Cairo Stela, Papyrus Rifeh, and other fragmentary manuscripts by K. A. Kitchen of the University of Liverpool. Translations and interpretations of the text have been done by C. Kuentz ("Deux versions d'un panégyrique royal," in *Studies Presented to F. Ll. Griffith*, pp. 97-110), John A. Wilson ("Egyptian Observations," ANET, p. 431), and G. Posener (*Littérature et politique dans l'Egypte de la XIIᵉ dynastie*, pp. 119-23).

4. Since the complete text of Sehetepibre has not yet been published, we have the actual text for the rubric in the first part only (Cairo Stela, 1. 35); Kuentz, "Deux versions," pp. 99-100). The clause that forms the rubric at the conclusion of the second part is cited by Posener (*Littérature et politique*, p. 120 [The Louvre Fragment, E4864]).

5. Posener, *Littérature et politique*, pp. 119-23; Kuentz, "Deux Versions," p. 109; Ronald J. Williams, "Literature as a Medium of Political Propaganda in Ancient Egypt," in *The Seed of Wisdom*, pp. 25-27.

6. For the text of this work see G. Posener, *Catalogue des ostraca hiératiques littéraires de Deir el Medineh*, 2, Plates 1-21. Translation and interpretation are given by W. C. Hayes, "A Much-Copied Letter of the Early Middle Kingdom," JNES 7 (1948): 1-10; Posener, *Littérature et politique*, pp. 4-7, 18-19.

7. To my knowledge Prov. 25 has never been treated as a wisdom book by any interpreter, even though individual parts of it have been considered to be related thematically. For a more detailed treatment of this wisdom book the reader is referred to the original study in the *Journal of Biblical Literature* 91, no. 2 (June 1972): 145-57. For recent studies of this chapter see also William McKane, *Proverbs*, pp. 577-93; Gerhard von Rad, *Wisdom in Israel*, p. 17, n6.

8. Prov. 25:16 and 24:13, 25:13 and 22:21, 25:6 and 22:29.

9. Crawford H. Toy, *A Critical and Exegetical Commentary on the Book of Proverbs*, pp. 457-71; B. Gemser, *Sprüche Salomos*, pp. 70-72; R. B. Y. Scott, *Proverbs, Ecclesiastes*, pp. 153-56.

10. This is particularly true of the second clause, which is variously translated as follows: "So the one who is a searcher of honor is overcome by glory" (*Sic qui scrutator est majestatis opprimetur a gloria*, Vulg.); "So *for men* to search out their own glory *is not* glory" (KJV); "But it is necessary to honor esteemed words" (τιμᾶν δὲ χρὴ λόγους ἐνδόξους. LXX); "So be sparing of complimentary words" (RSV).

11. LXX: ἐσθίειν μέλι πολὺ οὐ καλόν; Vulg.: *Sicut qui mel multum comedit, non est ei bonum.*

12. The correct form of the adverb is the infinitive absolute *hrbh*, meaning "greatly, exceedingly" (Francis Brown, S. R. Driver, and Charles A. Briggs, *A Hebrew and English Lexicon of the Old Testament*, p. 915).

13. In the verse in Job the parallelism is between "ear" and "palate," "examine" and "eat," and "words" and "food." Thus, as in Prov. 25:27, the act of eating is compared to mental activity or the act of judgment.

14. "I will not conceal anything from you. I have said, 'It is good to guard the secret of a king, but gloriously to reveal the works of God'." (RSV; Tobit 12:11, also v. 7). The Greek text of the manuscripts Vaticanus and Alexandrinus reads ἐνδόξως in v. 7. The Vulgate and some Greek manuscripts have the reading suggested in the text.

15. Cairo Stela, 1. 12; Kuentz, "Deux Versions," in the text. p. 98.

16. Gerhard von Rad, *Old Testament Theology*, 1: 430-31; *idem, Wisdom in Israel*, p. 17, n7. Paul Humbert connects the origins of Israelite wisdom with the intense development of the civil service in Israel at the time of King Solomon (*Recherches sur les sources égyptiennes de la littérature sapientäle d'Israël*, pp. 180-83. What ramifications this has for the history of Israel and the origin of wisdom may be surmised from a study of Posener's remarks about the need in Egypt during the Twelfth Dynasty to recruit and educate scribes in the service of the ruling house (*Littérature et politique*, pp. 7-20).

17. Prov. 16:10, 12, 13, 14, 15; 17:7; 19:10, 12; 20:2, 8, 26, 28; 21:1; 22:11, 29; 23:1; 24:21; 25:1, 2, 3, 5, 6, 7, 15. Prov. 25:1 is not properly a proverb, and 25:6-7 may be considered a single saying. In this case the number would be reduced to twenty-two sayings.

18. Fourteen verses with sayings concerning the king are found in the collection from 15:1-22:16. The book of "The Sayings of the Wise" (22:17-24:22) contains seventy verses; twenty-six form the wisdom book concerning the king and courtier (25:2-27). If we reduce the middle collection to the thirty sayings only, the total is somewhat less than one hundred. *These specific materials are not, of course, based simply upon the Egyptian analogy but grow out of careful scrutiny of Israelite sources* (Roland E. Murphy, "Assumptions and Problems in Old Testament Wisdom Research," CBQ 29 [1967]:412).

19. In Canaanite-Hebrew literature the words "wise" and "aged" are used in parallelism (Cyrus H. Gordon, *Ugaritic Textbook: Texts,* p. 171 (51 V 65-66); Ezek. 27:8-9 *(zqn);* Job 26:3 *(rb);* associated, respectively, in Ps. 105:22; Eccles. 4:13; Job 32:7, 9). When the word "aged" is used of a collective body, it designates the elders of Israel or a similar social group (1 Sam 8:4; Prov. 31:23). Although the elders are not specifically mentioned in either of the two collections studied, the phrase "the great men," used in Prov. 25:6, may include this group, since the word "great" may refer to age, wealth, or rank (Gen. 27:1; 2 Sam. 19:32; 2 Kings 10:6). The terms "elders" and "fathers" are also found in parallelism (Prov. 17:6). The elders gave counsel and were involved in political affairs (1 Kings 12). Some lived at the court and as friends of the king may have been invited to reside there (Ps. 105:22; 2 Sam. 19:33). Together with the young men, they formed councils that advised the king.

The special endowment of elders, advisors, and skilled personnel was wisdom and counsel. They may be correlative terms in some contexts. They are used together in synonymous parallelism (Jer. 49:7). Whereas Jeremiah associates counsel with the wise man (18:18), Ezekiel attributes it to the elders (7:26). Wisdom and counsel are also frequently associated and together with the term "understanding" *(tbwnh)* may form a triad or be used alternatively with a cluster of related ideas (Prov. 21:30; 19:20; Isa. 11:2). Like craftsmen, counselors are wise (Isa. 19:11). Ahitophel was such a man, and although wisdom is not specifically mentioned in relation to him, there is no doubt that he was regarded as a wise man. Thus King David prayed that the counsel of Ahitophel would be "made foolish" *(skl),* a word that is used in antithetical parallelism to "wise" (2 Sam. 15:31; Eccles. 2:13; 10:2; Isa. 44:25; R. N. Whybray, *The Intellectual Tradition of the Old Testament,* pp. 17, 148).

Moreover, in Israel the association of wise men, counselors, and scribes with the ruling groups suggests the outlines of a professional class. The prophets distinguish the wise men from others and associate them with the princes. The general distinction, wise man or elder, prophet, and priest, made in Jer. 18:18 and Ezek. 7:26, is usually followed in other prophetic contexts. This does not mean that the term "wise" cannot be applied to special religious personnel, as Isa. 3:3 may suggest, or be extended in parallelism to diviners, as Isa. 44:25 may be interpreted. On the other hand, usage elsewhere, in the light of which these passages may be interpreted, suggests a special group. In

Jer. 8:8-10 the wise men are separated from the priest and prophet. They are also distinguished from the warriors (Jer. 51:57; Isa. 3:3). Used of Israel and Babylon, the associated clusters are princes+wise men (Jer. 50:35; 51:57), scribes+wise men (Jer. 8:8-9), man of rank+counselor+wise man (?) (Isa. 3:3), contrasting with the association of prophet and priest. Although the distinction cannot be made on secular versus religious categories, the fact that the Old Testament uses the phrase "the wise men" of a professional class when referring to foreign nations is an indication of the categories that had been formulated in Hebrew thought in reference to social groups (R. N. Whybray, *The Intellectual Tradition*, pp. 15-16).

When used to designate or characterize persons in ancient Near Eastern literature, the terms "wise" or "skilled" may refer to specific social groups, including great men of the past who have become renowned as sages. At Ugarit the Akkadian term "wise" *(mudu)* was used to refer to certain persons who received a special appointment from the king (John Gray, *The Legacy of Canaan*, p. 232; Wolfram von Soden, *Akkadisches Handwörterbuch unter Benutzung des lexikalischen Nachlasses von BRUNO MEISSNER (1868-1947)*, 2:666). In certain contexts, then, this general term can have in it overtones of a social class. In Egypt, on the other hand, this attribute *(rḫ-yḫt)* is used to refer to the famous sages of the past, who are especially singled out as "those wise scribes," specifically Djedefhor, Imhotep, Neferti, Cheti, Ptah-em-Djehuti, Cha-cheper-Re-soneb, Ptahhotep, and Kaïrsu. Two general terms may be used to describe their writings, "instruction" *(sb3y·t)* and "prophecy" *(srw·t)*, although other designations may also apply. Of course, several literary genres are covered by these two terms. Yet, as Hellmut Brunner has suggested, they all have one thing in common, the use of one particular stylistic device. In all of these writings statements are articulated in the form of the saying or maxim ("Der zum Spruch 'geknotete' Satz"; "Die 'Weisen', ihre 'Lehren' und 'Prophezeiungen' in altägyptischer Sicht," ZÄS 93 [1966]:35). In this sense, then, we can refer to the wise men and the wisdom of Egypt.

Of course, wisdom or skill, which were prerequisites for association with great men or courtiers, could be gained through education. However, this enterprise was often controlled by or even confined to the upper classes. A study of five hundred school graduates in ancient Sumeria has revealed that all of these scribes were members of wealthy and ruling families (Samuel Noah Kramer, *The Sumerians,* p. 231). As for the Mesopotamian scribes, Benno Landersberger describes the class as a whole as a "poor aristocracy," attaining the highest administrative posts only during the Ur III period (*City Invincible*, p. 99). Later, however, during the Middle Assyrian and Neo-Assyrian period, city scribes are mentioned among the chief administrative officials (A. Leo Oppenheim, *Ancient Mesopotamia: Portrait of a Dead Civilization* [Chicago: University of Chicago Press, 1964], pp. 242-343). It was the scribe who played the central role in the preservation and revitalization of

Mesopotamian culture (*idem, Letters from Mesopotamia*, p. 8). In Egypt, during the earliest and latest period of its history, education was in the hands of royal and priestly families. Although a process of democratization was at work during the New Kingdom period, teachers and wise men often belonging to the middle classes, the goal of education was the production of administrators and scribes who would be loyal to the royal house. This is reflected in the conclusion of Amenemope, where the goal of the student and the highest attainment of an alumnus is asserted, becoming a courtier (27:16-17; Hellmut Brunner, *Altägyptische Erziehung*, pp. 23, 36, 42). From another point of view classic expression is given to this ideal in a maxim from the Instruction for Merikare: "A wise man is a storehouse for nobles" (P 33; R. J. Williams, "Literature as a Medium of Political Propaganda in Ancient Egypt," in *The Seed of Wisdom*, p. 16).

With reference to the post-exilic period in Palestine, it is worthy of observation that in Eccles. 8:1 "the wise man" is described in terms of his acquisition of special knowledge as one who knows the "interpretation of a thing" (*pšr dbr*), a phrase that in this context is more descriptive of Egyptian prophecy as delineated by Hellmut Brunner ("Die 'Weisen', ihre 'Lehren' und 'Prophezeihungen,'" pp. 33-35) than the kind of interpretation done by members of the Qumran Community. Moreover, such a man is found in the service of a king (vv. 2-5), a reference appertaining to foreign monarchs (Robert Gordis, *Koheleth—The Man and His World*, pp. 285-86; Elke Blumenthal and Siegfried Morenz, "Spuren ägyptischer Königsideologie in einem Hymnus auf den Makkabäerfürsten Simon," ZÄS 93 [1966]: 21-29). Given the difficulty that we have in identifying "the wise men" as a social class, what can be said is that royal and aristocratic associations are a constant factor, although, no doubt, this is not the only background out of which the wisdom literature arose.

20. Prov. 22:18; 23:3, 30; 24:13; 25:12, 11, respectively. Robert Gordis asserts, "It has not been hitherto observed how commonly precious stones are used as an object of comparison and value in Proverbs" ("The Social Background of Wisdom Literature," HUCA 18 (1943-44):92).

R. N. Whybray has isolated a small group of terms that he associates with an intellectual elite in Israel, represented by a group of literate and educated persons in Israel who "concerned themselves more than the majority of their contemporaries in an intellectual way with the problems of human life" (*The Intellectual Tradition in the Old Testament*, p. 70). Among the terms that belong to this tradition and are "apparently" exclusive to it are "understanding" (*bynh*), "stupid" (*b'r, ksyl*), "scoffer" (*lṣ*), "understanding" (*lqḥ*), "intelligent" (*nbwn*), "senseless" (*skl*), "prudent" (*'rwm*), and "wisdom" (*twšyh*). Together with the word for "wise" (*ḥkm*) and another cluster of terms appearing primarily in Proverbs, Job and/or Ecclesiastes (*'wyl, 'wlt, ḥnp, ḥqr, 'qš, 'rmh, pty, śkl, tbwnh,* and *twkḥt),* these expressions may be used to discover this intellectual tradition that appears elsewhere in the Old Testament (pp. 134-54). For another list of words associated with wisdom literature but with a more general semantic range, see R. B. Y. Scott, *The Way of Wisdom in the Old Testament,* pp. 121-22.

Unfortunately, the stringent methodology employed in Whybray's useful study limits its scope, particularly with respect to the literary contexts in which the social background of the wise men is reflected. Thus, the conclusion reached in the first part of the study, that the phrase "the wise men" *(hḥkmym)* may refer to a professional class when used of foreign social groups but does not include such a reference when used of Israelite society, is tenuous *(The Intellectual Tradition,* pp. 15-16, 31). To determine the meaning of the specific usage "the wise," it is necessary to study the semantic range of the term "wise" itself, its association with other words in both the singular and plural, and its parallels in Canaanite-Hebrew poetry, which may well reflect earlier traditions. Of course, this includes the attempt to reconstruct the social contexts that form the background for understanding the word. For example, in the two collections that have been studied in Proverbs, there is no way of knowing what general terms such as "wisdom," "counsel," "knowledge," and "righteous" mean until some hint of the social setting is available. Moreover, since wisdom literature was an international genre, it must be understood in its ancient Near Eastern context, not isolated or set over and against it. For another study of the criteria by which the influence of wisdom literature can be determined in other passages in the Old Testament, see J. L. Crenshaw, "Method in Determining Wisdom Influence upon 'Historical' Literature," JBL 88 (1969): 129-42.

21. This is an important consideration that suggests that wisdom does have its own independent setting and cannot be explained merely as an outgrowth of law of prophecy (G. Ernest Wright, *The Old Testament against Its Environment,* p. 44, n2; H. Wheeler Robinson, *Inspiration and Revelation in the Old Testament,* pp. 238, 241). Moreover, as against the strong stress upon law and prophecy found in the theological interpretation of men such as Wright and Robinson, wisdom itself involved a total integration of life in which morality and piety were extended to the realms of etiquette and rhetoric. The wise men are judged not only upon the basis of a breach of law but also as to whether their conduct is appropriate according to the correct canons of etiquette. For an aspiring courtier a breach of etiquette could be as serious as a breach of law!

22. W. Baumgartner, *Israelitische und altorientalische Weisheit,* p. 6; O. S. Rankin, *Israel's Wisdom Literature,* pp. 4-9; J. Fichtner, *Die altorientalische Weisheit in ihrer israelitisch-jüdischen Ausprägung,* p. 24.

23. H. H. Schmid, *Wesen und Geschichte der Weisheit,* p. 145; von Rad, *Old Testament Theology,* 1: 437, n40. For a summary of von Rad's position on the

subject of the relation of the secular and the profane in wisdom, see my comments in a review of *Wisdom in Israel* by Gerhard von Rad, *Theology To-day* 30 (1974): 436-42.

24. Similar advice is given in the Babylonian "Counsels of Wisdom." The passage dealing with the subject of disputes in law courts ends with the admonition: "Do not return evil to the man who disputes with you; requite with kindness your evil-doer." The book is addressed to a "son," in this case a young man aspiring to the service of a prince (W. G. Lambert, *Babylonian Wisdom Literature*, pp. 101 (ll. 41-46), 103 (l. 81).

25. von Rad, *Wisdom in Israel*, pp. 58-60.

26. von Rad, *Theology of the Old Testament*, 1: 420-22; *idem*, "Die ältere Weisheit Israels," KeDo 2 (1956): 55-57.

27. Ptahhotep 115-16 (Zbyněk Žába, *Les Maximes de Ptahhotep*, pp. 25, 121).

28. H. O. Lange, *Das Weisheitsbuch des Amenemope*, pp. 97-98; John A. Wilson, "Proverbs and Precepts," ANET, p. 423; Kurt Sethe, " 'Der Mensch denkt, der Gott lenkt' bei den alten Agyptern," in *Nachrichten von der Gesellschaft der Wissenschaften zu Göttingen aus dem Jahre 1925*, pp. 141-46.

29. Aksel Volten, *Studien zum Weisheitsbuch des Ani*, pp. 117-18.

30. This is a peculiar case where, with the help of the later Hebrew proverb contained in Prov. 16:1, we are better able to interpret the Egyptian original. My own proposal, to understand the Egyptian word $s(w)$ not as a pronoun but as the word for "man" (sing. s) and to restore a w', "another" (sw from $s. . .w'$) at the beginning of the second part, is not only simpler than Volten's reconstruction but also has the support of the parallel proverb of the same type in Amen. 19:16-17 (Volten, *Studien zum Weisheitsbuch*, pp. 124-25). Irene Grumach's translation of this saying supports my own conjecture (*Untersuchungen zur Lebenslehre des Amenope*, p. 126).

31. Merikare 123-24 (Aksel Volten, *Zwei altägyptische politische Schriften*, p. 66; John A. Wilson, "Proverbs and Precepts," ANET, p. 417.

32. Merikare 136-37; Alan H. Gardiner, "New Literary works from Ancient Egypt," JEA 1 (1914): 34-35.

33. von Rad, *Theology of the Old Testament*, 1: 453-59; *idem, Wisdom in Israel*, pp. 233-35; Robert Gordis, *Koheleth—The Man and His World*, p. 123. In view of this cluster of sayings that negate man's capacity to know the plan of God, found both in Egyptian and Israelite wisdom, the older view that Job and Ecclesiastes represent a "revolt" of the later writers against the excessive eudaemonism of the earlier wisdom literature must now be greatly modified. Wisdom literature must be seen as possessing this note of agnosticism in latent form from the very beginning, so that Job and Ecclesiastes are not as sharply antithetical to the earlier themes as Wright and Scott suggest (G. Ernest Wright and Reginald H. Fuller, *The Book of the Acts of God*, pp. 181-90; Scott, *The Way of Wisdom*, p. 140.

34. For a fuller discussion of this subject with bibliographical references see chapter 8.

Chapter 7

1. 5:9-14 (MT).

2. Hugo Gressmann, "Die neugefundene Lehre des Amen-em-ope und die vorexilische Spruchdichtung Israels," ZAW 42 (1924): 282-84, 293-94; Paul Humbert, *Recherches sur les sources égyptiennes de la littérature sapientiale d'Israël,* pp. 181-83; W. O. E. Oesterley, *The Book of Proverbs with Introduction and Notes,* p. xxii; Hilaire Duesberg, *Les Scribes inspirés,* 1: 141-88; W. Baumgartner, "The Wisdom Literature," in *The Old Testament and Modern Study,* p. 213; Albrecht Alt, "Die Weisheit Salomos," TLZ 76 (1951): 144; James A. Montgomery, *A Critical and Exegetical Commentary on the Books of Kings,* p. 139; O. S. Rankin, *Israel's Wisdom Literature,* pp. 6, 66; Martin Noth, "Die Bewährung von Salomos 'Göttlicher Weisheit'," in *Wisdom in Israel and in the Ancient Near East,* pp. 235-37; Norman W. Porteous, "Royal Wisdom," in *Wisdom in Israel and in the Ancient Near East,* pp. 249-50; Gerhard von Rad, *Old Testament Theology,* 1: 423-30; John Bright, *A History of Israel,* pp. 198-99; O. Eissfeldt, *The Hebrew Kingdom,* p. 66; *idem, The Old Testament,* pp. 85, 476; Ernst Sellin and Georg Fohrer, *Introduction to the Old Testament,* pp. 308-9; J. Liver, "The Book of the Acts of Solomon," Bib 48 (1967): 83-86; Bazalel Porten, "The Structure and Theme of the Solomon Narrative (1 Kings 3-11)," HUCA 38 (1967): 113-17; R. B. Y. Scott, *Proverbs, Ecclesiastes,* p. xxxiii; Sigmund Nowinckel, "Israelite Historiography," ASTI 2 (1963): 2, 7-8.

3. Alt, "Die Weisheit Salomos," p. 144.

4. 5:12-13 (MT).

5. R. B. Y. Scott, "Solomon and the Beginnings of Wisdom," in *Wisdom in Israel and in the Ancient Near East,* pp. 266-72.

6. Georges Posener, *Littérature et politique dans l'Egypte de la XIIᵉ dynastie, passim;* Eberhard Otto, "Weltanschauliche und politische Tendenzschriften," *Handbuch der Orientalistik,* 1 (pt. 2):111-19; R. J. Williams, "Literature as a Medium of Political Propaganda in Ancient Egypt," in *The Seed of Wisdom,* pp. 14-30.

7. Charles Kuentz, "Deux versions d'un panégyrique royal," in *Studies Presented to F. Ll. Griffith,* pp. 97-110; A. de Buck, "The Instruction of Amenemmes," in *Mélanges Maspero,* 1:847-52. Kuentz refers to propaganda that serves the interests of the throne (p. 109); de Buck describes the instruction of King Amenemmes as "a literary composition making propaganda for Sesostris and his cause" (p. 851).

8. For dates and a sketch of the period see William C. Hayes, *The Middle Kingdom in Egypt,* pp. 3-70, also R. O. Faulkner, *Egypt,* pp. 3-37.

9. John A. Wilson, "Egyptian Myths, Tales, and Mortuary Texts"; "Proverbs and Precepts"; "Egyptian Observations," ANET, pp. 18-23, 414-19, 431; Williams, "Literature as a Medium," *passim.*

10. Posener, *Littérature et politique,* pp. 121-22.

11. Aylward M. Blackman, *Middle-Egyptian Stories,* p. 18 (B47-49).

12. *Ibid.*, p. 21 (B 70).

13. Posener, *Littérature et politique*, p. 70.

14. Fr. Ll. Griffith, "The MILLINGEN Papyrus (teaching of Amenemhat)," ZÄS 34 (1896): 40 (1:6), 46 (2:12-3:1).

15. For a translation of the passages cited see John A. Wilson, "Proverbs and Precepts," ANET, pp. 418-19.

16. Williams, "Literature as a Medium," p. 16.

17. Posener, *Littérature et politique*, p. 64.

18. Eissfeldt, *The Old Testament*, p. 288; Sellin and Fohrer, *Introduction*, p. 231; R. K. Harrison, *Introduction to the Old Testament with a Comprehensive Review of Old Testament Studies an a Special Supplement on the Apocrypha*, p. 726; Mowinckel, "Israelite Historiography," pp. 7-8; Norman H. Snaith, "The First and Second Books of Kings," in *The Interpreter's Bible*, 3: 4; John Gray, *I and II Kings*, pp. 23-25; Liver, "The Book of the Acts," pp. 76-81, 85-86, 100; Porten, "The Structure and Theme," p. 113. Martin Noth has also suggested that the chronicle included literature of a wisdom type ("Die Bewährung," p. 226).

19. Blackman, *Middle-Egyptian Stories*, pp. 19-22 (B 50-75); Adolf Erman, *The Ancient Egyptians*, pp. 18-19.

20. G. Ernest Wright, *Biblical Archaeology*, pp. 130-42; Porten, "Structure and Theme," pp. 98, 100, 103, 110.

21. Scott, "Solomon and the Beginnings," p. 271; Martin Noth, *Überlieferungsgeschichtliche Studien*, p. 68.

22. Noth, "Die Bewährung," p. 228.

23. Siegfried Hermann, "Die Königsnovelle in Ägypten und in Israel," *Wissenschaftliche Zeitschrift der Karl-Marx-Universität*, 3: 51-62; Alfred Hermann, "Die ägyptische Königsnovelle," LÄS 10 (1938): 5-61.

24. Sellin and Fohrer, *Introduction*, p. 231; Hermann, "Die Königsnovelle," p. 54.

25. G. W. Ahlström, "Solomon, The Chosen One," HR 8 (1968): 100-103.

26. Noth, "Die Bewährung," pp. 226-27; Liver, "The Book of the Acts," pp. 84-85.

27. For a discussion of promise and fulfillment in the Deuteronomic history see Gerhard von Rad, *The Problem of the Hexateuch and Other Essays*, pp. 205-21.

28. Scott, "Solomon and the Beginnings," p. 268.

29. Noth, *Überlieferungsgeschichtliche Studien*, pp. 67-68, 71. "Die Bewährung," p. 227.

30. Exchanges of such women between Egypt and other countries were not so unusual as A. Malamat maintains when he asserts that "there is no other attested instance apart from that of Solomon, of a *daughter* of Pharaoh being given in marriage to a foreign ruler" ("Aspects of the Foreign Policies of David and Solomon," JNES 22 [1963]: 10). For evidence to the contrary see Claude F.-A. Schaeffer, ed., *Ugaritica III*, pp. 179-220 and Margaret S. Crower, *Ugarit*, p. 10.

31. Montgomery, *A Critical and Exegetical Commentary,* pp. 108-9.

32. North, "Die Bewährung," p. 279.

33. Horst Seebass suggests that the real reason for the rejection of Solomon by Ahijah the prophet was the building of the temple by Solomon, a repudiation of the religious traditions associated with his father, David, that Yahweh would dwell among the people (1 Kings 6:13; "Die Verwerfung Jerobeams I. und Salomos durch die Prophetie des Ahia von Silo," WO 4 [1967-68]: 173-79).

34. Horst Seebass, "Zur Königserhebung Jerobeams I," VT 17 (1967): 330, 332.

35. Martin Noth, *The History of Israel,* p. 233.

36. Shoshana R. Bin-Nun, "Formulas from the Royal Records of Israel and of Judah," VT 18 (1968): 422.

37. Bright, *A History of Israel,* p. 266; Noth, *The History of Israel,* pp. 265-69.

38. Noth makes reference to Josiah's restoration of the former dual monarchy in Judah and in Israel (*The History of Israel,* p. 27), and Bright speaks of the annexation of Israel to Judah (*A History of Israel,* p. 298).

Chapter 8

1. The use of terms such as "profane," "worldly," or "intellectual" continues to appear in recent discussions of wisdom literature (Hans Heinrich Schmid, *Wesen und Geschichte der Weisheit,* p. 145). R. B. Y. Scott suggests that among the wise men there were two groups, the moralists, who believed in a divinely established order, and the secularists, who "did not have (or at least did not show) any theological interest" (*The Way of Wisdom in the Old Testament,* p. 115). As statesmen, the wise men are characterized as those who relied on "hard-headed pragmatic procedures," not reposing the security of the state in "a theological assumption or article of faith" as the prophets apparently did (William McKane, *Prophets and Wise Men,* p. 127). According to Gerhard von Rad, the wise men were not priests and in fact showed "a decidedly enlightened intellectualism" in their attitude toward the cult. For them "the idea that God manifested himself in his world by means of miracles or other occasional incursions had lapsed" (*Wisdom in Israel,* pp. 188, 299, respectively). R. N. Whybray suggests that in Israel "there existed an educated class, albeit a small one, of well-to-do citizens who were accustomed to read for edification and for pleasure," and that from them men of literary ability produced the distinctive writings known as wisdom literature. They not only participated in the traditions of Israel concerned with daily and religious life, but also involved themselves in an "intellectual" way with the problems of life confronting ordinary citizens, family, community, justice, and destiny, but *not* the political problems of the nation (*The Intellectual Tradition in the Old Testament,* p. 69).

Reference to the "theologizing of wisdom," a phrase that Schmid uses as a rubric (*Wesen und Geschichte,* pp. 144-55), may merely reveal the concessions made by scholars to this particular perspective, although it has a rather wide usage, referring to various developments in the tradition (Roland E. Murphy, "Introduction to Wisdom Literature," *The Jerome Biblical Commentary,* 1:494).

2. G. Ernest Wright, *The Old Testament against its Environment,* p. 44, n2; H. Wheeler Robinson, *Inspiration and Revelation in the Old Testament,* pp. 241-42, 250; Gerhard von Rad, *Old Testament Theology,* 1:355. These views are not very different from that expressed by Gustav Oehler: "Upon the soil already formed by the facts of Divine revelation and the theocratic ordinances. . . springs up not merely a practical piety, but an *impulse for knowledge (Theology of the Old Testament,* p. 537). D. A. Hubbard, who emphasizes the importance of the religious aspects of wisdom, unfortunately does this too one-sidedly, making the linkage between wisdom and the covenant-faith of Israel too close ("The Wisdom Movement and Israel's Covenant Faith," *Tyndale Bulletin* 17 (1966):3-32). Bernhard W. Anderson, on the other hand, stresses the religious background of wisdom literature, yet maintains its distinctiveness from the religious traditions of Israel found in the Pentateuch (*Understanding the Old Testament,* pp. 490-91).

3. O. S. Rankin, *Israel's Wisdom Literature,* p. 1.

4. Artur Weiser, *The Old Testament,* p. 298.

5. von Rad, *Old Testament Theology,* 1: 434.

6. Martin Noth, "Die Bewährung von Salomos 'Göttlicher Weisheit,' " in *Wisdom in Israel and in the Ancient Near East,* pp. 232-37. Noth restricted his study, referring primarily to the term "wisdom" when other terms belonging to the "intellectual," i. e., the religious epistemological tradition, ought to have been included. For some of these see Whybray, *The Intellectual Tradition,* pp. 139-40, 149.

7. The quotation is from Thomas Mann's *Joseph and His Brothers.* Noth, "Die Bewährung," p. 233.

8. As the one who establishes and maintains righteousness, the king possesses wisdom like the gods. For a discussion of *Maat,* justice, in relation to the Egyptian kings, see Siegfried Morenz, *Egyptian Religion,* pp. 113-30; Henri Frankfort, *Kingship and the Gods,* pp. 51-60; Georges Posener, *Littérature et politique dans l'Egypte de la XIIᵉ Dynastie,* pp. 57-58, 130; Hans Bonnet, *Reallexikon der ägyptischen Religionsgeschichte,* p. 432; Eberhard Otto, "Prolegomena zur Frage der Gesetzgebung und Rechtssprechung in Ägypten," MDAIK 14 (1956): 151; Erik Hornung, "Zur geschichtlichen Rolle des Königs in der 18 Dynastie," MDAIK 15 (1957): 120-33. The terms *wise* and *just* are frequently use as epithets of the Babylonian kings. Ivan Engnell, *Studies in Divine Kingship in the Ancient Near East,* pp. 189-91; M.-J. Seux, *Epithètes royales akkadiennes et sumériennes,* p. 22; Geo. Widengren, *Religionsphänomenologie,* pp. 546-48.

9. H. Donner und W. Röllig, *Kanaanäische und aramäische Inschriften,* I:5;2:36 (no. 26, I 12-13). The noun *'bt* is best interpreted as an abstract noun meaning "father," and the phrase *p'l b* is probably similar in meaning to the Hebrew idiom *'sh b* as in Ezek. 23:25 and Jer. 18:23, where it means "to deal (or) treat with," since the Phoenician and Hebrew are parallel in meaning. For other interpretations see Charles-F. Jean and Jacob Hoftizer, *Dictionnaire des inscriptions sémitiques de l'Ouest,* p. 232 and Cyrus H. Gordon, "Azitawadd's Phoenician Inscription," JNES 8 (1949): 110.

10. Cyrus H. Gordon, *Ugaritic Textbook: Texts,* p. 193 (126, IV 3); *idem, Ugaritic Literature,* p. 80. In contrast to Gordon's translation, which reads "Thou art wise like Ṭor-Lṭpn," H. L. Ginsberg translates the names: "wisdom like Bull, the Kindly One" ("The Legend of King Keret: A Canaanite Epic of the Bronze Age," BASOR Supplementary Studies 2-3 [1946]: 29). The decree of El, that Baal is king, is "wise" (51 IV 41; Gordon, *Ugaritic Textbook: Texts,* p. 171; *idem, Ugaritic Literature,* p. 32).

11. W. F. Albright, *Yahweh and the Gods of Canaan,* pp. 248-49; Martin Noth, "Noah, Daniel und Hiob in Ezechiel XIV," VT 1 (1951): 253; Kalman Yaron, "The Dirge over the King of Tyre," ASTI 3 (1964): 46-47; H. J. van Dijk, *Ezekiel's Prophecy on Tyre (Ez. 26:1-28:19),* p. 99. John Gray believes that Ezekiel's depiction of Dan'el as wise is based upon the etymology of the name and not directly upon the Ugaritic text under consideration here *(The Legacy of Canaan,* p. 107).

12. Two kings of Israel, David and Solomon, and three foreign rulers, the kings of Egypt and Assyria and the prince of Tyre, are singled out as being wise.

13. Gordon, *Ugaritic Textbook: Texts,* p. 194 (127:41-53); *Ugaritic Literature,* pp. 82-83; Ginsberg, "The Legend of King Keret," p. 32; Gray, *The Legacy of Canaan,* p. 150.

14. Gordon, *Ugaritic Textbook: Texts,* p. 248 (2 Aqht 5, 6-8): *Ugaritic Literature,* p. 88; Gray, *The Legacy of Canaan,* p. 107; Engnell, *Studies in Divine Kingship,* p. 137.

15. For the religious significance of the threshing-floor as a cult place, see G. W. Ahlström, "Der Prophet Nathan und der Tempelbau," VT 11 (1961): 116-17.

16. P. A. H. de Boer, "The Counsellor," in *Wisdom in Israel and in the Ancient Near East,* pp. 58-60.

17. 1 Sam. 10:22 (lot); 22:10, 15 (priest), 23:2, 4 (Yahweh), 28:6 (dreams, Urim, prophets); Judges 18:5 (priest).

18. Noth, "Die Bewährung," p. 236.

19. Bonnet, *Reallexikon,* pp. 835-38; Adolph Leo Oppenheim, *The Interpretation of Dreams in the Ancient Near East,* pp. 184-244; Ernst Ludwig Ehrlich, *Der Traum im Alten Testament,* pp. 137-50.

20. Widengren, *Religionsphänomenologie,* pp. 546-48.

21. The description in Isaiah corresponds with what is known of the religion of Egypt in the late period when the institution connected with oracle-giving was greatly expanded (Adolf Erman, *Die ägyptische Religion*, pp. 166-68, 181, 197). Georges Posener has suggested that the Egyptian word *by3y·t* in Amen. 21:13 ought to be translated "oracle." Its parallel in Amen. 21:14, *sḫr-w* is the term used for counsel or advice, which in this context betrays its cultic associations ["Aménémopé 21, 13 et *bj3j·t* au sens d ≤oracle≥," ZÄS 90 (1963): 98-102].

22. "Although the exact forms of divination practiced by the prophets may be uncertain, one thing is clear: during the monarchical period, at least, it was recognized as an authoritative branch of the prophetic activity" (A. R. Johnson, *The Cultic Prophet in Ancient Israel*, p. 34).

23. Fritz Rudolph Kraus, "Babylonische Omina mit Ausdeutung der Begleiterungscheinungen des Sprechens," AfO 11 (1936):223 (l. 17). This reference includes Prov. 16:30 and 10:10. Parallels to the other three passages, respectively, will be found in Fritz Rudolph Kraus, "Ein Sittenkanon im Omen-form," *Zeitschrift für Assyriologie*, 43 (1936): 92 (ll. 28-29); Franz Köcher and A. L. Oppenheim, "The Old Babylonian Omen Text VAT 7525," AfO 18 (1957-58): 65 (ll. 21-22); Kraus, "Ein Sittenkanon," p. 98 (l. 36; similarity in form only). For a study of these parallels and their significance for the interpretation of Israelite wisdom, see my study "Omen-Wisdom in Ancient Israel," JBL 94, no. 1 (1975): 19-37. The Hebrew is my translation.

24. J. Fichtner, *Die altoreintalischen Weisheit in ihrer israelitisch-jüdischen Ausprägung*, pp. 35-45; W. Zimmerli, "Ort und Grenze der Weisheit im Rahmen der alttestamentliche Theologie," in *Les sagesses du Proche-Orient ancien*, pp. 130-31; von Rad, *Wisdom in Israel*, pp. 186-89; Sigmund Mowinckel, "Psalms and Wisdom," in *Wisdom in Israel and in the Ancient Near East*, pp. 206-8; Hans-Jürgen Hermisson, *Studien zur israelitischen Spruchweisheit*, pp. 129-33.

25. A. R. Johnson, *The Cultic Prophet*, p. 34 (citing his translation).

26. For a discussion of eudaemonism and the role of the deity in determining the future in Egypt and Israel, see Hartmut Gese, *Lehre und Wirklichkeit in der alten Weisheit*, pp. 45-50 and Udo Skaldny, *Die ältesten Spruchsammlungen in Israel*, p. 75, and von Rad, *Wisdom in Israel*, pp. 97-106.

27. Isa. 28:29. This passage contains a small wisdom book, beginning at v. 23 and ending at v. 29. It consists of two main parts (vs. 24-26, 27-29a), each of which advises its reader about a particular type of agricultural activity. Its introduction (v. 23) is typical of an instructional type of composition. Its conclusion (v. 29b) affirms God as the source of all counsels of perfection. For an example of this genre of literature in Sumerian circles, see Samuel Noah Kramer, *The Sumerians*, pp. 340-42 ("Farmers' Almanac").

28. de Boer, "The Counsellor," p. 47.

29. Helmer Ringgren, *Word and Wisdom*, pp. 90-92.

30. Ivan Engnell, *A Rigid Scrutiny*, pp. 41-42; Widengren, *Religionsphänomenologie*, pp. 548-49; *idem, Sakrales Königtum im Alten Testament und*

in Judentum, pp. 17-33, 53-58; G. W. Ahlström, *Psalm 89,* pp. 103-4; Helmer Ringgren, *Israelite Religion,* pp. 231-32. Although Engnell has been criticized for making too little allowance for imagery, he himself has admitted the existence of the interpretive problem with respect to figurative language (*A Rigid Scrutiny,* pp. 250-51). Nevertheless, he believed that cultic ideology lay behind statements such as are found in Ps. 2:7, where the king is said to have been "begotten" by the deity, and Ps. 51:7, where the king is called "god." For the ancient Near Eastern background of this motif, see Helmer Ringgren, *Religions of the Ancient Near East,* pp. 38, 101-2, 171-72.

31. Van Dijk, *Ezekiel's Prophecy,* pp. 93-96, 119.

32. J. A. Knudtzon, *Die El-Amarna-Tafeln,* 2:622-23 (no. 151:18-20); 636-37 (no. 155:46-47); 616-17 (no. 149:24-25).

33. Albrecht Alt, *Essays on Old Testament History and Religion,* pp. 217-19; Widengren, *Sakrales Königtum,* pp. 17-25; Sigmund Mowinckel, *He That Cometh,* pp. 80-84; A. R. Johnson, "Hebrew Conceptions of Kingship," in *Myth, Ritual and Kingship,* pp. 212-13; Ringgren, *Israelite Religion,* pp. 210-14; Gösta Werner Ahlström, *Aspects of Syncretism in Israelite Religion,* pp. 1-2.

34. McKane, *Prophets and Wise Men,* pp. 127-29.

35. The importance of the royal bureaucracy in the maintenance of the Egyptian state is discussed by Hellmut Brunner, *Altägyptische Erziehung,* pp. 16, 23,55; Georges Posener, *Littérature et politique,* pp. x. 3-4, 8-9, 16-17, 127; Eberhard Otto, "Bildung und Ausbildung im alten Ägypten," ZÄS 81 (1956): 41-48.

36. These activities would have been intensified during the reigns of Solomon, Rehoboam and Jeroboam, Omri, Hezekiah, and Josiah.

37. In his study of the social background of Wisdom Literature in the later period, Robert Gordis contrasts the social teaching of the wisdom type, which "was fundamentally the product of the upper classes in society," with that of the schools conducted by the Sopherim and Pharisees, who were primarily teachers in the professional schools for students of the Torah. Thus, he asserts that the wisdom literature reflects the conservative outlook of the upper classes, who were satisfied with the status quo and opposed to change ("The Social Background of Wisdom Literature," HUCA 18 (1943-44): 81-82.

38. McKane, *Prophets and Wise Men, passim.* From a theological viewpoint, Walther Eichrodt discusses the tension that the monarchy introduced into Israel's understanding of the covenant (*Theology of the Old Testament,* 1: 438-56). However, his discussion is limited by the fact that he did not sufficiently regard the covenant of Yahweh with David as a valid and independent expression of the kingdom of God in a different form. For discussion of the importance of the two covenants and their interrelationship in the context of Old Testament theology, see J. Coert Rylaarsdam, "Jewish-Christian Relationship: The Two Covenants and the Dilemmas of Christology," *Journal of Ecumenical Studies* 9 (1972): 249-70.

39. J. Coert Rylaarsdam, *Revelation in Jewish Wisdom Literature,* pp. 18-46.

List of Abbreviations

AJSL	The American Journal of Semitic Languages and Literatures
ANET	Ancient Near Eastern Texts Relating to the Old Testament
AnglTR	Anglican Theological Review
AfO	Archiv für Orientforschung
ASTI	Annual of the Swedish Theological Institute
BASOR	The Bulletin of the American School of Oriental Research
Bib	Biblica
BZ	Biblische Zeitschrift

BZTS	Bonner Zeitschrift für Theologie und Seelsorge
CBQ	Catholic Biblical Quarterly
DLZ	Deutsche Literaturzeitung
HR	History of Religions
HUCA	The Hebrew Union College Annual
JAOS	The Journal of the American Oriental Society
JB	The Jerusalem Bible
JBL	The Journal of Biblical Literature
JEA	Journal of Egyptian Archaeology
JNES	The Journal of Near Eastern Studies
JRel	The Journal of Religion
JSS	The Journal of Semitic Studies
KeDo	Kerygma und Dogma
LÄS	Leipziger ägyptologische Studien
MDAIK	Mitteilungen des Deutschen Archäologischen Instituts, Abteilung Kairo
Miz	Mizraim
NEB	New English Bible
OLZ	Orientalistische Literaturzeitung
Or	Orientalia
PB	Pastor Bonus
RB	Revue Biblique
RE	Revue d'Egyptologie
REJ	Revue des Etudes Juives
RSV	Revised Standard Version
SAB	Sitzungsberichte der Preussischen (Deutschen) Akademie der Wissenschaften zu Berlin.

Saec	Saeculum
ScEccl	Sciences Ecclésiastiques
TGl	Theologie und Glaube
TLZ	Theologische Literaturzeitung
TPQ	Theologisch praktische Quartalschrift
VT	Vetus Testamentum
WO	Die Welt des Orients
ZAW	Zeitschrift für die Alttestamentliche Wissenschaft
ZÄS	Zeitschrift für ägyptische Sprache und Altertumskunde
ZDMG	Zeitschrift der Deutschen Morgenländischen Gesellschaft
ZKT	Zeitschrift für katholische Theologie
ZSG	Zeitschrift für Semitisk und verwandte Gebiete

Bibliography

Books

Ahlström, Gösta Werner. *Aspects of Syncretism in Israelite Religion.* Horae Soederblomianae, vol. 5. Lund: C. W. K. Gleerup, 1963.

⸻. *Psalm 89: Eine Liturgie aus dem Ritual des leidenden Königs.* Translated by Hans-Karl Hacker and Rudolph Zeitler. Lund: C. W. K. Gleerups, 1959.

Aistleitner, Joseph. *Wörterbuch der ugaritischen Sprache.* Edited by Otto Eissfeldt. Berichte über die Verhandlungen der sächsischen Akademie der Wissenschaften zu Leipzig: Philologisch-historische Klasse, vol. 106, pt. 3. 3rd ed., rev. Berlin: Akademie Verlag, 1967.

Albrektson, Bertil. *History and the Gods: An Essay on the Idea of Historical Events as Divine Manifestations in the Ancient Near*

East and in Israel. Coniectanea Biblica, O. T. Series, no. 1. Lund: C. W. K. Gleerup, 1967.

Albright, William Foxwell. *Archeology and the Religion of Israel.* 5th ed. Garden City, N. Y.: Doubleday and Co., 1969.

————. *Yahweh and the Gods of Canaan: A Historical Analysis of Two Contrasting Faiths.* Jordan Lectures in Comparative Religion, no. 7. London: Athlone Press, 1968.

Alt, Abrecht. *Essays on Old Testament History and Religion.* Translated by R. A. Wilson. Oxford: Basil Blackwell, 1966.

————. *Israel und Aegypten: Die politischen Beziehungen der Könige von Israel und Juda zu den Pharaonen nach den Quellen untersucht.* Beiträge zur Wissenschaft vom Alten Testament, no. 6. Leipzig: J. C. Hinrichs'sche Buchhandlung, 1909.

Anderson, Bernhard W. *Understanding the Old Testament.* 2d ed. Englewood Cliffs, N. J.: Prentice-Hall, 1957.

Archer, Gleason L. *A Survey of Old Testament Introduction.* Chicago: Moody Press, 1964.

Assmann, Jan. *Liturgische Lieder an den Sonnengott: Untersuchungen zur altägyptischen Hymnik I.* Münchner ägyptologische Studien, no. 19. Berlin: Bruno Hessling, 1969.

Barucq, André. *Le Livre des Proverbes.* Sources Bibliques. Paris: J. Gabalda, 1964.

Baumgartner, Walter. *Israelitische und altorientalische Weisheit.* Sammlung gemeinverständlicher Vorträge und Schriften aus dem Gebiet der Theologie und Religionsgeschichte, no. 166. Tübingen: J. C. B. Mohr, 1933.

Bezold, C., and Budge, E. A. Wallis, eds. *The Tell El-Amarna Tablets in the British Museum with Autotype Facsimiles.* London: The British Museum, 1892.

Biblia Sacra juxta Vulgatam Clementinam. Rome: Desclée et Socii, 1947.

Bissing, Fr. W. Freiherr von. *Altägyptische Lebensweisheit.* Die Bibliothek der Alten Welt, Reihe der Alte Orient. Zürich: Artemis Verlag, 1955.

Blackman, Aylward M. *Middle-Egyptian Stories*. Bibliotheca Aegyptiaca, no. 2. Brussels: La Fondation égyptogique reine Elisabeth, 1932.

Bonnet, Hans. *Reallexikon der ägyptischen Religionsgeschichte*. Berlin: Walter de Gruyter and Co., 1952.

Briggs, Charles Augustus, and Briggs, Grace Emilie. *A Critical and Exegetical Commentary on the Book of Psalms*. The International Critical Commentary on the Holy Scriptures of the Old and New Testaments. 2 vols. New York: Charles Scribner's Sons, 1906-7.

Bright, John. *A History of Israel*. Philadelphia: Westminster Press, 1959.

Brockelmann, Carl. *Hebräische Syntax*. Neukirchen: Kreis Moers, 1956.

Brown, Francis, Driver, S. R., and Briggs, Charles A. *A Hebrew and English Lexicon of the Old Testament*. 2d ed. Oxford: Clarendon Press, 1955.

Brunner, Hellmut. *Altägyptische Erziehung*. Wiesbaden: Otto Harrassowitz, 1957.

Budge, E. A. Wallis. *The Book of the Dead: The Papyrus of Ani in the British Museum. The Egyptian Text with Interlinear Transliteration and Translation, A Running Translation, Introduction, Etc.* 1895. Reprint. New York: Dover Publications, 1967.

————. *Facsimiles of Egyptian Hieratic Papyri in the British Museum with Descriptions, Summaries of Contents, Etc.* Second Series. London: Harrison and Sons, 1923.

————. *The Teaching of Amen-em-Apt, Son of Kanekht: The Egyptian Hieroglyphic Text and an English Translation, with Translations of the Moral and Religious Teachings of Egyptian Kings and Officials Illustrating the Development of Religious Philosophy in Egypt During a Period of About Two Thousand Years.* London: Martin Hopkinson and Co., 1924.

Burchhardt, Max. *Die altkanaanäischen Fremdeworte und Eigennumen im Aegyptischen*. Leipzig: J. C. Hinrichs'sche Buchhandlung, 1909.

Buttenweiser, Moses. *The Psalms: Chronologically Treated with a New Translation.* Chicago: University of Chicago Press, 1938.

Caminos, Ricardo A. *Late-Egyptian Miscellanies.* Brown Egyptological Studies, no. 1. London: Oxford University Press, 1954.

Cowley, A. *Aramaic Papyri of the Fifth Century* B.C. Oxford: Clarendon Press, 1923.

Dahood, Mitchell. *Proverbs and Northwest Semitic Philology.* Scripta Pontificii Instituti Biblici, no. 113. Rome: Pontificium Institutum Biblicum, 1963.

Dijk, H. J. van. *Ezekiel's Prophecy on Tyre (Ez. 26,1-28, 19): A New Approach.* Biblica et Orientalia, no. 20. Rome: Pontifical Biblical Institute, 1968.

Dijk, J. J. A. van. *La sagesse suméro-akkadienne: Recherches sur les genres littéraires des textes.* Commentationes Orientales, vol. 1. Leiden: E. J. Brill, 1953.

Donner, H., and Röllig, W. *Kanaanäische und aramäische Inschriften.* 3 vols. Wiesbaden: Otto Harrassowitz, 1962-64.

Driver, G. R. *Canaanite Myths and Legends.* Old Testament Studies, no. 3. Edinburgh: T. and T. Clark, 1956.

Driver, S. R. *Notes on the Hebrew Text and the Topography of the Books of Samuel with an Introduction on Hebrew Paleography and the Ancient Versions and Facsimiles of Inscriptions and Maps.* 2d ed., rev. Oxford: Clarendon Press, 1913.

Drower, Margaret S. *Ugarit.* The Cambridge Ancient History, vol. 2, chap. 21. 2d ed., rev. Fascicle no. 63. Cambridge: At the University Press, 1968.

Duesberg, Hilaire. *Les scribes inspirés: Introduction aux livres sapientiaux de la Bible.* 2 vols. Paris: Desclée de Brouwer, 1938.

Ehrlich, Ernst Ludwig. *Der Traum im Alten Testament.* Beihefte zur Zeitschrift für die alttestamentliche Wissenschaft, no. 73. Berlin: Alfred Töpelmann, 1953.

Eichrodt, Walther. *Theology of the Old Testament.* Translated by J. A. Baker. The Old Testament Library. 2 vols. Philadelphia: Westminster Press, 1967.

Eissfeldt, O. *The Hebrew Kingdom.* The Cambridge Ancient History, vol. 2, chap. 34. 2d ed., rev. Fascicle no. 32. Cambridge: At the University Press, 1965.

————. *The Old Testament: An Introduction including the Apocrypha and Pseudepigrapha, and also the Works of Similar Type from Qumran, The History of the Formation of the Old Testament.* Translated by Peter R. Ackroyd. New York: Harper and Row, 1965.

Ember, Aaron. *Egypto-Semitic-Studies: Aus den Überresten Originalmanuscripts hergestellt und nach älteren Arbeiten des Verfassers ergänzt von Frida Behnk.* Veröffentlichungen der Alexander Kohut Memorial Foundation, Philologische Reihe, vol. 2. Leipzig: Verlag Asia Minor G. M. B. H., 1930.

Engnell, Ivan. *A Rigid Scrutiny: Critical Essays on the Old Testament.* Edited and translated by John T. Willis. Nashville, Tenn.: Vanderbilt University Press, 1969.

————. *Studies in Divine Kingship in the Ancient Near East.* Uppsala: Almqvist and Wiksell, 1943.

Erman, Adolf. *Die ägyptische Religion.* Berlin: Georg Reimer, 1905.

————. *The Ancient Egyptians: A Sourcebook of Their Writings.* Translated by Aylward M. Blackman. 1927. Reprint. New York: Harper and Row, 1966.

————. *Neuägyptische Grammatik.* Edited by W. Erichsen. 2d ed., rev. Hildesheim: Georg Olms Verlagsbuchhandlung, 1968.

Erman, Adolf, and Grapow, Hermann. *Aegyptisches Handwörterbuch.* Berlin: Reuther and Reichard, 1921.

————, eds. *Wörterbuch der aegyptischen Sprache im Auftrage der Deutschen Akademien.* 5 vols. 1926-1931. Reprint. Berlin: Akademie Verlag, 1971.

————, eds. *Wörterbuch der aegyptischen Sprache im Auftrage der Deutschen Akademien: Die Belegstellen.* 5 vols. 1938-1953. Reprint. Berlin: Akademie Verlag, 1971.

————, eds. *Wörterbuch der aegyptischen Sprache im Auftrage der deutschen Akademien,* vol. 6, *Deutsch-aegyptisches Wörterverzeichnis im alphabetischer und sachlicher Ordnung nebst Ver-*

zeichnissen der koptischen, semitischen und griechischen Wörter. Berlin: Akademie Verlag in Arbeitsgemeinschaft mit dem J. C. Hinrichs Verlag, 1950.

Faulkner, Raymond O. *A Concise Dictionary of Middle Egyptian.* Oxford: At the University Press, 1962.

—————. *Egypt.* The Cambridge Ancient History, vol. 2, chap. 23. 2d ed., rev. Fascicle no. 52. Cambridge: At the University Press, 1966.

Fichtner, Johannes. *Die altorientalische Weisheit in ihrer israelitisch-jüdischen Ausprägung: Eine Studie zur Nationalisierung der Weisheit in Israel.* Beihefte zur Zeitschrift für die alttestamentliche Wissenschaft, no. 62. Geissen: Alfred Töpelmann, 1933.

Field, Fridericus. *Origenis Hexaplorum quae supersunt; sive veterum interpretum Graecorum in totum Vetus Testamentum fragmenta. Post Flaminium Nobilium, Drusium, et Montefalconium, adhibita etiam versione Syro-Hexaplari, concinnavit, emendavit, et multis partibus auxit Fridericus Field.* 2 vols. Oxford: E Typographeo Clarendoniano, 1925.

Frankfort, Henri. *Kingship and the Gods: A Study of Ancient Near Eastern Religion as the Integration of Society and Nature.* Chicago: University of Chicago Press, 1948.

Frost, Stanley Brice. *Old Testament Apocalyptic: Its Origins and Growth.* London: Epworth Press, 1952.

Gardiner, Alan H. *The Admonitions of an Egyptian Sage from a Hieratic Papyrus in Leiden (Pap. Leiden 344 Recto).* Leipzig: J. C. Hinrichs'sche Buchhandlung, 1909.

—————. *Egypt of the Pharaohs: An Introduction.* 1961. Reprint. New York: Oxford University Press, 1966.

—————. *Egyptian Grammar: Being an Introduction to the Study of Hieroglyphs.* 3rd ed., rev. London: Oxford University Press, 1957.

—————, ed. *Egyptian Hieratic Texts, Transcribed, Translated and Annotated.* Ser. 1, *Literary Texts of the New Kingdom,* pt. 1, *Papyrus Anastasi I and Papyrus Koller.* Leipzig: J. C. Hinrichs'sche Buchhandlung, 1911.

———. *Late-Egyptian Stories*. Bibliotheca Aegyptiaca, no. 1. Brussels: La Fondation égyptologique reine Elisabeth, 1932.

Gauthier, Henri. *Le personnel du dieu Min*. Recherches d'archéologie de philologie et d'histoire, no. 3. Cairo: L'Institut français d'archéologie orientale, 1939.

Gelb, Ignace J.; Jacobsen, Thorkild; Landsberger, Benno; and Oppenheim, A. Leo, eds. *The Assyrian Dictionary of the Oriental Institute of the University of Chicago*. Vols. 1, 2,3,5,16. Chicago: Oriental Institute, 1956-.

Gemser, B. *Sprüche Salomos*. Handbuch zum Alten Testament, 1st ser., vol. 16. Tübingen: J. C. B. Mohr (Paul Siebeck), 1937.

Gese, Hartmut. *Lehre und Wirklichkeit in der alten Weisheit: Studien zu den Sprüchen Salomos und zu dem Buch Hiob*. Tübingen: J. C. B. Mohr (Paul Siebeck), 1958.

Gevirtz, Stanley. *Patterns in the Early Poetry of Israel*. Studies in Ancient Oriental Civilization, no. 32. Chicago: University of Chicago Press, 1963.

Glanville, S. R. K. *Catalogue of Demotic Papyri in the British Museum*, vol. 2, *The Instructions of 'Onchsheshonqy (British Museum Papyrus 10508)*, pt. 1, *Introduction, Transliteration, Translation, Notes and Plates*. London: Trustees of the British Museum, 1955.

Gordis, Robert. *The Biblical Text in the Making: A Study of the Kethib-Qere*. Philadelphia: Dropsie College for Hebrew and Cognate Learning, 1937.

———. *Koheleth—The Man and His World: A Study of Ecclesiastes*. 3rd ed. New York: Schocken Books, 1968.

Gordon, Cyrus H. *Ugaritic Literature: A Comprehensive Translation of the Poetic and Prose Texts*. Scripta Pontificii Instituti Biblici, no. 98. Rome: Pontificium Institutum Biblicum, 1949.

———. *Ugaritic Textbook: Grammar, Texts in Transliteration, Cuneiform Selections, Glossary, Indices*. Analecta Orientalia, vol. 38. Rome: Pontificium Institutum Biblicum, 1965.

Gray, John. *I and II Kings.* The Old Testament Library. Philadelphia: Westminster Press, 1963.

———. *The Legacy of Canaan: The Ras Shamra Texts and Their Relevance to the Old Testament.* Supplements to Vetus Testamentum, vol. 5. 2d ed., rev. Leiden: E. J. Brill, 1965.

Gressmann, Hugo. *Israel's Spruchweisheit im Zusammenhang der Weltliteratur: Kunst und Altertum.* Alte Kulturen im Lichte neuer Forschung, vol. 6. Berlin: Carl Curtius, 1925.

Groll, Sarah Israelit. *Non-Verbal Sentence Patterns in Late Egyptian.* London: Oxford University Press, 1967.

Grumach, Irene. *Untersuchungen zur Lebenslehre des Amenope.* Münchner ägyptologische Studien, vol. 23. Berlin: Deutscher Kunstverlag, 1972.

Gunkel, Hermann, and Begrich, Joachim. *Einleitung in die Psalmen: Die Gattungen der religiösen Lyrik Israels.* 2nd ed. Göttingen: Vandenhoeck und Ruprecht, 1966.

Hamp, Vinzenz. *Das Buch der Sprüche.* Die Heilige Schrift in deutscher Übersetzung, Echter-Bibel, Das Alte Testament, vol. 8. Würzburg: Echter-Verlag, 1949.

Harrison, R. K. *Introduction to the Old Testament with a Comprehensive Review of Old Testament Studies and a Special Supplement on the Apocrypha.* Grand Rapids, Mich.: Wm. B. Eerdmans Publishing Co., 1969.

Hassan, M. Sélim. *Hymnes religieux du Moyen Empire.* Cairo: L'Institut français d'archéologie orientale, 1928.

Hatch, Edwin, and Redpath, Henry A. *A Concordance to the Septuagint and Other Greek Versions of the Old Testament (Including Apocryphal Books).* 2 vols. Oxford: Clarendon Press, 1897.

Hayes, William C. *The Middle Kingdom in Egypt.* The Cambridge Ancient History, vol. 1, chap. 20. 2d ed., rev. Fascicle no. 3. Cambridge: At the University Press, 1964.

Hermisson, Hans-Jürgen. *Studien zur israelitischen Spruchweisheit.* Wissenschaftliche Monographien zum Alten und Neuen Testament, vol. 28. Neukirchen-Vluyn: Neukirchener Verlag, 1968.

Humbert, Paul. *Recherches sur les sources égyptiennes de la littérature sapientiale d'Israël.* Mémoires de l'Université de Neuchatel, vol. 7. Neuchatel: Secrétariat de l'Université, 1929.

Jean, Charles-F., and Hoftijzer, Jacob. *Dictionnaire des inscriptions sémitiques de l'Ouest.* Leiden: E. J. Brill, 1965.

Johnson, Aubrey R. *The Cultic Prophet in Ancient Israel.* Cardiff: University of Wales Press, 1962.

―――. *Sacral Kingship in Ancient Israel.* Cardiff: University of Wales Press, 1955.

Jones, Edgar. *Proverbs and Ecclesiastes: Introduction and Commentary.* Torch Bible Commentaries. London: SCM Press, 1961.

Kapelrud, Arvid S. *Baal in the Ras Shamra Texts.* Copenhagen: G. E. C. Gad, 1952.

Kautzsch, E., and Cowley, A. E., eds. *Gesenius' Hebrew Grammar as Edited and Enlarged by the Late E. Kautzsch.* 2d ed., rev. Oxford: Clarendon Press, 1910.

Kayatz, Christa B. *Studien zu Proverbien 1-9: Eine form- und motivgeschichtliche Untersuchung unter Einbeziehung ägyptischen Vergleichsmaterials.* Wissenschaftliche Monographien zum Alten und Neuen Testament, vol. 22. Neukirchen-Vluyn: Neukirchener Verlag, 1966.

Kevin, Robert Oliver. *The Wisdom of Amen-em-apt and its Possible Dependence upon the Hebrew Book of Proverbs.* Austria: Adolf Holzhausen's Successors, 1931.

Kittel, Rudolf, ed. *Biblia Hebraica.* 3rd ed. Stuttgart: Privilegierte württembergische Bibelanstalt, 1937.

―――, ed. *Geschichte des Volkes Israel.* 2d ed. 3 vols. Stuttgart: W. Kohlhammer, 1929.

Knudtzon, J. A., ed. *Die El-Amarna-Tafeln mit Einleitung und Erläuterungen.* Vorderasiatische Bibliothek, part 2. 2 vols. Leipzig: J. C. Hinrichs'sche Buchhandlung, 1915.

Kramer, Samuel Noah. *The Sumerians: Their History, Culture and Character.* Chicago: University of Chicago Press, 1963.

Kuhn, Gottfried. *Beiträge zur Erklärung des Salomonischen Spruchbuches.* Beiträge zur Wissenschaft von Alten und Neuen Testament, 3rd ser., no. 16. Stuttgart: W. Kohlhammer, 1931.

Lambert, W. G. *Babylonian Wisdom Literature.* Oxford: Clarendon Press, 1960.

Lange, H. O. *Das Weisheitsbuch des Amenemope aus dem Papyrus 10,474 des British Museum herausgegeben und erklärt.* Det Kgl. Danske Videnskabernes Selskab. Historisk-filologiske Meddelelser, vol. II, no. 2. Copenhagen: Andr. Fred. Høst and Søn, 1925.

The Later Historical Records of Ramses III by Epigraphic Survey, vol. 2, *Medinet Habu.* Oriental Institute Publications, vol. 9. Chicago: University of Chicago Press, 1932.

Lefebvre, Gustave. *Grammaire de l'Egyptien classique.* Bibliothèque d'étude, vol. 12. Cairo: L'Institut français d'archéologie orientale, 1940.

Lévi, Israel, ed. *The Hebrew Text of the Book of Ecclesiasticus.* Study Series, no. 3. 1904. Reprint. Leiden: E. J. Brill, 1969.

Lexa, Francois. *Papyrus Insinger: Les enseignements moraux d'un scribe egyptien du premier siècle après J.-C. Texte démotique avec transcription, traduction française, commentaire, vocabulaire et introduction grammaticale et littéraire.* 2 vols. Paris: Librairie orientaliste Paul Geuthner, 1926.

McKane, William. *Prophets and Wise Men.* Studies in Biblical Theology, 1st ser., no. 44. London: SCM Press, 1965.

———. *Proverbs: A New Approach.* The Old Testament Library. Philadelphia: Westminster Press, 1970.

Mercer, Samuel A. B., ed. *The Tell El-Amarna Tablets.* 2 vols. Toronto: Macmillan Company of Canada, 1939.

Montet, Pierre. *L'Egypte et la Bible.* Cahiers d'archéologie biblique, no. 11. Neuchatel: Delachaux et Niestlé, 1959.

Montgomery, James A. *A Critical and Exegetical Commentary on the Books of Kings.* Edited by Henry Snyder Gehman. The International Critical Commentary. New York: Charles Scribner's Sons, 1951.

Morenz, Siegfried. *Egyptian Religion.* Translated by Ann E. Keep. Ithaca, N. Y.: Cornell University Press, 1973.

Mowinckel, Sigmund. *He That Cometh.* Translated by G. W. Anderson. New York: Abingdon Press, 1956.

———. *The Psalms in Israel's Worship.* Translated by D. R. Ap-Thomas. 2 vols. Oxford: Basil Blackwell, 1962.

Noth, Martin. *The History of Israel.* Translated by Stanley Godman. New York: Harper and Brothers, 1958.

———. *Überlieferungsgeschichtliche Studien.* 2d ed. Tübingen: Max Niemeyer Verlag, 1957.

Nougayrol, Jean; Laroche, Emmanuel; Virolleaud, Charles; and Schaeffer, Claude F. A., eds. *Ugaritica V.* Mission de Ras Shamra, vol. 16. Paris: Librairie orientaliste Paul Geuthner, 1968.

Oehler, Gustave Friedrich. *Theology of the Old Testament.* Revised by George E. Day. Grand Rapids, Mich.: Zondervan Publishing House, 1883.

Oesterley, W. O. E. *The Book of Proverbs with Introduction and Notes.* Westminster Commentaries. London: Methuen and Co., 1929.

———. *The Wisdom of Egypt and the Old Testament in the Light of the Newly Discovered 'Teachung of Amen-em-ope'.* London: Society for Promoting Christian Knowledge, 1927.

Oppenheim, Adolph Leo. *The Interpretation of Dreams in the ancient Near East with a Translation of an Assyrian Dream-Book, Transactions of the American Philosophical Society,* n.s. vol. 46, pt. 3. Philadelphia: American Philosophical Society, 1956.

———. *Letters from Mesopotamia: Official, Business, and Private Letters on Clay Tablets.* Chicago: University of Chicago Press, 1967.

Otto, Eberhard. *Die biographischen Inschriften der ägyptischen Spätzeit: Ihre geistesgeschichtliche und literarische Bedeutung.* Edited by Hermann Kees. Probleme der Ägyptologie, vol. 2. Leiden: E. J. Brill, 1954.

Posener, Georges. *Catalogue des ostraca hiératiques littéraires de Deir el Medineh.* Documents de fouilles publiés par les membres de l'Institut français d'archéologie orientale du Caire sous la direction de M. Charles Kuentz, vol. 18. Cairo: L'Institut français d'archéologie orientale, 1951.

———. *De la divinité du Pharaon.* Cahiers de la Société asiatique, vol. 15. Paris: Imprimerie Nationale, 1960.

———. *Littérature et politique dans l'Egypte de la XIIᵉ dynastie.* Paris: Librairie ancienne Honoré Champion 1956.

Rad, Gerhard von. *Deuteronomy: A Commentary.* Translated by Dorothea Barton. The Old Testament Library. Philadelphia: Westminster Press, 1966.

———. *Old Testament Theology.* Translated by D. M. G. Stalker. 2 vols. New York: Harper and Brothers, 1962.

———. *The Problem of the Hexateuch and Other Essays.* Translated by E. W. Trueman Dicken. New York: McGraw-Hill Book Co., 1966.

———. *Wisdom in Israel.* Translated by James D. Martin. Nashville, Tenn.: Abingdon Press, 1972.

Rahlfs, Alfred, ed. *Septuaginta: Id est, Vetus Testamentum Graece iuxta LXX interpretes.* 5th ed. Stuttgart: Privilegierte württembergische Bibelanstalt, 1952.

Rankin, O. S. *Israel's Wisdom Literature: Its Bearing on Theology and the History of Religion.* The Kerr Lectures Delivered in Trinity College, Glasgow, 1933-36. Edinburgh: T. and T. Clark, 1954.

Richter, Wolfgang. *Recht und Ethos: Versuch einer Ortung des weisheitlichen Mahnspruches.* Studien zum Alten und Neuen Testament, vol. 15. München: Kösel-Verlag, 1966.

Ringgren, Helmer. *Israelite Religion.* Translated by David E. Green. Philadelphia: Fortress Press, 1966.

———. *Religions of the Ancient Near East.* Translated by John Sturdy. Philadelphia: Westminster Press, 1973.

———. *Word and Wisdom: Studies in the Hypostatization of Divine Qualities and Functions in the Ancient Near East.* Lund: Hakan Ohlssons Boktryckeri, 1947.

O. O. Ringgren, Helmer, and Zimmerli, Walther. *Sprüche, Prediger.* Das Alte Testament Deutsch, vol. 16, no. 1. Göttingen: Vandenhoeck and Ruprecht, 1962.

Robinson, H. Wheeler. *Inspiration and Revelation in the Old Testament.* 1946. Reprint. Oxford: Clarendon Press, 1962.

Roeder, Günther, ed. and trans. *Die ägyptische Religion in Text und Bildern,* vol. 4, *Der Ausklang der ägyptischen Religion mit Reformation, Zauberei und Jenseitsglauben.* Die Bibliothek der Alten Welt, Reihe der Alte Orient. Zürich: Artemis Verlag, 1961.

————, ed. and trans. *Altägyptischen Erzählungen und Märchen.* Jena: Eugen Diederichs, 1927.

Roth, W. M. W. *Numerical Sayings in the Old Testament: A Form-Critical Study.* Supplements to Vetus Testamentum, vol. 13. Leiden: É. J. Brill, 1965.

Rowley, H. H. *The Relevance of Apocalyptic: A Study of Jewish and Christian Apocalypses from Daniel to the Revelation.* London: Lutterworth Press, 1944.

Russel, D. S. *The Method and Message of Jewish Apocalyptic 200 BC-AD 100.* The Old Testament Library. Philadelphia: Westminster Press, 1964.

Rylaarsdam, J. Coert. *The Proverbs, Ecclesiastes, The Song of Solomon.* The Layman's Bible Commentary, vol. 10. Richmond, Va.: John Knox Press, 1964.

————. *Revelation In Jewish Wisdom Literature.* Chicago: University of Chicago Press, 1946.

Schaeffer, Claude F.-A., ed. *Ugaritica III: Sceaux et cylindres hittites, épée gravée du cartouche de Mineptah, tablettes chypro-minoennes et autres découvertes nouvelles de Ras Shamra.* Mission de Ras Shamra, vol. 8. Paris: Librairie orientaliste Paul Geuthner, 1956.

Scharff, Alexander. *Aegyptische Sonnenlieder.* Berlin: Karl Curtius, 1922.

Schechter, S. and Taylor, C., eds. *The Wisdom of Ben Sira: Portions of the Book of Ecclesiasticus from Hebrew Manuscripts in the Cairo Geniza.* Cambridge: At the University Press, 1899.

Schmid, Hans Heinrich. *Wesen und Geschichte der Weisheit: Eine Untersuchung zur altorientalischen und israelitischen Weisheitsliteratur.* Beihefte zur Zeitschrift für die altestamentliche Wissenschaft, no. 101. Berlin: Alfred Töpelmann, 1966.

Schneider, Heinrich. *Die Heilige Schrift für das Leben erklärt,* vol. 7, pt. 1, *Die Sprüche Salomos, Das Buch des Predigers, Das Hoheleid.* Herders Bibelkommentar. Freiburg: Herder, 1962.

Schollmeyer, P. Anastasius. *Sumerisch-babylonische Hymnen und Gebete an Samas.* Studien zur Geschichte und Kultur des Altertums, vol. 1. Paderborn: Ferdinand Schöningh, 1912.

Schott, Siegfried. *Altägyptische Liebeslieder mit Märchen und Liebesgeschichten.* Die Bibliothek der Alten Welt, Reihe der Alte Orient. Zürich: Artemis-Verlag, 1950.

Scott, Melville. *Textual Discoveries in Proverbs, Psalms, and Isaiah.* London: Society for Promoting Christian Knowledge, 1927.

Scott, R. B. Y. *Proverbs, Ecclesiastes.* The Anchor Bible, vol. 18. New York: Doubleday and Co., 1965.

―――. *The Way of Wisdom in the Old Testament.* New York: Macmillan Co., 1971.

Sellin, Ernst. *Geschichte des israelitisch-jüdischen Volkes.* 2 vols. Leipzig: Quelle und Meyer, 1924-32.

Sellin, Ernst, and Fohrer, Georg. *Introduction to the Old Testament.* Translated by David E. Green. Nashville, Tenn.: Abingdon Press, 1968.

Sethe, Kurt. *Von Zahlen und Zahlworten bei den alten Ägyptern und was für andere Völker und Sprachen daraus zu lernen ist: Ein Beitrag zur Geschichte von Rechenkunst und Sprache.* Schriften der wissenschaftlichen Gesellschaft Strassburg, vol. 25. Strassburg: Karl J. Trübner, 1916.

Seux, M.-J. *Epithètes royales akkadiennes et sumériennes.* Paris; Letouzey et Ané, 1967.

Skladny, Udo. *Die ältesten Spruchsammlungen in Israel.* Göttingen: Vandenhoeck and Ruprecht, 1962.

Soden, Wolfram von. *Akkadisches Handwörterbuch unter Benutzung des lexikalischen Nachlasses von BRUNO MEISSNER (1868-1947).* 2 vols. Wiesbaden: Otto Harrassowitz, 1965-.

———. *Grundriss der akkadischen Grammatik.* Analecta Orientalia, no. 33. Rome: Pontificium Institutum Biblicum, 1952.

Stadelmann, Rainer. *Syrisch-palästinenische Gottheiten in Ägypten.* Probleme der Ägyptologie, vol. 5. Leiden: E. J. Brill, 1967.

Stummer, F. *Der kritische Wert der altaramäischen Aḥiḳartexte aus Elephantine.* Alttestamentliche Abhandlungen, vol. 5, no. 5. Münster: Druck der Aschendorffschen Buchdruckerie, 1914.

Toy, Crawford H. *A Critical and Exegetical Commentary on the Book of Proverbs.* The International Critical Commentary on the Holy Scriptures of the Old and New Testaments. Edinburgh: T. and T. Clark, 1899.

Voegelin, Eric. *Israel and Revelation.* Order and History, vol. 1. Baton Rouge, Louisiana: Louisiana State University Press, 1958.

Volten, Aksel. *Studien zum Weisheitsbuch des Anii.* Det Kgl. Danske Videnskabernes Selskab. Historisk-filologiske Meddelelser, vol. 23, no. 3. Copenhagen: Levin and Munksgaard (Ejnar Munksgaard), 1937.

———. *Zwei altägyptischen politische Schriften: Die Lehre für König Merikarê (Pap. Carlsberg VI) und die Lehre des Königs Amenemhet.* Analecta Aegyptiaca, vol. 4. Copenhagen: Einar Munksgaard, 1945.

Wainwright, G. A. *The Sky-Religion in Egypt: Its Antiquity and Effects.* Cambridge: At the University Press, 1938.

Weiser, Artur. *The Old Testament: Its Formation and Development.* Translated by Dorothea M. Barton. New York: Association Press, 1961.

———. *The Psalms: A Commentary.* Translated by Herbert Hartwell. The Old Testament Library. Philadelphia: Westminster Press, 1962.

Whybray, R. N. *The Intellectual Tradition in the Old Testament.* Beiheft zur Zeitschrift für die alttestamentliche Wissenschaft, no. 135. Berlin: Walter de Gruyter, 1974.

——. *The Succession Narrative: A Study of II Samuel 9-20, I Kings 1 and 2.* Studies in Biblical Theology, 2d ser., no. 9. Naperville, Ill.: A R. Allenson, 1968.

Widengren, Geo. *Religionsphänomenologie.* Translated by Rosmarie Elgnowski. Berlin: Walter de Gruyter and Co., 1969.

——. *Sakrales Königtum im Alten Testament und im Judentum.* Stuttgart: W. Kohlhammer, 1955.

Winckler, Hugo. *The Tell-el-Amarna Letters.* Translated by John M. P. Metcalf. New York: Lemcke and Buechner, 1896.

Worrell, William H., ed. *The Proverbs of Solomon in Sahidic Coptic according to the Chicago Manuscript.* The University of Chicago Oriental Institute Publications, vol. 12. Chicago: University of Chicago Press, 1931.

Wright, G. Ernest. *Biblical Archaeology.* 2d ed., rev. Philadelphia: Westminster Press, 1962.

——. *God Who Acts: Biblical Theology as Recital.* Studies in Biblical Theology, no. 8. London: SCM Press, 1952.

——. *The Old Testament against Its Environment.* Studies in Biblical Theology, no. 2. Longon: SCM Press, 1950.

Wright, G. Ernest, and Fuller, Reginald H. *The Book of the Acts of God: Christian Scholarship Interprets the Bible.* Garden City, N. Y.: Doubleday and Co., 1957.

Würthwein, Ernest. *Die Weisheit Ägyptens und das Alte Testament.* Schriften der Philipps-Universität, vol. 6. Marburg: N. G. Elwert Verlag, 1960.

Young, Edward J. *An Introduction to the Old Testament.* London: Tyndale Press, 1949.

Žába, Zbyněk. *Les Maximes de Ptahhotep.* Prague: L'Académie tchécoslovaque des sciences, 1956.

Articles and Periodicals

Ahlström, G. W., "Der Prophet Nathan und der Tempelbau." *Vetus Testamentum: Quarterly Published by the International Organization of Old Testament Scholars* 11 (1961): 113-27.

———. "Solomon, The Chosen One." *History of Religions: An International Journal for Comparative Historical Studies* 8 (1968): 93-110.

Albright, William Foxwell. "Akkadian Letters." In *Ancient Near Eastern Texts Relating to the Old Testament,* edited by James B. Pritchard. 2d ed., rev. Princeton, N. J.: Princeton University Press, 1955.

———. "The Egyptian Correspondence of Abimilki, Prince of Tyre." *Journal of Egyptian Archaeology* 23 (1937): 190-203.

———. "Notes on Egypto-Semitic Etymology," and "Notes on Egypto-Semitic Etymology. II." *American Journal of Semitic Languages and Literatures* 34 (1917-18): 81-98, 215-55.

———. "Notes on Egypto-Semitic Etymology, III." *Journal of the American Oriental Society* 47 (1927): 198-237.

———. "A Set of Egyptian Playing Pieces and Dice from Palestine." *Mizraim: Journal of Papyrology, Egyptology, History of Ancient Laws, and Their Relations to the Civilizations of Bible Lands* 1 (1933): 130-34.

———. "Some Canaanite-Phoenician Sources of Hebrew Wisdom." In *Wisdom in Israel land in the Ancient Near East: Presented to Professor Harold Henry Rowley.* Edited by M. Noth and D. Winton Thomas. Supplements to Vetus Testamentum, vol. 3. Leiden: E. J. Brill, 1955.

Alt, Albrecht. "Hic Murus aheneus esto." *Zeitschrift der Deutschen Morgenländischen Gesellschaft* 86 (1933): 33-48.

———. "Die Weisheit Salomos." *Theologische Literaturzeitung: Monatsschrift für das gesamte Gebiet der Theologie und Religionswissenschaft* 76 (1951): 139-44.

———. "Zur literarischen Analyse der Weisheit des Amenemope." In *Wisdom in Israel and in the Ancient Near East: Presented to Professor Harold Henry Rowley,* edited by

M. Noth and D. Winton Thomas. Supplements to Vetus Testamentum, vol. 3. Leiden: E. J. Brill, 1955.

Baumgartner, W. "The Wisdom Literature." In *The Old Testament and Modern Study: A Generation of Discovery and Research, Essays by Members of the Society for Old Testament Study,* edited by H. H. Rowley. 1951. Reprint. London: Oxford University Press, 1961.

Biggs, Robert D. "Akkadian Didactic and Wisdom Literature." In *The Ancient Near East: Supplementary Texts and Pictures Relating to the Old Testament, Consisting of Supplementary Materials for* The Ancient Near East in Pictures *and* Ancient Near Eastern Texts, edited by James B. Pritchard. Princeton, N. J.: Princeton University Press, 1969.

Bin-Nun, Shoshana R. "Formulas from Royal Records of Israel and of Judah." *Vetus Testamentum: Quarterly Published by the International Organization of Old Testament Scholars* 18 (1968): 414-32.

Boer, P. A. H. de. "The Counsellor." In *Wisdom in Israel and in the Ancient Near East,* edited by M. Noth and D. Winton Thomas. Supplements to Vetus Testamentum, vol. 3. Leiden: E. J. Brill, 1955.

Böhl, Franz M. Th. "Die Sprache der Amarnabriefe mit besonderer Berucksichtigung der Kanaanismen," *Leipziger semistische Studien* 5 (pt. 2) (1909): 1-96.

Brunet, Achille. "Proverbes (XXII, 17-XXIV, 22) et la possibilité d'une source égyptienne." *Sciences ecclésiastiques: Revue théologique et philosophique* 1 (1948): 19-40.

Brunner, Hellmut. "Der freie Wille Gottes in der ägyptischen Weisheit." In *Les sagesses du Proche-Orient ancien.* Colloque de Strasbourg, 17-19 mai 1962. Travaux du Centre d'études spécialisé d'historie des religions de Strasbourg. Paris: Presses universitaires de France, 1963.

———. "Die religiöse Wertung der Armut im Alten Aegypten." *Saeculum: Jahrbuch für Universalgeschichte* 12 (1961): 319-44.

———. "Die 'Weisen', ihre 'Lehren' und 'Prophezeiungen' in

altägyptischer Sicht." *Zeitschrift für ägyptische Sprache und Altertumskunde* 93 (1966): 29-35.

——. "Die Weisheitsliteratur." *In Handbuch der Orientalistik,* edited by Bertold Spuler, vol. 1 (pt. 2), *Ägyptologie.* Leiden: E. J. Brill, 1952.

Bryce, Glendon E. "Another Wisdom-'Book' in Proverbs." *Journal of Biblical Literature* 91 (1972): 145-57.

——. "'Better'-Proverbs: An Historical and Structural Study." In *The Society of Biblical Literature One Hundred Eighth Annual Meeting: Book of Seminar Papers,* edited by Lane C. McGaughy. 2 vols. Society of Biblical Literature 1972 Proceedings. Missoula, Mont.: Society of Biblical Literature, 1972.

——. "Omen-Wisdom in Ancient Israel." *Journal of Biblical Literature* 94, no. 1 (March 1975): 19-37.

——. Review of *Wisdom in Israel,* by Gerhard von Rad. *Theology Today* 30 (1974): 436-42.

Buck, A. de. "The Instruction of Amenemmes." *Mélanges Maspero,* vol. 1. Mémoires de l'Institut français d'archéologie orientale, no. 66. Cairo:L'Institut français d'archéologie orientale, 1935-38.

Cadbury, Henry J. "Egyptian Influence in the Book of Proverbs." *Journal of Religion* 9 (1929): 99-108.

Couroyer, B. "Mettre sa main sur sa bouche en Egypte et dans la Bible." *Revue Biblique* 67 (1960): 197-209.

——. "L'origine égyptienne de la sagesse d'Amenemopé." *Revue Biblique* 70 (1963): 208-24.

Cross, Frank Moore. "The Development of Jewish Scripts." In *The Bible and the Ancient Near East: Essays in Honor of William Foxwell Albright,* edited by G. Ernest Wright. Garden City, N. Y.: Doubleday and Co., 1961.

Dahood, Mitchell. "The Phoenician Contribution to Biblical Wisdom Literature." In *The Role of the Phoenicians in the Interaction of Mediterranean Civilizations,* edited by William A. Ward. Papers Presented to the Archaeological Symposium at the American University of Beirut, March 1967. Beirut: American University of Beirut, 1968.

Döller, Joh. "Das Buch der Sprüche und die Lehre des Amen-em-ope." *Theologisch-praktische Quartalschrift* 79 (1926): 305-14.

Drioton, Etienne. "Une colonie israélite en Moyenne Egypte à la fin de VIIe siècle av. J.-C." In *A la rencontre de Dieu: Mémorial Albert Gelin.* Bibliothèque de la faculté catholique de theologie de Lyon, vol. 8. Le Puy: Xavier Mappus, 1961.

———. "Le Livre des Proverbes et la sagesse d'Aménémopé." In *Sacra Pagina: Miscellenea Biblica Congressus internationalis Catholici de Re Biblica,* edited by J. Coppens, A. Descamps, E. Massaux, vol. 1. Bibliotheca ephemeridum theologicarum Lovaniensium, vol. 12-13. Gembloux: J. Duculot, 1959.

———. "Un livre hébreu sur couverture égyptienne." *La Table ronde* (October 1960), pp. 81-91.

———. "Sur la sagesse d'Aménémopé." In *Mélanges bibliques rédigés en l'honneur de André Robert.* Travaux de l'Institut catholique de Paris, no. 4. Paris: Bloud and Gay, 1957.

Dunsmore, Marion Hiller. "An Egyptian Contribution to the Book of Proverbs." *Journal of Religion* 5 (1925): 300-308.

Dürr, Lor. "Hebr. נפש =akk. napištu=Gurgel. Kehle." *Zeitschrift für die alttestamentliche Wissenschaft und die Kunde des nachbiblischen Judentums* 43 (1925):262-69.

Erman, Adolf. "Eine ägyptische Quelle der 'Sprüche Salomos.'" *Sitzungsberichte der Preussischen Akademie der Wissenschaften zu Berlin: Phil.-hist. Klasse* 15 (1924):86-93.

———. "Das Weisheitsbuch des Amen-em-ope." *Orientalistische Literaturzeitung: Monatsschrift für die Wissenschaft vom ganzen Orient und seinen Beziehungen zu den angrenzenden Kulturkreisen* 27 (1924): 241-52.

Fichtner, J. "Zum Problem Glaube und Geschichte in der israelitisch-jüdischen Weisheitsliteratur." *Theologische Literaturzeitung: Monatsschrift für das gesamte Gebiet der Theologie und Religionswissenschaft* 76 (1951): 145-50.

Fox, Michael V. "Aspects of the Religion of the Book of Proverbs." *Hebrew Union College Annual* 39 (1968): 55-69.

Fritsch, Charles T. "The Book of Proverbs." In *The Interpreter's Bible,* edited by George Arthur Buttrick, vol. 4. New York Abingdon-Cokesbury Press, 1952.

Gardiner, Alan H. "New Literary Works from Ancient Egypt." *Journal of Egyptian Archaeology* 1 (1914): 20-36.

———. "Writing and Literature." In *The Legacy of Egypt,* edited by S. R. K. Glanville. Oxford: Clarendon Press, 1942.

Gevirtz, Stanley. "On Canaanite Rhetoric: The Evidence of the Amarna Letters from Tyre." *Orientalia* n. s. 42 (1973): 162-77.

Ginsberg, H. L. "The Legend of King Keret: A Canaanite Epic of the Bronze Age." *Bulletin of the American Schools of Oriental Research, Supplementary Studies* 2-3 (1946): 4-50.

Gordis, Robert. "The Social Background of Wisdom Literature." *Hebrew Union College Annual* 18 (1943-44): 77-118.

Gordon, Alex R., trans. "The Book of Proverbs." In *The Complete Bible: An American Translation,* edited by J. M. Powis Smith and Edgar J. Goodspeed. Chicago: University of Chicago Press, 1923.

Gordon, Cyrus H. "Azitawadd's Phoenician Inscription." *Journal of Near Eastern Studies: Continuing the American Journal of Semitic Languages and Literatures* 8 (1949): 108-15.

Gray, John. "Canaanite Kingship in Theory and Practice." *Vetus Testamentum: Quarterly Published by the International Organization of Old Testament Scholars* 2 (1952): 193-200.

———. "The Kingship of God in the Prophets and Psalms." *Vetus Testamentum: Quarterly Published by the International Organization of Old Testament Scholars* 11 (1961): 1-29.

Gressmann, Hugo. "Ägypten im Alten Testament." *Vossische Zeitung,* 22 June 1924, pp. 2, 11.

———. "Hadad und Baal nach den Amarnabriefen und nach ägyptischen Texten." In *Abhandlungen zur semitischen Religionskunde und Sprachwissenschaft: Wolf Wilhelm Grafen von*

Baudissin zum 26. September 1917. Beihefte zur Zeitschrift für die alttestamentliche Wissenschaft, no. 33. Giessen: Alfred Töpelmann, 1918.

————. "Die neugefundene Lehre des Amen-em-ope und die vorexilische Spruchdichtung Israels." *Zeitschrift für die alttestamentliche Wissenschaft und die Kunde des nachbiblischen Judentums* 42 (1924): 272-96.

Griffith, F. Ll. "Bibliography 1922-23: Ancient Egypt." *Journal of Egyptian Archaeology* 9 (1923): 201-25.

————. "The MILLINGEN Papyrus (teaching of Amenemhat): With Note on the Compounds Formed with Substantivised *n*." *Zeitschrift für ägyptische Sprache und Altertumskunde: Mit Unterstützung der Deutschen Morgenländischen Gesellschaft* 34 (1896): 35-51.

————. "The Teaching of Amenophis the Son of Kanakht. Papyrus B. M. 10474." *Journal of Egyptian Archaeology* 12 (1926): 191-231.

Grimme, Hubert. "Wieteres zu Amen-em-ope und Proverbien." *Orientalistische Literaturzeitung: Monatsschrift für die Wissenschaft vom ganzen Orient und seinen Beziehungen zu den angrenzenden Kulturkreisen* 28 (1925): 57-62.

Gunn, Battiscombe. "Some Middle-Egyptian Proverbs." *Journal of Egyptian Archaeology* 12 (1928): 282-84.

Hayes, William C. "A Much-Copied Letter of the Early Middle Kingdom." *Journal of Near Eastern Studies: Continuing the American Journal of Semitic Languages and Literatures* 7 (1948): 1-10.

Hermann, Alfred. "Die ägyptische Königsnovelle." *Leipziger ägyptologische Studien* 10 (1938): 5-61.

Hermann, Siegfried. "Die Königsnovelle in Ägypten und in Israel." *Wissenschaftliche Zeitschrift der Karl-Marx-Universität: Gesellschafts- und sprachwissenschaftliche Reihe* 3 (1953-54): 51-62.

Herzog, D. "Die Sprüche des Amen-em-ope und Proverbien Kapp. 22,17-24,35." *Zeitschrift fur Semitistik und verwandte Gebiete* 7 (1929): 124-60.

Heyes, H. J. "Das Buch der Sprüche und das altägyptische Weisheitsbuch des Amen-em-ope." *Bonner Zeitschrift für Theologie und Seelsorge* 3 (1926): 1-11.

Hornung, Erik. "Zur geschichtlichen Rolle des Königs in der 18. Dynastie." *Mitteilungen des Deutschen Archäologischen Instituts, Abteilung Kairo* 15 (1957): 120-33.

Hubbard, D. A. "The Wisdom Movement and Israel's Covenant Faith." *Tyndale Bulletin* 17 (1966): 3-33.

Johnson, A. R. "Hebrew Conceptions of Kingship." In *Myth, Ritual and Kingship: Essays on the Theory and Practice of Kingship in the Ancient Near East and in Israel,* edited by S. H. Hooke. Oxford: Clarendon Press, 1958.

Keimer, Ludwig. "The Wisdom of Amen-em-ope and the Proverbs of Solomon." *American Journal of Semitic Languages and Literatures* 43 (1926-27): 8-21.

Köcher, Franz, and Oppenheim, A. L. "The Old-Babylonian Omen Text VAT 7525." *Archiv für Orientforschung: Internationale Zeitschrift für die Wissenschaft vom Vorderen Orient* 18 (1957-58): 62-77.

Kopf L. "Arabische Etymologien und Parallelen zum Bibelwörterbuch." *Vetus Testamentum: Quarterly Published by the International Organization of Old Testament Scholars* 8 (1958): 161-215.

Kraus, Fritz Rudolph. "Babylonische Omina mit Ausdeutung der Begleiterungscheinungen des Sprechens." *Archiv für Orientforschung: Internationale Zeitschrift für die Wissenschaft vom Vorderen Orient* 11 (1936): 219-30.

———. "Ein Sittenkanon in Omenform." *Zeitschrift für Assyriologie und verwandte Gebiete* 43 (1936): 77-113.

Kuentz, Charles. "Deux versions d'un panégyrique royal." In *Studies Presented to F. Ll. Griffith,* edited by S. R. K. Glanville. London: Oxford University Press, 1932.

Lacau, M. Pierre. "Sur le parallélisme dans les textes des pyramides et ailleurs." In *The Pyramid Texts,* edited by Samuel A. B. Mercer, vol. 4, *Excurses.* New York: Longmans, Green and Co., 1952.

Lanczkowski, Günter. "Reden und Schweigen im ägyptischen Verständnis, vornehmlich des Mittleren Reiches." In *Ägyptologische Studien,* edited by O. Firchow. Deutsche Akademie der Wissenschaften zu Berlin, Institut für Orientforschung, vol. 29. Berlin: Akademie-Verlag, 1955.

Landsberger, Benno. "Scribal Concepts of Education." In *City Invincible,* edited by Carl H. Kraeling and Robert M. Adams. A Symposium on Urbanization and Cultural Development in the Ancient Near East, Held at the Oriental Institute of the University of Chicago, December 4-7, 1958. Chicago: University of Chicago Press, 1960.

Leclant, Jean. "Les relations entre l'Egypte et la Phénicie du voyage d'Ounamon à l'expédition d'Alexandre." In *The Role of the Phoenicians in the Interaction of Mediterranean Civilizations,* edited by William A. Ward. Papers Presented to the Archaeological Symposium at the American University of Beirut, March 1967. Beirut: American University of Beirut, 1968.

Linder, Josef. "Das Weisheitsbuch des Amen-em-ope und die 'Sprüche von Weisen' (Prov. 22,17-23,11)." *Zeitschrift für katholische Theologie* 49 (1925): 138-46.

Liver, J. "The Book of the Acts of Solomon." *Biblica* 48 (1967): 75-101.

Löhr, Max. Review of "Eine ägyptische Quelle der Sprüche Salomos," by Adolf Erman. *Orientalistische Literaturzeitung: Monatsschrift für die Wissenschaft vom ganzen Orient und seinen Beziehungen zu den angrenzenden Kulturkreisen* 28 (1925): 72-73.

Malamat, Abraham. "Aspects of the Foreign Policies of David and Solomon." *Journal of Near Eastern Studies: Continuing the American Journal of Semitic Languages and Literatures* 22 (1963): 1-17.

———. "Kingship and Council in Israel and Sumer: A Parallel." *Journal of Near Eastern Studies: Continuing the American Journal of Semitic Languages and Literatures* 22 (1963): 247-53.

Mallon, Alexis. "La 'sagesse' de l'égyptien Amen-em-opé et les 'Proverbes de Salomon'." *Biblica* 8 (1927): 3-30.

Mercer, Samuel A. B. "A New-Found Book of Proverbs." *Anglican Theological Review* 8 (1925-26): 237-44.

Morenz, Siegfried. "Feurige Kohle auf dem Haupt." *Theologische Literaturzeitung: Monatsschrift für das gesamte gebiet der Theologie und Religionswissenschaft* 78 (1953): 187-92.

Mowinckel, Sigmund. "Israelite Historiography." *Annual of the Swedish Theological Institute* 2 (1963): 4-26.

———. "Psalms and Wisdom." In *Wisdom in Israel and in the Ancient Near East: Presented to Professor Harold Henry Rowley,* edited by M. Noth and D. Winton Thomas. Supplements to Vetus Testamentum, vol. 3. Leiden: E. J. Brill: 1955.

Murphy, Roland E. "Assumptions and Problems in Old Testament Wisdom Research." *Catholic Biblical Quarterly* 29 (1967): 407-18 (101-12).

———. "Introduction to Wisdom Literature." In *The Jerome Biblical Commentary,* edited by Raymond E. Brown, Joseph A. Fitzmyer, and Roland E. Murphy. 2 vols. Englewood Cliffs, N. J.: Prentice-Hall, 1968.

Nims, Charles F. "Second Tenses in Wenamūn." *Journal of Egyptian Archaeology* 54 (1968): 161-64.

Noth, Martin. "Die Bewährung von Salomos 'Gottlicher Weisheit.'" In *Wisdom in Israel and in the Ancient Near East: Presented to Professor Harold Henry Rowley,* edited by M. Noth and D. Winton Thomas. Supplements to Vetus Testamentum, vol. 3. Leiden: E. J. Brill, 1955.

———. "Noah, Daniel und Hiob in Ezechiel XIV." *Vetus Testamentum: Quarterly Published by the International Organization of Old Testament Scholars* 1 (1951): 251-60.

Oppenheim, Leo. "Mesopotamian Mythology II." *Orientalia* n. s. 17 (1948): 17-58.

Otto, Eberhard. "Bildung und Ausbildung im alten Agypten." *Zeitschrift fur ägyptische Sprache und Altertumskunde* 81 (1956): 41-48.

————. "Prolegomena zur Frage der Gesetzgebung und Rechtssprechung in Ägypten." *Mitteilungen des Deutschen Archäologischen Instituts, Abteilung Kairo* 14 (1956): 150-59.

————. "Weltanschauliche und politische Tendenzschriften." In *Handbuch der Orientalistik,* edited by Bertold Spuler, vol. 1, pt. 2, *Ägyptologie.* Leiden: E. J. Brill, 1952.

Peterson, Bengt Julius. "A New Fragment of *The Wisdom of Amenemope.*" *Journal of Egyptian Archaeology* 52 (1966): 120-28.

Plumley, J. M. "The Teaching of Amenemope." In *Documents from Old Testament Times,* edited by D. Winton Thomas. London: Thomas Nelson and Sons, 1958.

Porten, Bezalel. "The Structure and Theme of the Solomon Narrative (1Kings 3-11)." *Hebrew Union College Annual* 38 (1967): 93-128.

Porteous, Norman W. "Royal Wisdom." In *Wisdom in Israel and in the Ancient Near East,* edited by M. Noth and D. Winton Thomas. Supplements to Vetus Testamentum, vol. 3. Leiden: E. J. Brill, 1955.

Posener, Georges. "Aménémopé 21,13 et *bj3j t* au sens d' ≤oracle≥." *Zeitschrift fur ägyptische Sprache und Altertumskunde* 90 (1963): 98-102.

————. "Une nouvelle tablette d'Aménémopé." *Revue d'Egyptologie* 25 (1973):251-52.

————. "Ostraca inédits du Musée de Turin (Recherches littéraires III)." *Revue d'Egyptologie* 8 (1951): 171-89.

————. "Quatre tablettes scolaires de basse époque (Aménémopé et Hardjédef)." *Revue d'Egyptologie* 18 (1966): 45-65.

————. Review of *Recherches sur les sources égyptiennes de la littérature sapientiale d'Israël,* by Paul Humbert. *Revue des études juives: Publication trimestrielle de la Société des études juives* 88 (1929): 97-101.

————. "Les richesses inconnues de la littérature égyptienne (Recherches littéraires I)." *Revue d'Egyptologie* 6 (1951): 27-48.

Rad, Gerhard von. "Die ältere Weisheit Israels." *Kerygma und Dogma: Zeitschrift für theologische Forschung und kirchliche Lehre* 2 (1956): 54-72.

Rainey, A. F. "The Soldier-Scribe in 'Papyrus Anastasi I.' " *Journal of Near Eastern Studies: Continuing the American Journal of Semitic Languages and Literatures* 26 (1967): 58-60.

Ramoroson, Léonard. " 'Charbons ardents': 'sur la tête' ou 'pour le feu'?" *Biblica* 51 (1970): 230-34.

Ranke, Hermann, "Ägyptische Texte." In *Altorientalische Texte zum Alten Testament,* edited by Hugo Gressmann. 2d ed., rev. Berlin: Walter de Gruyter and Co., 1926.

Rylaarsdam, J. Coert. "The Proverbs." In *Peake's Commentary on the Bible,* edited by Matthew Black and H. H. Rowley. London: Thomas Nelson and Sons, 1962.

———. "Jewish-Christian Relationship: The Two Covenants and the Dilemmas of Christology." *Journal of Ecumenical Studies* 9 (1972): 249-70.

Scott, R. B. Y. "Solomon and the Beginnings of Wisdom in Israel." In *Wisdom in Israel and in the Ancient Near East: Presented to Professor Harold Henry Rowley,* edited by M. Noth and D. Winton Thomas. Supplements to Vetus Testamentum, vol. 3. Leiden: E. J. Brill, 1955.

Seebass, Horst. "Zur Königserhebung Jerobeams I." *Vetus Testamentum: Quarterly Published by the International Organization for the Study of the Old Testament* 17 (1967): 325-33.

———. "Die Verwerfung Jerobeams I. und Salomos durch die Prophetie des Ahia von Silo." *Die Welt des Orients: Wissenschaftliche Beitrage zur Kunde des Morgenlandes* 4 (1967-68): 163-82.

Sellin, Ernst. "Die neugefundene. 'Lehre des Amen-em-ope' in ihrer Bedeutung für jüdische Literatur- und Religionsgeschichte." *Deutsche Literaturzeitung für Kritik der internationalen Wissenschaft* 45 (1924): 1873-84.

———. Review of "Eine ägyptische Quelle der 'Sprüche Salomos,' " by Adolf Erman. *Deutsche Literaturzeitung für*

Kritik der internationalen Wissenschaft 45 (1924): 1325-29.

Selms, A. van. "The Origin of the Title 'The King's Friend.'" *Journal of Near Eastern Studies: Continuing the American Journal of Semitic Languages and Literatures* 16 (1957): 118-23.

Sethe, Kurt. "'Der Mensch denkt, der Gott lenkt' bei den alten Ägyptern." In *Nachrichten von der Gesellschaft der Wissenschaften zu Göttingen aus dem Jahre 1925: Philologisch-historische Klasse.* Berlin: Weidmannsche Buchhandlung, 1926.

Simpson, D. C. "The Hebrew Book of Proverbs and the Teaching of Amenophis." *Journal of Egyptian Archaeology* 12 (1926): 232-39.

Simpson, William Kelly, trans. "The Instruction of Amenemope." In *The Literature of Ancient Egypt: An Anthology of Stories, Instructions, and Poetry,* edited by William Kelly Simpson. New Haven, Conn.: Yale University Press, 1972.

Snaith, Norman H. "First and Second Books of Kings." In *The Interpreter's Bible,* edited by George Arthur Buttrick, vol. 3. New York: Abingdon-Cokesbury Press, 1952.

Speiser, E. A. "The Epic of Gilgamesh." In *Ancient Near Eastern Texts Relating to the Old Testament,* edited by James B. Pritchard. 2d ed., rev. Princeton, N. J.: Princeton University Press, 1955.

Spiegelberg, Wilhelm. Review of *Facsimiles of Egyptian Hieratic Papyri in the British Museum,* by E. A. Wallis Budge. *Orientalistische Literaturzeitung: Monatsschrift für die Wissenschaft vom ganzen Orient und seinen Beziehungen zu den angrenzenden Kulturkreisen* 27 (1924): 182-91.

Story, Cullen I. K. "The Book of Proverbs and Northwest Semitic Literature." *Journal of Biblical Literature* 64 (1945): 319-37.

Theis, Johannes. "Die Lehre des Amen-em-ope, eine ägyptische Quelle des biblischen Spruchbuches." *Pastor Bonus* 36 (1925): 256-69.

Vergote, Joseph. "La notion de Dieu dans les livres de sagesse égyptiens." In *Les sagesses du Proche-Orient ancien.* Colloque de Strasbourg, 17-19 mai 1962. Travaux de Centre d'études spécialisé d'histoire des religions de Strasbourg. Paris: Presses universitaires de France, 1963.

Ward, William A. "Comparative Studies in Egyptian and Ugaritic." *Journal of Near Eastern Studies: Continuing the American Journal of Semitic Languages and Literatures* 20 (1961): 31-40.

Wente, Edward F., Jr., trans. "The Contendings of Horus and Seth," "The Report of Wenamon." In *The Literature of Ancient Egypt: An Anthology of Stories, Instructions, and Poetry,* edited by William Kelly Simpson. New Haven, Conn.: Yale University Press, 1972.

Widengren, Geo. "King and Covenant." *Journal of Semitic Studies* 2 (1957): 1-32.

Wiesman, H. "Eine ägyptische Quelle der Sprüche Salomos?" *Biblische Zeitschrift* 17 (1926): 43-50.

Williams, Ronald J. "The Alleged Semitic Original of the 'Wisdom of Amenemope.'" *Journal of Egyptian Archaeology* 47 (1961): 100-106.

―――. "Literature as a Medium of Political Propaganda in Ancient Egypt." In *The Seed of Wisdom: Essays in Honour of T. J. Meek,* edited by W. S. McCullough. Toronto: University of Toronto Press, 1964.

―――. "Some Egyptianisms in the Old Testament." In *Studies in Honor of John A. Wilson.* Studies in Oriental Civilization, no. 35. Chicago: University of Chicago Press, 1969.

Wilson, John A. "Egyptian Historican Texts," "Egyptian Hymns and Prayers," "Egyptian Myths, Tales, and Mortuary Texts," "Egyptian Observations," and "Proverbs and Precepts." In *Ancient Near Eastern Texts Relating to the Old Testament,* edited by James B. Pritchard. 2d ed., rev. Princeton, N. J.: Princeton University Press, 1955.

Yaron, Kalman. "The Dirge over the King of Tyre." *Annual of the Swedish Theological Institute* 3 (1964): 28-57.

284   A LEGACY OF WISDOM

Zimmerli, Walther. "Ort und Grenze der Weisheit im Rahmen der alttestamentliche Theologie." In *Les sagesses du Proche-Orient ancien.* Colloque de Strasbourg, 17-19 mai 1962. Travaux du Centre d'études spécialisé d'histoire des religions de Strasbourg. Paris: Presses universitaires de France, 1963.

―――. "Zur Struktur der alttestamentlichen Weisheit." *Zeitschrift für die alttestamentliche Wissenschaft und die Kunde des nachbiblischen Judentums* 51 (1933): 177-204.

Zimmermann, Friedrich. "Altägyptische Spruchweisheit in der Bibel." *Theologie und Glaube: Zeitschrift für den katholischen Klerus* 17 (1925): 204-17.

Unpublished Material

McGlinchey, James M. "The Teaching of Amen-em-ope and the Book of Proverbs." D.S.T. Dissertation. The Catholic University of America, Washington, D. C., 1938.

Proulx, Pierre. "Ugaritic Verse Structure and the Poetic Syntax of Proverbs." Ph.D. Dissertation. Johns Hopkins University, Baltimore, Md., 1956.

Ruffle, John. "The Teaching of Amenemope." Master's Thesis. University of Liverpool, Liverpool, England, 1965.

Sassaman, William Henry. "The Influence of the Wisdom of Amenemopet on the Book of Proverbs." B.D. Dissertation. University of Chicago, 1925.

The thirtieth chapter and colophon of Amenemope (27:1-28:1), sixth century B.C. *Courtesy of the British Museum* (B. M. Papyrus 10474).
1. The Turin Writing-Tablet of Amenemope (24:1-25:9), seventh or sixth century B.C. *Courtesy of Georges Posener* (Cat. 6237).
2. The Stockholm Fragment of Amenemope (10:18-14:5), eleventh to the eighth centuries B.C. *Courtesy of Bengt Julius Peterson* (MM 18416).

3. The Hieroglyphic Transcription of Amenemope (9:1-20) by E. A. Wallis Budge. *Courtesy of the British Museum.*

4. Advice to Scribes in chapters fourteen to seventeen of Amenemope (17:1-18:23), sixth century B.C. *Courtesy of the British Museum* (B. M. 10474).

General Index

Abel, 195

Abimilki, King of Tyre, 59

Abimilki, letter of: adaptation in, 59-65, 75; Akkadian text of, 60; Canaanitized Akkadian of, 59, 61; Canaanite glosses in, 221, n9; Canaanite orthography of, 220, n6; Egyptian *Vorlage* of, 60-61, 221, n7; Egyptian motifs in, 63-64, 59, 61-62; Egyptianisms in 59, 62, 221, n10. *See also* Adaptation, Egyptian, in the Amarna Letters

Absalom, 193

Acrostic, 86, 124-25, 129

"Adam," 200

Adaptation, Egyptian; date of, 42; of Hebrew materials, 42-53; rejection of theory of, 53-56 (*see also* Rejection of Egyptian dependence, reasons for); in the Amarna Letters, 58-65

Adaptation, Israelite; creating new proverbs, 75; definition of 57-59; dependence on number "thirty," 81-85; final stage, in process of, 130; in Israelite schools, 87; of Egyptian literary forms, 75-78; of Egyptian literary genres, 78-87; of Jewish wisdom book, 52; of lost Hebrew source, 19; rejection of, 33-37. *See also* Adaptive Stage; Dependence, criteria for; Dependence, Egyptian; Dependence Israelite; Parallels between

tions; Theological bases of Israelite wisdom, in covenant faith

Creation, 158-59. *See also* Glory

Cult: as place of judgment, 194-95; attitude of wise men toward, 245, n1 (*see also* Secularism of Israelite wisdom); centers of, in Israel, 179, 194-95; royal, development of, 179, 204; divination in, 195-96; high places of, 179; Jebusite, 194; king as leader of, 194, 201-2; of Baal, 194; oracles of, 195 (*see also* Oracle); personnel of, 150; prophets in, 194 (*see also* Prophets, criticism of cult by); relation of wise men to, 195, 197-99; rites of, controlled by Yahweh, 188-89; rites of, ecstasy in, 195; revelation in, 194-95(*see also* Revelation); royal, 204; sacrifices in, 173, 175. *See also* Egyptian wisdom, associated with cult; Revelation; Religion of Egypt; Religion of Israel

Culture: idioms in, 99; Egyptian, 50-51 (see also Amenemope, the teaching of, Egyptian background of); Israelite, 152, 166, 202-5. *See also* Royal Court

Dahood, Mitchell, 110, 231, n28

Daniel, the Book of, 192

Dan'el, 161, 192-94. *See also* Hierophants; Ugaritic wisdom

David, 30, 82-83, 193-94, 249, n38. *See also* Kings, ancient Near Eastern, David

Dead, 77. *See also* Weighing of the heart

Death, 47, 77, 93-95, 127

de Boer, P. A. H., 199

Deborah, 195. *See also* Lot

de Buck, A., 243

Deities: Amon Re, 54, 60-63, 201, 221, n12; Baal, 64, 194; El, 192, 199; El Elyon, 199; Elohim, 83; Hadad, 60, 64; Horus, 63; Osiris, 31, 168; Seth, 63-64; Shamash, 120, 221, n10; Sia, 148, 167; Yahweh, 51, 73, 77, 83, 124-26, 129, 178, 184, 188, 194, 199-200, 205, 207. See also *Deus Absconditus*; God; Hiddenness of God

Democratization of wisdom, 32.*See also* Reformation of Israelite wisdom

Demotic wisdom, 74, 94-95

Dependence, criteria for: agreement of persons, 62; ancestry of phrases, 49; approximate correspondence, 89; association of content and form, 74-75; borrowing of words, 62; by intermediary source, 123, 127; clusters of parallels, 65-66, 74-75, 97, 128, 132, 156; cognate usage, 110-11; coincidences, 101; conglomeration of materials, 96-97; consecution of parallels, 42; context, 37, 111, currency of idioms, 50, 65-66, 221, n10; difference in idioms, 99; Egyptianisms, 59, 221, n10; environmental differences, 50-51, 54; equivalent ideas, 61-63, 67, 71, 98-99, 103; figurative interpretation, 47; foreign words, 51, 61, 65; form, 66, 75-76 (*see also* Comparative proverb; Literary genres); grammatical usage, 50, 99, 101, 103, 107; *hapax legomenon*, 101; ideological correspondence, 65, 89; imagery, 20, 107, 109-10; key words, 105, 139; literary genres, 75, 123, 133-34; motifs, 61-66; naturalization, 59, 89; order of words, 46, 66, 99-101, 103-4, 110, 128; parallelism, 91, 100, 104, 112, 115; paraphrasing, 75; phraseology, 46, 109; poetic stereotypes, 109; precise correspondence, 103; proximity to parallelisms, 158; Semiticization, 48-49; Semitisms, 42-43, 48, 217, n6, 218, n20, 218, n31; se-

General Index

94-95 (*see also* Egyptian ethics; Poverty; Riches); British Museum Papyrus 10474, 15 (*see also* Budge, E. A. Wallis); change in literary genres of, 171; characterization of, 32, 240, n19; comparative proverb in, 71-72, 75, 92; conception of king in, 136-37, 148, 159, 167-69 (*see also* Egyptian king; Political wisdom of Egypt); conception of God in, 41, 63, 155-58 (*see also* God; Religion of Egypt); contextual interpretation of, 92; cool man in (*see* Cool man, the); creative use of traditions of, 95; democratization of, 240, n 19; Demotic, 74, 94-95; dependence on Semitic sources (*see* Dependence, Egyptian); development of traditions of, 31, 95, 118, 171; distribution of forms in, 79; Egyptian word for, 78, 136, 171, 239, n19; encyclopedic character of, 164; enemy in (*see* Enemy); ethics of, 41, 92 (*see also* Egyptian ethics); etiquette in, 108, 152; first parallels of Amenemope and Proverbs observed, 16; forms of, 78-80, 171 (*see* Comparative proverb; Literary genres); glorification of king in, 136 (*see also* Egyptian king; Political wisdom of Egypt); government in (*see* Government); hiddenness of the god in, 62, 155-58 (*see also* Hiddenness of God); hybrid forms of, 171-72; idiom "coals of fire" in relation to, 130-31; importance of, for Israelite wisdom, 133-36, 138-39, 166, 187, 189, 204; influence of, 31; internationalism of, 29-30, 57 (*see also* Internationalism, Israelite); Kagemni, 108, 150, 171; Kemyt, 63, 137-39, 147; Khety, 150, 170, 239, n19; *Königsnovelle* of, 175; legacy of, in the Old Testament, 210; lists of

parallels to Proverbs, 101, 105; lists of famous scribes of, 239, n19; literary genres of, 136, 171-72; literary genres of, differences between, 171; literary genres of, international, 78, 80-81, 164-65; loyalism in, 137, 148, 167, 171 (*see also* Political wisdom of Egypt); mediated through Canaan, 30, 225, n50; mediated through intermediary form, 19; model schoolbook of, 138; *Naturweisheit* of, 164-65; 'Onchsheshonqy, 94-95; onomastica of, 164-65; ostraca of Amenemope, 54; panegyrics in, 78, 136, 167, 177; Papyrus 10474 of the British Museum, 15 (*see also* Amenemope, The Teaching of); parallels in, between Amenemope and Jeremiah, 122-23; parallels in, between Amenemope and Proverbs (*see* Parallels between Amenemope and Proverbs); parallels in, between Amenemope and Proverbs 25, 130-31; parallels in, between Amenemope and the Psalms, 120-21, 126-28; 234, n16; penetration of, into Israel, 28-31, 40; persons in, (*see* Persons, types of); plagiarization in, 172; political gonre of (*see* Political wisdom of Egypt); politicization of literature in (*see* Politicization of literature, in Egypt); popularity of, 54, 136-37; possessors of (*see* Possessors of wisdom); poverty in (*see* Poor man, the; Poverty); professional ethic of, 32 (*see also* Egyptian ethics); propaganda in, 78, 137, 166, 170 (*see also* Political wisdom of Egypt); Ptahhotep (*see* Ptahhotep, The Instruction of); purpose of, 172, 240, n19; quasi-philosophical discourse in, 155-56; reformulation of, by Israelite piety, 22; reformula-

ration; Masoretic Text; Reformulation of Israelite wisdom

Intellectual tradition, in the Old Testament, 241, n20. *See also* Professional class

Intellectualization, process of, 196, 203, 245, n1. *See also* Secularism of Israelite wisdom

Internationalism, Israelite, 29-30, 57, 98-99, 164-65, 202

Intermediary source. See Adaptation, of lost Hebrew source; Dependence, Israelite, through intermediary source

Irony, 179, 192

Isaiah, 31, 192, 196, 199-200, 248, n27

Israel: as mother, 182; attempt to legitimate, 185; child as symbol of, 181-82; Deuteronomic history of, 176-85; Deuteronomic use of term, 177; division of kingdom in, 181-85; fulfillment of promise to, 178-80; ideal sense of term, 177; legitimacy of kingdom of, 185, rejection of 182; relation of Jerusalem to, 201-2; relations with Assyria, 40; relations with Egypt, 31, 40, 51-52, 179; relations with Judah, 184-86; represents kingdom, 181-82; role of, in tale of harlots, 182; Solomon's relation to, 178-79; tragedy of, 183, 187; worship of Baal in, 194. *See also* Political relations

Israelite king: achievements of, 164, 170-71, 178, 186, 201-2; as a diviner, 196, 198; as a priest, 201-3; as agent of disaster, 127; as agent of God, 127; as ideal figure, 175; as Messiah, 192; as patron of wisdom, 207; as revealer of hidden, 160-62, 205; as son of God, 200-201, 205; birth of, 249, n30; called "god," 249, n30; choice of, 176; development of wisdom under, 30-31, 149;

different from mortals, 160; divine, 154, 160-61, 175, 193, 200-201; dreams of, 174-75, 196; dynastic succession of, 186; endowment of, 145, 161-62, 200-201, 205-6; enthronement of, 176; fear of, 127, 201; formulation of policies of, 195-96, 202-3, 206-7; glory of, in searching, 161; in loyalist texts, 148; in older wisdom, 149; in Prov. 25, 148; in the *Königsnovelle*, 175-76; inerrancy of, 159, 198; Jerusalem as the royal center of, 201-2; judicial functions of, 180, 193-94, 201; investigative role of, 148; legitimation of, 185; limitations of wisdom of, 145, 178, 207; manifests sacral reality, 159; mind of, 148, 193, 201, 205; mystery of, 160, 201, nothing hidden from, 161; number of references to, 149, 237, n17, 238, n18; obedience to, 126; oracular powers of, 159; personnel of, 150, 196, 203-4; political reforms of, 186; powers of, 195-98, 201, 204-6; prophets of, 194, 196; punishment of, 178; references to, in Proverbs, 142-43, 198, 149, 159, 238, n18; regnal formulas of, 185; rejection of, 182, 207; relation of the courtier to, 24, 108, 148, 154; relation to the royal court, 162, 202-3, 206; relation to elders, 150; relation to the wicked, 142, 145; religious personnel of, 196; responsibility to fulfill covenant, 178; revelation through, 148, 159-61, 194-96, 198, 205-6; role in the cult, 194-95, 198-99, 201-3; role contrasted to God, 159; special relation to God, 160; threat to theocracy in, 207; throne of, 201; transcendence of, 193, 200, 205-6; wisdom of, 145, 160-61, 192-93, 200; wisest of all

men, 160-61. *See also* King, the;
Kings, ancient Near Eastern; Solomon, King
Israelite kingship: as manifest destiny,
209; as new institution, 202; as rejection of theocracy, 207; characterized, 148, 159-62, 201-3; development of culture under, 203-4;
effect of decline of, 118, 207-8;
glorification of, 159, 204; ideology
of, 148, 200-201, 205-6, 249, n30;
inscriptions relating to, 200, 209;
internationalism of, 202 (*see also* Internationalism); isolation of, 201-2;
locus of revelation in, 160 (*see also*
Israelite king, revelation through);
model of, 203; nature of covenant
of, 249, n38; negative aspect of,
183; novel religious ideology of,
202; origins of wisdom under, 31,
164-65, 203-4; patron of wisdom,
210; political ideology of, 185-86,
203-4; political resistance toward,
207; proverbs relating to, 149; relationship to theocratic traditions,
201-2, 210; sacral imagery of 201-2;
secularization under, 154; skepticism toward, 118; struggle of, for
legitimacy, 185; syncretism in,
202-3; succession in, 176; tension
introduced by, 249, n37; theology
of, 205; throne of God in, 201;
unity of religious and political in,
202-3. *See also* Israelite king;
Chronicle of Solomon
Israelite literary genres. See Literary
genres
Israelite wisdom: adaptation of Egyptian wisdom, 57-59 (*see also* Adaptation; Adaptive stage); admonition
in, 75-79 (*see also* Admonition); aes-
thetical imagery of, 151-52 (*see also*
Ethics of Israelite wisdom); agnosticism in, 160 (*see also* Agnosticism);

aim of, 147-48 (*see also* Education,
Israelite); antithesis of human and
divine in, 159 (*see also* Antithesis of
human and divine); arrangement
of literary forms in, 79-80, 85-87,
147 (*see also* Collections of wisdom;
Oldest Collections of Israelite wisdom); as part of international
movement, 29 (*see also* Internationalism, Israelite); as rationale
of Solomon, 164 (*see also* Solomon,
King); assimilation in 89-90 (*see also*
Assimilation; Assimilative stage);
associated with judicial function of
kings, 193-95 (*see also* Judgment,
legal); attribution of, 150 (*See
also* Possessors of wisdom);
authority of, 191, 206 (*see
also* Theological bases of Israelite
wisdom); books of, 29, 134-35 (*see
also* Israelite wisdom books); causal
clauses in, 76-78; centers of, 195 (*see
also* Cult); central figure in, 149 (*see
also* Israelite king; Israelite kingship); characterized 33, 191, 206-7,
249, n37; cleverness in, 192; coals
of fire in, 130-31; combined with
political history, 172-73 (*see also*
Political wisdom of Israel); comparative proverb in, 71-75 (*see also*
Comparative proverb); compared
with apocalyptic, 126-27 (*see also*
Apocalyptic); conception of God in,
127, 159, 192, 198-99, 206 (*see also*
God; Hiddenness of God); cool
man in, 68 (*see also* Cool Man, the);
created by Yahweh, 200 (*see also*
God, wisdom of); date of, 30-32 (*see
also* Oldest Collections of Israelite
wisdom; Origin of Israelite wisdom); democratization of, 23; dependence of, 22 (*see also* Dependence, criteria for; Dependence, Israelite); dependence

aesthetics, 151-52; relation to customary law, 180, 194; religious bases of, 194-95; role of king in, 193-96

Kagemni, 108, 150, 171, *See also* Egyptian wisdom books; Wisdom books, ancient Near Eastern

Kemyt, 69, 137-39, 147. *See also* Egyptian wisdom books; Wisdom books, ancient Near Eastern

Keret, 99, 192-93. *See also* Hierophants

Kethib, 82, 86, 114. *See also* Masoretic text

Kings, the First Book of. See Chronicle of Solomon; Solomon, King

Kevin, Robert Oliver, 40, 42-45

Khety, 150, 170, 239, n19. *See also* Merikare, The Instruction of

King, the: as "Adam," 200; as patron of wisdom, 149, 225, n50; compositions to, 149-50, 225, n50; divine, 148, 200-201, 249, n30; in relation to the people, 148; judicial role of, 193-94; life-giving power of, 201; loyalist texts for, 148; mythological imagery of, 200; revelation through, 148, 195; righteousness of, 246, n8; sacral imagery surrounding, 200-201; self-exaltation of, 200; wisdom of, 160-61, 192-94, 247, n10. *See also* Egyptian king; Israelite king; Kings, ancient Near Eastern; Merikare, The Instruction of; Solomon, King

Kingdom, the divided, 180-86. *See also* Israel; Judah

Kingdom of God, 182, 249, n38. *See also* Theocracy, the traditions of

Kings, ancient Near Eastern: Abimilki of Tyre, 59, 75; Akhenaton, 59; Ammenemes I, 150, 168-69, 172; Azitawadda, 192; Ben Hadad, 194; Dan'el, 161, 192-94, 247, n11,

David, 30, 82, 181, 183-85, 194, 201-2, 238, n19, 247, n12; 249, n38; Hadad, 179; Haremhab, 225, n50; Hezekiah, 30-32, 40, 139, 165, 186; Hiram of Tyre, 174, Jehoram, 194, 245, n38; Jeroboam, 179-82, 185; Josiah, 186-87, 245, n38; Keret, 99, 192-93; Khety III, 150, 170; king of Assyria, 200; king of Babylon, 195, 246, n8, king of Egypt, 200, 246, n8; king of Tyre, 61, 192, 200, 247, n12; king of Ugarit, 247, n10; Merikare, 150, 158, 167, 170; Omri, 249, n36; Ramses II 63; Ramses III 167; Rehoboam, 182, 185; Saul, 196; Sesostris I, 168-71; Solomon, 247, n12 (*see also* Solomon, King)

Kittel, Rudolph, 32-33, 117, 220, n3

Knudtzon, J. A., 221, n10

Königsnovelle, 175-176. *See also* Succession to the throne

Kuentz, Charles, 243, n7

Lacau, M. Pierre, 228, n4

Land (of Palestine), 125

Landsberger, Benno, 239, n19

Lange, H. O., 216, n44

Late Egyptian texts, 49, 54. *See also* Demotic wisdom, Egyptian literature

Latin Vulgate, The: conjectural emendation in, 102; omission of words in, 102; parallelism in, 102; preservation of rubric, 140; support of Masoretic Text by, 84, 140; "thirty" in, 84, 95, 226-27, n53; translation of rubrics, 237, nn10, 11. *See also* Masoretic Text; Jerome

Law: as priestly torah, 118; as Pentateuch, 152, 208; authority of, 191; 234, n10; concept of revelation in, 207; customary, 180, 194; Deuteronomic development of, 208; difference from wisdom, 151-52, 191, 206; fusion of, with

pendence, criteria for; Dependence, Israelite; Parallels between Amenemope and Proverbs
Relationship of Israelite wisdom: to apocalyptic, 127; to cult, 195, 197-99, 204; to Deuteronomic traditions, 152, 208; to history, 126-27, 129, 173 (*see also* History); to kingship, 149, 154, 164, 203; to Judaism, 208, 210; to prophecy, 190, 206, 241, n21, 246, n2; to the Pentateuch, 206, 241, n21, 246, n2; to political events, 164, 187; to the Psalms, 119-20, 124-25, 127-28; to the faith of Israel, 190-91; to the theocratic traditions, 190, 201-2, 205-6, 246, n2; to the Torah, 152, 190, 206, 208, 241, n21. *See also* Origin of Israelite Wisdom, Reformulation of Israelite wisdom
Religion of Egypt: antithesis of human and divine in, 155-57; Canaanite influence upon, 64-65; conception of God in, 41, 155-58; conception of man in, 155-57; conception of reality in, 157; expansion of oracles in, 248, n21; idolatry in, 196; influence on Jews in Egypt, 51; Isaiah's description of, 248, n21; judgment of the dead in, 47; Semitic influence upon, 50-52; uniqueness of ideas, in Amenemope, 41; weighing of the heart in, 47, 77, 120-21. *See also* Deities; Egyptian king
Religion of Israel: as concern of Deuteronomist, 172 (*see also* Deuteronomist); as rationale of wisdom, 32, 154 (*see also* Israelite wisdom, religious background of); assimilative capacity of, 210; basis of law in, 194-95 (*see also* Revelation, by divination); development of, 190; effect of monarchy upon 202 (*see also* Israelite kingship): in rela-

tion to Judaism, 207-8; Jebusite contribution to, 201-2; judgment of the dead in, 47; personnel of, 196; place of wisdom in, 190-91, 206; prophetic description of, 196; relationship to literary paradigm, 189-90, 209 (*see also* Adaptive stage; Assimilative stage); role of cult place in, 194 (*see also* Cult); secular in relation to, 154, 206 (*see also* Secularism of Israelite wisdom); sun worship in, 51; superior ethics of, 40, 92; syncretism of, 201-2; tension of, 207; theology of kingship in, 204-5; two centers of, 206-7, 210 (*see also* Theological bases of Israelite religion, independent of theocracy). *See also* Divination, Israelite; Judgment, legal
Revelation: as concealment of meaning, 154, 159, 205; as counsel, 194-95; as enterprise of the royal court, 161-62; basis of belief in, 162; by divination, 195-98, 248, n22 (*see also* Cult); by dream, 174-75, 196; concept of God in, 159-60, 207-8; criterion of true, 202; honor in seeking, 147, 162; in creation, 158-59; in the Pentateuch, 206-8; in Tobit, 141; inerrancy of the king in, 159, 198; lapse of divine action in, 245, n1; locus of, 160; loss of, 160; mystery of, 154, 198; negation of, 242, n33; no divine self-disclosure in, 205-6; prophetic conception of, 207; relation of proverbial counsel to, 206; role of the king in, 148, 157-62, 194-96, 198, 204-5; sacralization of political order in, 162, 202, 205; tension in conceptions of, 206-7; through dreams, 174-75; through structures of kingship, 202. *See also* God; Hiddenness of God; Theological bases of Israelite wisdom

Scriptural Index

THE OLD TESTAMENT AND THE APOCRYPHA

Pss.			71:2	230, n24

Pss.

1	120, 123-24, 234, n16
1:3	121
2:7	200, 249, n30
6:1	222, n20
10:10	234, n6
17:6	34, 229, n20, 230, n24
31:2	230, n24
31:5	50
37	124-25, 127-28, 209, 235, n28
37:1-3	125
37:1	125
37:6	119
37:7	126
37:8	128-29, 222, n20
37:9	129
38:10	127-28
37:13	130
37:16	93, 124, 129, 224, n39
37:21	126
37:25	129, 235, n24
37:26	126
37:27	126
37:30-31	126
37:31	126
37:34	126, 129
37:35	235, n20
37:35-36	129
37:36	128
37:39	126
45:1	106-7, 232, n41
45:6-7	200
45:6	201
45:10	229, n20
45:13	230, n25
48:13	230, n25
51:7	249, n30
62:10	230, n25
62:10	230, n25

71:2	230, n24
72:1	228, n5
76:10	223, n20
78:38	222, n20
86:1	230, n24
86:15	228, n3
88:2	230, n24
89:7	200
89:14	228, n5
90:7	223, n20
102:2	230, n24
103:6	228, n5
103:8	228, n3
103:16	128
105:22	238, n19
106:3	228, n5
111:10	120
119:44	234, n10
119:55	234, n10
119:136	234, n10
120:1	231, n27
135:3	231, n29
145:8	228, n3
147:1	231, n29

Prov.

1-9	45, 79
1:4	234, n7
1:8	231, n28
1:33	117
2:1	231, n28
3:1	231, n28
4:1-2	231, n28
4:4-5	231, n28
4:20	230, n24, 231, n28
4:21	35
4:25	197
5:1	230, n24, 231, n28
5:7	231, n28
5:13	229, n20
6:12-15	197

17	234, n16	JOEL	
17:5-8	122, 235, n20		
17:6	122	2:13	228, n3
18:18	238, n19		
18:23	247, n9		
25:4	229, n20	JON.	
29:17	110		
34:14	229, n20	4:2	228, n3
35:15	229, n20		
37:29	231, n30		
49:7	238, n19	MIC.	
50:35	239, n19		
51:57	239, n19	3:5-7	196
EZEK.			
7:26	238, n19	NAH.	
8:6	51		
8:16	51	1:2	222, n20
14:14	193	1:3	228, n3
14:20	193		
23:25	247, n9		
27:8-9	238, n19	ZECH.	
28	161		
28:3	161, 192-93, 200	14:6	234, n6
28:6	200		
28:12-13	200	TOBIT	
28:14	200		
		1:15	49
DAN.		12:7	237, n14
		12:11	237, n14
2:20	192		
9:18	229, n20, 230, n24		
		ECCLUS.	
HOS.			
		30:14	92-93, 224, n39
3:4	196	31:12	27, 232, n42
9:1-2	194	31:16	233, n45, 233, n46

NEAR EASTERN INDEX
ANCIENT NEAR EASTERN TEXTS